MENTAL HYGIENE
(A SCIENCE OF ADJUSTMENT)

MENTAL HYGIENE
(A SCIENCE OF ADJUSTMENT)

Dr. S.S. CHAUHAN
M.A. Psy., Ed., Ph. D.
Himachal Pradesh University,
Summerhill, Shimla-171 005 (HP)

ALLIED PUBLISHERS PRIVATE LIMITED
NEW DELHI MUMBAI KOLKATA CHENNAI NAGPUR
AHMEDABAD BANGALORE HYDERABAD LUCKNOW

ALLIED PUBLISHERS PRIVATE LIMITED

1/13-14 Asaf Ali Road, **New Delhi**–110002
Ph.: 011-23239001 • E-mail: delhi.books@alliedpublishers.com

87/4, Chander Nagar, Alambagh, **Lucknow** - 226005
Ph.: 0522-4012850 • E-mail: appltdlko9@gmail.com

17 Chittaranjan Avenue, **Kolkata**–700072
Ph.: 033-22129618 • E-mail: cal.books@alliedpublishers.com

15 J.N. Heredia Marg, Ballard Estate, **Mumbai**–400001
Ph.: 022-42126969 • E-mail: mumbai.books@alliedpublishers.com

60 Shiv Sunder Apartments (Ground Floor), Central Bazar Road,
Bajaj Nagar, **Nagpur**–440010
Ph.: 0712-2234210 • E-mail: ngp.books@alliedpublishers.com

F-1 Sun House (First Floor), C.G. Road, Navrangpura,
Ellisbridge P.O., **Ahmedabad**–380006
Ph.: 079-26465916 • E-mail: ahmbd.books@alliedpublishers.com

751 Anna Salai, **Chennai**–600002
Ph.: 044-28523938 • E-mail: chennai.books@alliedpublishers.com

Hebbar Sreevaishnava Sabha, Sudarshan Complex - 2
No. 24/1, 2nd Floor, Seshadri Road, **Bangalore** - 560009
Ph.: 080-22262081 • E-Mail: bngl.books@alliedpublishers.com

3-2-844/6 & 7 Kachiguda Station Road, **Hyderabad**–500027
Ph.: 040-24619079 • E-mail: hyd.books@alliedpublishers.com

Website: www.alliedpublishers.com

First Edition, 1986

Second Edition, 1991

Reprinted, 1999, 2001, 2005, 2009, 2011, 2016

ISBN 81-7023-094-2

Published by Sunil Sachdev and printed by Ravi Sachdev at Allied Publishers Private Limited, Printing Division, A-104 Mayapuri Phase II, New Delhi - 110064

Preface

The science of Mental Hygiene has undergone great changes since its development in the beginning of the present century. Several factors have been responsible for the changes in the outlook and interest of people in mental hygiene. More specifically, the rapid growth in population, scientific researches, and tremendous increase in mental disorders have effected changes in the recent past in all developing countries of the world. The problems of mental health have caused great concern in the minds of those who are engaged in human welfare. It is a well-known fact that in a democracy, every citizen is expected to contribute, according to his maximum capacity, to the development and welfare of the country. But mentally disordered people are not only a liability on the national exchequer but consume the time and energy of other citizens that would have otherwise been utilized for the welfare of the nation.

The author felt a great need to write a book which would acquaint readers with the problems of mental health of children, adolescents and adults so that the increasing number of problems may be minimized by developing preventive measures.

The main purpose of the present book is to provide a complete elementary knowledge of the field of mental hygiene within a reasonable number of pages. In order to achieve this aim, I have ordered and systematized the information that is basic and indispensable to such a study,

The straightforward, simple language and style of the book permits it to be used both with graduate and postgraduate classes in Education and Psychology of Indian universities and also by those who are interested in the mental health problems of the general population.

It is a great pleasure to express my gratitude to all my colleagues in the Department of Education who have contributed through their suggestions to the improvement of the manuscript of the book. I am indebted to all authors whose books I consulted. I specially thank Mrs. Chauhan who encouraged me to complete the book inspite of her chronic illness of the last thirty years. But for her constant motivation the book would not have been written.

S. S. Chauhan

CONTENTS

SECTION — A

1. Introduction to Mental Hygiene
2. The Concept of Mental Health
3. Factors Affecting Mental Health
4. Adjustment and Adjustment Problems
5. Adjustment Demands (Stresses)
6. Adjustment Mechanisms
7. Psychoneurotic Adjustment Mechanisms
8. Psychotic Adjustment Mechanisms
9. Conduct Disorders
10. Assessing Psychological Adjustment

CHAPTER 1

Introduction to Mental Hygiene

The problems of mental disorders have been increasing tremendously for the last two decades all over the world. Our country is no exception. We have witnessed a rapid growth in mental disorders of all types during this period. The incidences of mental disorders are acquiring unusual dimensions every year, causing great concern to educationists, psychologists, sociologists, social workers and all those who are closely connected with the welfare of the individual and the society as a whole. The mentally disordered persons have become a great liability on the nation.

The extent of mental disorders in the general population, according to a survey which was conducted by Dr. Suria in 1962-63 was 9.5 persons for every one thousand. According to another survey conducted by Dr. Dube in 1964, it was 21.3 person for every one thousand. Even if we agree with Dr. Suria, at least 7 lac people need mental treatment (population 68 crores vide 1981 census). Since then conditions in our society have changed greatly and subsequently the percentage of mental disorders has also increased in the last two decades. According to a recent survey conducted by the National Institute of Mental Health, Bangalore, the number of people who need immediate attention is 15 lacs.

The major factors responsible for this are rapid growth of population, conflict of values, social alienation, industrialization, competition, unemployment communal disharmony, and the materialistic attitude of the people.

There is a great need to check the rapidly growing menace of mental disorders in order to maximally develop the potentialities of our population for the progress and benefit of the country.

Mental disorders have been referred to in our ancient scriptures since the dawn of civilization. If we go through the *Atharva-Veda*, the *Chrak Samihita*, the *Surut Samihita*, and other documents, we find a number of mental diseases referred to in these ancient books. Also a full-fledged system of treatment has been given which affirms the fact that our 'Rishis' had a deep knowledge of mental disorders But the treatment given to mentally disordered people in the past was inhuman. They were left to the mercy of God. Mental abnormality was considered God's wrath on the afflicted person and other people were unable to do any service to the sufferes.

However, as scientific investigations on human behaviour were conducted, people came to know the reality about mental disorders. Gradually a body of scientific knowledge was systematically developed to prevent and cure mental disorders. The attitude of the general public towards mentally disordered persons has undergone a change in recent years resulting in better understanding and treatment of their problems.

Meaning of Mental Hygiene

Mental hygiene is a science which deals with the process of attaining mental health and preventing mental illness in society. It is a life-long process which begins in early childhood and continues till the death of an individual. It covers all phases of life right from infancy to old age.

Before we trace the development of the mental hygiene movement, let us differentiate between the two terms : "mental hygiene", and "mental health" which often confuse the readers. Mental hygiene and mental health may be differentiate as means and ends. Mental hygiene is a means of mental health meaning thereby that the main objective of mental hygiene is to attain mental health In other words mental hygiene is a systematic body of knowledge which aims at attaining mental health.

Definition

Several definitions of mental hygiene have been given by clinicians, psychologists and educationists from different points of view. It is not possible here to reproduce all of them, so we will follow a sample approach.

Klien has defined mental hygiene as, "an endeavour to aid people to ward off trouble as well as to furnish ways of handling trouble in intelligent fashion when it cannot be warded off. What people call their 'troubles' can be classified into a series of conventional categories as illness, religion, finances, sex, social position, economic security, safety from accident, old age, fire and inadequate shelter."

Rivillin defined mental hygiene as, "the application of a body of hygienic information and technique culled from the sciences of Psychology, Child Psychology, Education, Sociology Psychiatry, Medicine and Biology, for the purpose (a) of the preservation and improvement of mental health of the individual and of the community and (b) for the prevention and cure of minor and major mental diseases and defects of mental, educational and social maladjustment."

It is very difficult to trace the history of mental hygiene because no one can be pinpointedly called its propounder. Mental hygiene was present in some form since the dawn of civilization. In India, thousands of years ago, the wise Rishis and saints had evolved a full-fledged system of *Ayurveda* which successfully treated mental disorders of different natures. But the system of *Ayurveda* was dealt a death blow by the continuous invasions of foreigners and was completely relegated during the British rule which annihilated the system and established its own system of Allopathic treatment.

The beginning of the mental hygiene movement in the West may be traced to the first decade of the present century when Clifford Beers, a graduate of Yale University, being frustrated with his life attempted to commit suicide in the year 1908 by jumping from the roof of a building. But he was saved and treated for his mental illness. After recovery, he wrote about his experiences and the type of treatment he had received during his illness in a book entitled, "*A Mind That Found Itself*". The book revolutionized the concept of mental ill-health and created awareness in the general public for the necessity of mental hygiene. The first society for mental hygiene was established in 1908 and the National Society for mental hygiene was formed after a decade in 1919 which gradually grew into the International Committee for Mental Hygiene. The committee publishes a journel "Mental Hygiene" to coordinate and disseminate the findings of researches being conducted all over the world and to facilitate understanding and cooperation among workers in the field. In India, an Institute of Mental Health was established at Bangalore in 1937 which has been doing pioneering work in training mental hygienists for mental hospitals and other institutions. Since then several institutions to train personnel in the field of mental hygiene have been opened. But there is a great need to open more institutions for training workers in view of the large population of the country and the increasing percentage of mental disorders.

Goals of Mental Hygiene

The specific goals of mental hygiene fall into the following four categories :

(i) Realization of Potentialities

The main goal of mental hygiene is to provide opportunity to the individual to develop his potentialities to the maximum. Every individual has some inherent potentialities which remain repressed through want of proper opportunities. Such individuals feel frustrated and consequently become the victims of menta illness.

(ii) Happiness

Happiness is a subjective criterian which is very difficult to define in operational terms. Here it means that the goal of mental hygiene is to develop a positive attitude towards life and work so that the individual may lead an efficient life by utilizing maximally his potential abilities.

(iii) Harmonious Development

Mental hygiene aims at the harmonious development of the physical, mental and spiritual capacities of the individual so that he may properly adjust to his social environment and contribute to the welfare of society.

(iv) Effective Existence

The last goal of mental hygiene is to prepare the individual for effective existence in society. Indian society is moving very rapidly towards industrialization which is fraught with many problems of adjustment. Mental hygiene prepares the individual for effective adjustment in home, school, work and society. The scope of mental hygiene includes all behaviour problems from infancy to old age.

Functions of Mental Hygiene

Mental hygiene is a recently developed science whose functions have not yet been clearly defined and delineated in our country. However, the following four functions have been given by mental hygienists in the literature on mental hygiene:

(i) Training

The first function of mental hygiene is to train mental health personnel who can understand people's psychological problems and can help them to meet their needs.

(ii) Prevention

The second important function of mental hygiene is to prevent mental health problems by developing such programmes as may check and reduce mental disorders in the population.

(iii) Cure of Mental Disorders

The third function is to develop programmes for those who have already become the victims of mental illness. Such programmes of counselling/psychotherapy may be developed for the individual or the group as may help in curing the patients.

(iv) Preservation

All people are not mentally ill. A good majority of people possess sound mental health. One function of mental hygiene is to preserve and maintain their mental health through education programmes.

Principles of Mental Hygiene

No two individuals are alike. Even identical twins who are born out of the same cell differ to a great extent in physical, intellectual, emotional, social, moral and religious dimensions of development. These differences are caused by the interactional process of the factors of Nature and Nurture. These differences influence adaptability of the individuals to their environment and affect their mental health.

Now a simple question which arises here is : can we formulate general principles of mental hygiene which may be applied to all human beings irrespective of wide difference in their personality? Apparently, it appears impossible, because of the following difficulties in the formulation of the general principles of mentalhy giene. The first difficulty is the multiplicity of needs

Human beings have multiple needs which grow in the course of development. These needs are contradictory in nature. The second difficulty is the lack of absolute standards. It is a very difficult task to decide the absolute standard of mental health against which the mental health of people can be evaluated. It is like the ideal of goodness, beauty and truth which is an "El Dorado" and is never achieved. But inspite of the above difficulties we can formulate some general principles of mental hygiene which may be used by parents and teachers to prevent mental disorders in children and to enhance and preserve their mental health. The broad principles are :

Adjustment in home

Early interaction of the child with parents has great influence on his later development. The behaviour patterns developed in early childhood leave permanent impressions on the child A child begins life in a state of virtually complete helplessness (a big, buzzing, blooming confusion) and is completely dependent on his parents or significant others who gratify his needs which are physiological in nature.

It is the duty of the mother to give plentiful mothering for the conducive development of the child. It has been reported by Spitz that a close bond between the child and the mother foster security and confidence in the child which help better adjustment in later life. Parents must develop in the r children a basic sense of thrust and the sense of indepen-dece should be inculcated gradually in children. But it does not mean that dependence should be rooted out as if it were inherently evil.

A child from the age of six months develops his repertory of actions by manipulating all objects within his reach. He explores and manipulates his environment in order to gain knowledge about it and to deal with it competently.

The attainment of competence beings in playful exploration and experimentation with one's physical and human surroundings. The process continues to important through all stages of development.

Parents should develop competency in children by allowing their initiatives full play as far as is practiceable and safe.

Parents should inculcate desirable traits in their children and develop competence, security, adequacy, self-esteem and discipline by catering to their basic needs. If desirable characteristics develop during early childhood, children do not experience any difficulty in the process of adjustment during adolescence.

Adjustment to School

After home, the school plays a crucial role in the development of personality. School through its various activities can help in preventing mental disorders and preserving the mental health of students. It can also correct emotional disturbances caused by the home environment by developing remedial programmes for emotionally disturbed and socially alienated students. The role of education for mental health has been dealt with in detail in a subsequent chapter.

Adjustment to Society

Man is a social animal. He is born and brought up in a society. A human being from his birth to his death remains in close association with society. We cannot imagine the harmonious development of personality of an individual without social interaction. In the process of social adjustment, normal reaction to feeding appears to be essential for mental health. In the words of W. Brown, "It is a mistake to hold feeling in contempt; it is in feeling that values reside, and the life of feeling has a logic of its own, distinct from the logic of pure reason and not necessarily inferior to it." Therefore for mental health normal expression is essential. There should be no repression of feelings because it leads to mental abnormality. Burnham says, "The wholesome personality is characterized by normal expression of emotion and by control of emotion". Parents, teachers and society must provide socially acceptable channels for the release of pent-up emotional feelings so that children and adolescents may properly adjust themselves to the society which presents situations in which the emotions find no expression but rather have to be suppressed.

Adjustment to Work

Work is worship, says an old proverb. It means that the individual must absorb himself in his work like a worshipper only then he can get pleasure and satisfy himself. It is work; through which an individual makes contribution to society and gets pleasure in proportion to the recognition of his contribution. Therefore it becomes essential for parents and teachers to develop positive attitudes in children to whatever work is assigned to them. According to Freud, one is mentally healthy if one can work successfully and love successfully. Children should be provided opportunities for self-directed activities which create confidence and adequacy to stand on their own feet. School, through its programmes, should develop proper mental set towards work in children

Adjustment to Self

'Know thyself' is the first maxim of Mental Hygiene. This maxim is equally applicable to children, adolescents and adults. Parents and teachers should help the child to understand himself, meaning thereby that the child must know about his own body and mind. The child must also know the realities of life which is full of difficulties. Children should be led to understand the problems of sex, and mental ill health etc.

Headfield says that mere knowing oneself is not enough; it must be supplemented by accepting oneself and being oneself. It is the duty of the teacher to develop an objective attitude in children to appraise themselves. Children should be helped to set life goals in accordance with their potentialities to avoid frustration.

In brief, the basic principles of mental hygiene have been outlined. There is no doubt that if these principles are followed faithfully we can reduce the mental health problems of children and can help them in better adjustment to society.

Limitations of Mental Hygiene

Interest in mental hygiene is gradually acquiring importance in our country and in all developing countries of the world because of the increasing number of mental patients every year. Educationists, psychologists and social workers are convinced that the increasing percentage of mental disorders should be checked as early as possible by involving parents, teachers, social workers and professionals working in the field of mental health. Parents and the general public should be educated through the mass media in the fundamental principles of mental hygiene and schools make mental hygiene an integral part of the curriculum.

There are certain limitations in the way of implementing the principles of mental hygiene in our country. The majority of parents in our country are illiterates. They are not familiarised with the fundamental principles of mental hygiene. Moreover, they are conservative and traditional in their outlook. They are not easily prepared to give up their old traditions which clash with the new philosophy of life which is fast emerging in the transitional period, challenging the old. Parents in the present circumstances cannot be held responsible for the mental health of their sons and daughters. As regards school, it can do a lot to prevent mental disorders in students but in the present circumstances our teachers are overloaded with academic work and cannot devote enough time to organize activities conductive to mental health. A detailed description of the activities which a teacher can uudertake in school for the mental health of the students has been given in a subsequent chapter.

The greatest obstacle is the lack of trained personnel who may deal with the mental health problems of our population which according to 1981 census report ha reached the mark of 78 crores approximately. There is a great need to train sufficient number of persons for early detection and correction of behaviour disorders before they become more severe.

The researches in the field of mental health are very few because sufficient funds are not provided. There is great need to make provision for adequate funds with which programmes for conducting research studies in different areas may be carried out for the welfare of society.

QUESTIONS FOR DISCUSSION

1. Differentiate between mental hygiene and mental health. Describe the functions of mental hygiene.
2. What are the basic principles of mental hygiene ? Describe them.
3. Describe the history of the movement of mental hygiene.
4. Discuss the functions of mental hygiene in the present conditions of our country

SUGGESTED READINGS

1. Beers, C. W.: A mind That Found Itself, Longmans, NY, 1935.
2. Kirkpatrick, F. A. : Mental Hygiene for Effective Living, Appleton Century, NY, 1934.
3. Klien : Mental Hygiene, Henry Holt, NY.
4. Redl, Fritz, et. al. : Mental Hygiene in Teaching Harcourt Brace, NY, 1951.
5. Rue, D. W. La. : Mental Hygiene, MacMillan, NY, 1972

CHAPTER 2

The Concept of Mental Health

The concept of mental health is as old as human beings. Our ancient scriptures are full of references to mental diseases and their treatment. The *Atharva-Veda*, the *Chrak Samihita*, the *Surut Samihita*, and the *Astangh Sangrah* have described several diseases of the mind with specific methods of treatment. They have also given the concept of mental health and how to maintain and promote it.

In the west, the concept of mental health is a comparatively recent one. A number of studies have been conducted to list the characteristics of mentally healthy individuals. Burnham, who emphasized the importance of integration or wholeness of personality said, "A mentally healthy person is one who has a wholesome balanced personality free from schisms and inconsistencies, emotional and nervous tensions, discorders and conflicts. He does not compart himself like a series of compartmentalized seleves, a series of Dr. Jekylls and Mr. Hydes, honest on Sunday, dishonest on Monday, generous to-day, crabbed tomorrow, reasonable and logical at times, at other times, confused and inconsistent."

"The balanced personality", according to Professor Hamley, "is like the balanced physical system; it stands firm in the nidst of strain and stress. There can be no balance of personality, where there is no possibility of conflict. We do not seek the balanced personality in the cloister or in the retreat, although it is often to be found there but in the tempests and storms of life."

If we minutely examing the above two concepts of a mentally healthy personality we can say that a mentally healthy person is firm in his intentions and is not disturbed by the strain and stress of life.

Mental health is a condition of psychological maturity—a relatively constant and enduring function of personality. It is a condition of personal and social functioning with a maximum of effectiveness and satisfaction. Mental health involves positive feelings and attitudes toward the self and toward others.

The following are the five behaviour patterns that a mentally healthy person may evidence.

Sense of responsibility : The person who is mentally healty has a sense of responsibility and is sensitive to the needs of others and attempts to satisfy those needs for the welfare of others.

A sense of self-reliance : The mentally healthy person has confidence in his judgement and abilities and views setback as problems to be solved rather than an occassion for the display of anger and emotional outbursts.

A sesne of direction : The mentally healthy individual has a clear concept of his life goals. He directs his efforts, energy and creativeness toward the attainment of these goals.

A set of personal values: The mentally healthy individual has a philosophy of life that is based on convictions, beliefs and goals that contribute to his happiness and the happiness of those around him. His philosophy of life will tend to increase his social status and his contribution to society.

A sense of individuality : The mentally healthy individual recognizes himself as a person who is separate and distinct from others. He endeavours to develop attitudes and patterns of behaviour that entail neither blind conformity to the demands and desires of others nor a rebellious detachment and isolation from others.

Saul has described the mentally healthy individual as, "The mature adult is both predominantly independent and responsible with little need to regress, and also is giving and productive, although still able to relax and to receive normally, he is cooperative rather than egotistical and competitive; he is in relative harmony with his conscience which easily integrates with his mature feelings and behaviour, his sexuality is free and integrated with mating and responsible productive activity both sexual and social; his hostility toward others and towards himself is minimal but is freely available for defenses and constructive use, he is discriminating and highly adaptable...his anxiety is at a minimum."

Jacky Roy in his book '*Abnormal Psychology*' has given the following conditions for good mental health.

1. Good physical health

That a sound mind can only exist in a sound body is an old proverb. The psycho-bio-social approach to the understanding of behaviour emphasizes that the physical health of the organism is of importance in its adaptation to and survival in the world.

2. Satisfying social relation

Harry Stack Sullivan defined a human being as the totality of his real and imagined relations. Satisfactory social intercourse is a pre-requisite not only for a person's mental health but also for his very humanity. A mentally, healthy person is he who has good social relations.

3. A confident

Each individual needs at least one other person in whom he can confide his intnermost secrets and problems. Without such a confident a person can feel all alone, even while immersed in a continual round of superficial social activity, A thousand cquaintances cannot fill the need felt for one close intima te friend. It is with his intimate confident that a person is able to realize his full potential to love and be loved.

4. Personal Worth

Important in mental health is a feeling of self-esteem. A person must be able to accept himself as a person of worth and to give himself the respect due to such a person. We will see in a subsequent chapter that feelings of inferiority and insecurity are typical of neurotic individuals. These are the very feelings that prevent and block the development of self-esteem.

5. Insight

A person must learn to evaluate realistically all behaviours. A mentally healthy person must have insight into his actions.

6. Philosophy of Life

A well adjusted person has a sound philosophy of life built upon the following :

(i) First a person must live in the world in the sense of active social participation and commitment.

(ii) Life is worth living. It has meaning which can be understood in terms of either religion or humanism.

(iii) "No man". as John Donne put it, "is an island entire of itself." Each man is a vital part of every other person in terms of Erich Fromm's philosophy, "All men are brothers and are capable of productive love."

Each individual's philosophy must meet his unique personal needs as well as the demands made on him by the society.

Criteria for Mental Health

Jahoda (1963) proposes the following six characteristics of the mentally healthy individual.

1. Environment mastery, including the ability to love; adequacy in interpersonal relationships; efficiency in meeting situation requirements; capacity for adaption and adjustment, efficiency in problem solving and adequacy in love, work and play.

2. Undistorted perception of reality including empathy and social sensitivity.

3. Integration, meaning a balance of psychic forces in the individual, a unifying outlook on life and resistance of stress.

4. Autonomy, referring to the decision-making process, regulation from within and independent action.

5. Growth, self-development and self actualization including conceptions of self, motivational processes and investment in living.

6. Attitude towards self, including accessibility of the self to consciousness, correctness of the self-concept and a sense of identity.

Different authors emphasize different characteristics as they define acquisition and maintenance of mental health. Harry Stack Sullivan says that a mentally healty individual would place a major value on efficient social functioning. Freudians lay emphasis on an awareness of one's unconscious motivations and subsequent self-control, based on that awareness.

Erich Fromm focusses on a person's connections with the social environment, stressing humanism, freedom, relationality and individualism.

Perls emphasizes a person's accepting responsibility for directing his/her own life.

It can be seen that these criteria overlap to some extent. However, Jahoda states that in examining the literature on positive mental health, she found that all of the ideas presented could be assigned to one of these six categories. Researches in the field of mental hygiene assign priority to different variables for mental health. There are some who consider self-actualization as the essence of mental health; still others regard attitude toward self as the basic criterion for mental health; some regard the individual reality-orientation and his ability to master his environment as the primary criterion for mental health.

INDIAN CRITERIA

The Indian concept of mental health is available in the *Atharva-Veda* which provides detailed information on mental disorders and their treatment. According to the *Atharva-Veda*, human personality on the physical side has three components or gunas as *Vata, pitta* and *Kaph.* These three gunas are universal in nature and are found in every human body from birth, varying in different degrees but maintaining a certain equilibrium. So far as this equilibrium is present, it indicates physical normality and no disease arises. But when there is increase or decrease in any of these, it gives rise to different diseases.

The mental personality also constitutes three *gunas* or characteristics *Sattav, Rajas* and *Tamas.* According to the *Atharva-Veda* the imbalance of these gunas cause mental disorders. These gunas are in *Manas* (mind) since birth but they keep a certain equilibrium in a normal person. So normal mental health means living in *Rajas* and *Tamas* to a certain degree.

The *Charak Sam hita* and Susrut have also given the concept of mental health but they do not differ significantly from the Atharva-Vedic concept of mental health. Here we describe the concept of physical and mental health as given by Susrut.

Susrut while defining the health of the body laid the following characteristics of it:

— *Sumadasa*—The equilibrium of the body humours.

—*Samagni*—Uniform health digestor.

— *Samadhatu* —Normal in body tissues.

— *Mala kriva*—Normal process of excretion.

— *Prasanatmendryamana* —Whose organic functions of mind and soul, are healthy and happy.

The above definition of health is the most comprehensive ever given in and discipline of knowledge. The last characteristic has been included in the Ayurveda in which the mental and spiritual happiness have been made part and parcel of health.

In Ayurveda health means the state of *Dhatusamya*. Charaka, a great Ayurvedic physician, holds that the concordance of *dhatu* is said to be normal health and it is the end sought in the employment of medicines as also in the observance of wholesome habits so that the equilibrium of dhatu may be achieved. This principle of *Dhatusamya* resemble to a great extent the modern approach to Homeostasis.

The term homeostasis is currently used in physiology and indicates that the organism takes action to protect or to restore certain favourable steady states. Ross Stagner, in his book '*Psychology of Personality*', wrote that many bodily Functions tend toward constancy and any disturbance leads to active effort aimed at restoring the steady state.

The following indications are given to the state of *dhatusamya* (Homeostasis).

— Allevation of pain

— Accession of voice and complexion

— Plumpness of the body

— Increase of strength

— Desire for food

— Relish to eat

— Timely and proper digestion of food

— Timely sleep

— Freedom from frightful dream

— Happy awakening

— The proper elimination of urine, feces and semen

— Freedom from impairment of any kind of the mind intellect and sense organ,

MEASURES TO ATTAIN IDEAL HEALTH

According to Ayurveda, the following are the measures to attain ideal health.

1. Diet

The body is the product of food; disease is born of food. The distinction of happiness and sorrow results from the distinction of wholesome diet. Therefore one should take balanced diet for good health.

2. Use of rasayana

Great importance has been given to the Rejuvenation therapy in Ayurveda and it is regarded as one of the specialized branches of medicine. Charaka observes that he who makes use of *Rasayana* in the prescribed manner not only attains longevity on the earth but after dying goes the auspicious way of the divine sages and reaches the immutable *Brahma* itself.

3. Tri-upasthambha of life

(a) Proper *Ahara* (diet) (b) Proper *Nidra* (sleep) and (c) *Brahmacharya* (celibacy).

4. Following the regimen of life according to Desa, Kala and Prakrti.

5. Following dietic and behaviouristic regimen according to Rtu (season) and to following the health rules.

6. Dinacarya and Ratricarya (Day and Night routine). A great emphasis has been laid in Ayurveda in these aspects of personal hygiene for the improvement of health.

7. Follow up of *Dharaniya* and *adharaniya Vegas* (Suppressable and unsuppressable urges).

8. Avoidance of *Sahasa* (excess or overwork).

9. Right conduct moral and ethical duties. These are regarded promoters of health.

10. Mental and intellectual methods. A brief description of the methods is given below.

(*a*) *Satmya-indriyartha-Samyoga*

(b) The right use of *manas* (psyche) and intellect, as the excessive, deficient and erroneous use of mental and intellectual factors causes diseases.

(c) Charaka summarizing the ways and means of keeping *arogya* (healthy) observes "One, who is accustomed to suitable diet and habit, who always acts after proper reflection, who does not entangle himself in the objects of the senses, who is charitable, who behaves equally towards all living creatures, who is devoted, who is forgiving, who serves with humility, who is wise or who is contented with what he possesses is never attacked by diseases. One who has a happy combination of thought speech and action, who has his mind under control, who has his intellect clear and who posseses knowledge of the soul and is devoted to austerities and yoga, never suffers from any disease. Caraka says that the entire activity of every individual is directed to the goal of happiness. The man desirous of happiness should observe the rules related to the prevention of unborn diseases and the cure of those which have already arisen. Health is the supreme foundation of virtue, wealth, enjoyment and salvation and a wish man should be ever vigilant in the case of his own *Sarira* (Physique) like the lord of a city in the affair of his city and a charioter in the management of his chariot. Leaving everything else, one should take care of the body, for in the absence of the body, there is the total extinction of all that characteristic embodied beings."

SOME CONCLUSIONS

We have discussed above the western and Indian concepts and criteria of mental health. Now we shall list a few very relevant and important observations on mental health. They are as follows :

1. The concept of mental health is purely subjective. It

pertains to the inner frame of reference of the individual.

2. The measurement of mental health is very difficult because there is no absolute mental health standard against which the mental health of an individual may be measured. We cannot measure mental health as in physical science in which the zero base line is a reference.

3. Criteria of mental health may differ from country to country and culture to culture.

4. Mental health is a dynamic concept. It is a state of equilibrium which is dynamic and not static.

5. Consistency in behaviour is an important characteristic of sound mental health.

6. There can be a variety of normal and integrative adjustments just as there is a variety of abnormal behaviour from simple anxiety to psychosis.

7. Adjustment during adulthood is largely a question of values which are the product of a matrix of attitudes.

8. A sound mind in a sound body is an old proverb which means that mental health to a lare extent is dependent on sound physical health. Therefore, it becomes essential to promote the physical health of individuals for sound mental health. Recent researches in the field of psychology have established the fact that food plays an important role in developm:nt of behaviour.

Lord Krishna, thousands of years ago in his celestial song 'Gita' declared that as is grain (food) so is our psyche (Mana).

QUESTIONS FOR DISCUSSION

1. **What do you mean by the concept of mental health ?**

2. What are the characteristics of a mentally healthy person ?
3. What is the Indian concept of mental health ?

SUGGESTED READINGS

1. Bhan, Suraj and Dutt, N. K. : Mental Health through Education, Vision Books, New Delhi, 1978.

2. Bianchi, L. : Foundations of Mental Health, Appleton, London, 1930.

3. Compbell, G. M. : Towards Mental Health' Harvard Uni-Press, 1933.

4. Howard, F. E. (ed.) : Mental Health, Basic Book, NY, 1950.

5. Ress, J. R. : The Health of Mind, Faber and Feber, London, 1936.

6. Singh H. G. : Psychotherapy in India, NPC, Agra, 1970.

CHAPTER 3

Factors Affecting Mental Health

It has unanimously been agreed upon by all experts that mental health plays a crucial role in the development of personality. It is impossible to imagine harmonious development of human beings without sound mental health. In the preceding chapter we described the concept of mental health from Indian and Western points of view. The present chapter deals with the various factors which may influence the mental health of human beings. It is very difficult to list all the factors that effect mental health because there are wide individual differences among human beings which may create variation in causal factors. However, an effort will be made to describe common factors.

Differing View Points

The information which we have about human behaviour is not sufficient to predict accurately how given circumstances will affect a given individual. The process of social interaction is made complex by a number of variables operating simultaneously in the environment to cause a specific behaviour. Neverthelesss, contemporary research findings in the areas of biological and social sciences have greatly enhanced our knowledge of the factors that may affect the mental health of human beings.

Mental ill-health has been a subject of study for a long time. Several approaches have been advanced by professionals to explain the causal factors affecting it. Therefore it will be helpful to review them briefly. Following are some of the important models which explain the causes of mental disorders from different angles.

The first model is the medical model which emphasizes the role of various organic conditions that can affect brain functioning and lead to mental disorder.

Another model is the psychoanalytic model of human behaviour which is concerned primarily with stress situations that involve a threat to the individual by causing anxiety. This in turn functions as both a warning of danger and an acutely unpleasant condition demanding immediate remedial measures. If the individual copes effectively with the stress situation, anxiety is eliminated, However, if the anxiety and stress continue, the individual typically resorts to various ego-defense mechanisms which have been described in chapter 6 and his mental health is affected. The psychoanalytic model gives importance to early childhood experiences in the family which are repressed due to malhanding by parents.

According to the behaviouristic model, the key factor is faulty learning. Mental-health is greatly affected by failure to learn necessary adaptive behaviour or competencies to handle social situations successfully. Maladaptive behaviour is learned like other skills from the environment.

Humanistic-existential models give importance to blocked or distorted personal growth as the major factor affecting mental health. According to these models, emphasis is laid on maintenance Vs. growth motivation and the necessity of being and shaping one's self. If the individual is denied opportunities for personal growth and self-fulfilment, he experiences anxiety, despair and frustration which ultimately lead to maladjustment. Distortion of human nature, which is basically cooperative and constructive, by unfavourable environmental conditions, causes maladjustment.

The interpersonal model concentrates on unsatisfactory interpersonal relationship among human beings as being at the root of maladaptive behaviour.

The socio-cultural viewpoint emphasizes the role of pathological social conditions such as poverty, discrimination, casteism, favouritism and violence as the major factors which affect the mental health of the individuals and the community.

The indian view of human nature is quite different from that of the western philosophers. Here we will only refer to ths Upnishadic view of human nature. The upnishadas believe in the philosophy of *Brahma* and *Atma*. It believes that the individual *Atma* (psyche) is a part of the Supreme energy called Brahma from which it has temporarily been separated due to illusion, though as a matter of fact it is always connected with Brahma When this oneness with Brahma is realized one derives enormous energy from Him through one's own individual psyche. Mental illness is caused by disturbances in the equilibrium of ita, *Vat* and *kaph* and also in the *Rajas*, *Tamas* and *Sattav gunas* of the human personality.

To understand the factors which affect the mental health of human beings, it is helpful not only to keep the preceding models in mind but also to note certain more general ways of viewing causal rleationship.

There are four different types of causes namely: primary, predisposing, precipitating and reinforcing which are important to consider while analysing the factors affecting mental health. The primary cause is the condition without which the mental disorder would have not occurred such as shyphilis of the brain in the case of general paresio.

A predisposing cause is a condition that comes before and paves the way for later maladjustment : an example is the parental rejection of the child. If a child is rejected by his parents in early childhood, he may develop a mental disorder in later years. A precipitating cause is a condition that proves to much to bear for the individual and triggers maladaptive behaviour. For example, due to a severe disappointment in love, an individual may become mentally disturbed or the sudden death of a loved one may cause mental disorder. A reinforcing cause is a condition that tends to maintain the maladaptive behaviour already present such as being provided with a 'sick role' and being relieved of unwanted responsibility for the family.

With the recent introduction of the concept of self-regulating system (Bio feedback), the causation of maladaptive behaviour is often viewed as being more complex than a simple cause-effect relationship.

Now we will describe the various factors that may affect the mental health of human beings. The factors will be dealt with under separate headings.

A. HEREDITARY FACTORS

Heredity is the foundation on which the structure of human personality is built. Hereditary factors influence all aspects of our behaviour including our intellectual capabilities, basic temperament, primary reaction tendency, stress tolerance and adaptive resources. A wide range of biological conditions, such as faulty genes, diseases, endocrine imbalances, malnutrition, injuries and other conditions interfere with the growth, development and functioning of the organisms and these become the potential causes of maladaptive behaviour. The following are the important hereditary factors :

(i) *Genetic Defects* : It is well-known that our behavour is inevitably influenced by our biological inheritance. Genetic defects are clearly a potential cause ot maladaption. The three genetic defects of major concern are as follows :

(a) *Chromosomal Aberrations* : It is a well known fact that great progress has been made in the field of genetics during the last decade which has enabled us to detect chromosomal aberrations and to study their implications for development and behaviour. The first major breakthrough in this area was the identification of the complement of 46 chromosomes in the nucleus of each normal cell and the discovery that encoded in the chromosomes is the hereditary plan -- the over-all strategy or information for guiding development. When fertilization takes place, the normal inheritance of the new individual consists of 23 pairs of chromosomes — one of each pairs being from the mother and the father. Twety two of these chromosome pairs are called autosomes. They determine body characteristics. The remaining pair, the sex chromosomes, determine the individual's sex and certain other characteristics.

Research in the developmental genetics has shown that abnormalities in the structure or number of the chromosomes are associated with a wide range of congential malformations and deficient in specific genetic information, the result may be colour blindness, hemophillia, and mongolism etc. in children.

(b) *Faulty Genes* : An important and major discovery in modern genetics has been the development of ultra microscopic techniques – for example, the combined use of the electron microscope and X-ray diffraction—which make it possible to study the actual structure of the chromosomes. Each chromosome is made up of a long molecule of DNA arranged in two strands linked together at regular intervals to form a double spiral or helix, that looks like a ladder curving round and round. In a series of epic experiments, scientists have shown that our genetic instructions are stored in this DNA ladder or book, The sentences in this DNA book of instructions are the genes which follow one another like beads strung together to from a necklace. Genes carry the instructions for specific body traits.

The breaking of the genetic code has enabled us to study loss, gains or changes of material in the gene itself, thus introducing a more precise approach relating genetic factors to physical and mental disorders.

(c) *Genetic peedisposition to specific mental disorders* : Great progress has been made in the identification of faulty genes as the cause of transmitting diseases. Most of the information concerning the role of genes in mental disorders is based on the study of family trees.

Kallmann (1958) studied the inheritance of schizophrenia. It has been statistically analysed that incidence of schizophrenia is much higher among blood relations than in the general population. The following figures confirm his conclusions.

Relationship	*Percentage of Schizophrenia*
Identical	86.2
Fraternal	14.5
Siblings	14.2
Half-siblings	7.1
General Population	0.85

All studies confirm that the genetic factor plays an important role in the inheritance of schizophrenia. Most researchers take the position that only a predisposition to mental disorders can be inherited.

Constitutional Liabilities

The term constitution is used to denote the bodily make-up of the individual resulting from both genetic and environmental influences.

(*i*) *Physique*

Since ancient times, attempts have been made to classify people into types and to predict personality traits on the basis of body build. Sheldon and his associates attempted to relate physique to personality and psychopathology. They concluded that there are three types of body bulid : ectomorphic, mesomorphic and endomorphic, each associated with particular temperamental and other personality characteristics.

Though physique is not directly related to psychopathology it does influence the type of disorder the individual is likely to develop under stress.

Most significant is the view we take of our own physical

appearance. A conception of one's own body as being too different from the standards valued by one's group can be self-devaluating and may cause anxiety in the mind of the person.

(ii) Physical Handicap

Deformities and imperfections of body such as lameness, deafness, blindness, and crookedness etc. whether inborn or accidental affect the mental health of the individual. Such physical defects may result from genetic defects or from environmental conditions operating before or after birth. However, the singnificance of a physical impairment depents primarily on the way the individual evaluates and adjusts to it. One of the obstacles that a handicapped person faces is the tenency to accept the role of a cripple which society often seems to expect and subtly encourages. This picture is often complicated by family members who either encourage such a sick role or expect performance beyond the individual's capacity. Other common and undersirable reactions to physical handicaps are feelings of inferiority, self-pity and hostility. As a consequence of such obstacles, the individual, whether child, adoleseent, or adult may develop psychological handicaps that are much more disabling than his physical impairment.

(iii) Vulnerability to Stress

The primary reaction tendencies such as sensitivity, temperament and activity level affect interactions with the environment. Several researches have reported that primary tendencies have relation with stress vulnerability and mental maladaptation. Primary reaction tendencies also include characteristic ways of reacting to stress.

Physical Deprivation

Physical deprivation greatly affects mental health and the functioning of the physique and the mind of organism. Here we will describe the effects of malnutrition, sleep deprivation and fatigue on individuals.

(*i*) *Malnutrition*

It has been established by several research findings that severe malnutrition in infancy not only impairs physical development and lowers resistance to diseases, but also stunts brain growth and results in markedly lowered intelligence. The fact that malnutrition in early childhood affects the intellectual development of children has been reported by the International Commission on Education in their report entitled, "Learning to Be."

(*ii*) *Sleep deprivation and fatigue*

Sleep deprivation over a long period of time may affect mental health. According to Adelson, two out of three hospitalized mental patients have suffered severe sleep disturbances before being hospitalized.

(*iii*) *Disruptive emotional processes*

Emotional processes like fear and anger represent the mobilization of body resources to meet emergency situations. Such mobilization enables a threatened organism either to fight or flee more effectively.

Mild emotions may be constructive in their overall effect by reinforcing our actions toward worthwhile goals. But as we get into the intermediate range of intensity, emotions are typically detrimental to problem solving and task performance and as the level of emotional tension increases, it becomes increasingly disruptive to organized behaviour. Prolonged emotional mobilization produces physiological changes that are not only useless but actually harmful to the organism.

(*iv*) *Brain Pathology*

There are some typical organic disturbances which directly affect the central nervous system. It is estimated that fifty per cent of patients suffer from mental disorders associated with organic brain pathology. Brain pathology may be temporary as in the case of drug intoxication or it may be permanent as in the case of syphilitic infection of the brain.

B. PSYCHOSOCIAL FACTORS

Psychosocial factors affecting mental health are numerous. It is difficult to list all the factors. Therefore, we will list only the major ones.

(i) Mental Deprivation

Faulty development has often been observed in infants deprived of mental stimulation (mothering) as a consequence of (a) separation from the mother and placement in an institution (b) lack of adequate mothering at home. All these conditions affect the mental health of children.

(ii) Institutionalization (Foster Homes)

In an institution infants do not get warmth, physical contact, intellectual, social and emotional stimulation necessary for healthy development. There is lack of encouragement and help in positive learning for children who are institutionalized in cary childhood. The long-rang effects of severe early deprivation of maternal love and stimulation are suggested by the findings of Beres and Overs (1950) in their study of 38 adolescents, 3 weeks 13 years institutionlized. At the time of the study 16 to 18 year after discharge from the orphanage 4 were diagnosed as psychotic, 21 had character disorder, 4 were mentally retarded, 2 neurotic and only 7 were normal.

(iii) Deprivation in Home

Home plays an important role in the development of personality. Maternal deprivation during infancy affects future development, if children get inadequate and distorted care, for instance negligence of the child, lack of proper attention and rejection of the child etc. Rubble 1945 reported that rejecting indifferent, or punishing mothers may cause tense, unsatisfied and negativistic behaviour among their infants even at a very early stage.

Severe and sustained maternal deprivation of children within the home can seriously retared intellectual, emotional, social and physical developments. The actual nature and extent of the damage resulting from maternal deprivation appears to depend on (a) the age at which deprivation occurs; (b) the extent and duration of such deprivation; (c) the constitutional make-up of the child; and (d) the substitute care.

(iv) Pathogenic Family Pattern

As already mentioned, the family plays a very crucial role in development during infancy. There are certain pàtterns of family relationship that affect the mental health of children. A brief description of the major ones is given below :

(a) Faulty Parent-Child Relationship

There are many faulty parent child relationship patterns that are harmful for the mental health of children.

(i) Rejection : Parents who reject their children do great harm to their proper development. Rejection may be physical neglect, denial of love and affection, lack of interest in the child's activities and achievements, harsh, inconsistent punishment and failure to spend time with the child.

(ii) Overprotection and Restrictiveness: Mental overprotection of the child from the slightest risk may hamper the child's growth. Jenkins reported in a study that children referred to clinics had overanxious, infantilizing mothers. Overprotective children suffer from exeessive fears. In the process of overprotection from every danger, the mothers deny neened opportunities for reality testing and development of essential competencies. In the same way over-restriction does not provide necessary freedom.

(iii) Over Permissiveness and Indulgence: Over indulged, over-permissive children are characterized as spoiled, selfish, inconsiderate and demanding. Seers reported that high permissiveness and low punishment in the home were correlated positively with antisocial aggressive behaviour.

(iv) Unrealistic Demands : Parents who place excessive pressure on their children to live upto unrealiftically high standards, also cause anxiety in the minds of children.

(*v*) *Faulty Discipline* : Severe or harsh discipline may have a variety of harmful effects on children. Faulty discipline may cause fear, hatred toward the punishing person and less friendly feelings towards others.

(*vi*) *Communication Failure* : Parents can discourage a child from asking questions and in other ways fail to foster the information exchange essential for healthy development.

(*vii*) *Undesirable Parental Model* Emotionally disturbed parents addicted to alcohol or drugs or otherwise maladjusted may provide undesirable model for children.

(*b*) *Maladaptive Family Structures*

Maladaptive behaviour may be fostered in children by general family environment as well as by the child's relationship with one or both parents Here we will describe four different patterns of family structures which may be detrimental to the healthy development of children.

(*i*) *The Inadequate Family*: This type of family is characterized by inability to cope with the ordinary problems of family living. It lacks the resources, physical and psychological, for meeting demands with which most families can cope. Such families rely heavily on continued outside assistance and support in resolving their problems.

The incompetency of such a family may stem from immaturity, lack of education, mental retardation or other shortcomings of the parents. Such families cannot give feelings of safety and security to their children.

(*ii*) *The Disturbed Family*: Parents with grossly eccentric and abnormal abilities may keep the home in constant emotional turmoil. Disturbed families are characterized by (a) the presence of parents who fight to maintain their own equilibrium and who fail to give the child needed love and guidance (b) exposure of the child to irritationality and faulty parental models and (c) almost inevitably, the enmeshment of the child in the emotional conflicts of the parents.

(*iii*) *The Antisocial Family*: Such a family inculcate values not accepted by the wider community. Children in such families are encouraged in dishonesty, deceit and other undesirable behaviours.

(*iv*) *The Disrupted Family* : Disrupted families are incomplete whether as a result of death, divorce, separation or some other conditions. The disrupted family fails to inculcate feelings of security and adequacy in children.

(*c*) *Early Psychic Trauma*

Every one of us has had traumatic experiences (death; seperation partition, flood, etc.) that shatter our feelings of security. adequacy and worth and are important in influencing our later behaviour.

(*d*) *Pathogenic Interpersonal Relationship*

It is a well-known fact that no two individuals are alike in their ability to give and receive love Marital and other intimate relationship fulfil many of our needs. In this section of the chapter we will describe the role of marital instability and other damaging interpersonal relationship in maladaptive behaviour.

(*i*) *Marital Instability*: It is the desire of most of the people in society to lead a happy married life but unfortunately this goal is not attained by the majority of the people. This is evident from the high rate of divorce, dowry-deaths and marital separation, bickering etc. in our society. Marital dissatisfaction and instability are not only frustrating to the parents but also place the children under additional stress often leading to dysfunctional parenting.

It is relevant to note that traditionally the Indian marriage system was based on certain moral principles and the authority was vested in the husband. But in morden society, marriage is viewed as a mutually need-fulfilling relationship.

To add to the difficulty, modern urbanization has led to the decline and disorganization of the old joint family system with its stable network of relationship and support. Thus it can be said that the old marital stability has been threatened in moderen society, leading a good majority of people to experience maladjustment.

TYPES OF PATHOGENIC RELATIONSHIP

Interpersonal relationships may be conducive either to need satisfaction and mental health or to personal distress maladaptive behaviour. There may be three types of pathogenic relationships that have serious detrimental effects on one or both partners.

(a) Fraudulent interpersonal contracts

This involves the terms of relationship being violated by one person in such a way as to exploit the other. The wife/husband may develop illicit relations with some other person to cause mental agony to the partner.

(b) Collusion

In this relationship the partners enter into a conspiracy to follow certain maladaptive rules and norms of their own choosing rather than socially established adaptive ones.

(c) Discordant interpersonal patterns

Serious and continued dissensions, disagreement, quarrels, and conflicts are detrimental to the quality and stability of the relationship as well as to the persons involved. Such types of discordant interactions may result when one or both partners do not play their agreed-upon roles in the relationship.

In other cases, one or both partners who are not gaining satisfaction from the relationship may express feelings of frustration in hostile ways such as nagging, teasing, belittling and doing things purposely to annoy the other partner. A common source of conflict and dissatisfaction stems from value differences of partners which may lead to serious disagreement on a variety of topics, including sexual behaviour and how money is spent. It has been observed that immature and maladjusted persons are likely to find it especially difficult to maintain successful intimate relations.

Severe stress

We have given above some of the sources of stressees which may cause maladaptive behaviour. There are certain other common sources of stress in our modern society which are directly relevant to the understanding of maladaptive behaviour. In our developing society, there are a number of frustrations that lead to self-devaluation. The important are :

(*i*) *Failure* : Cut throat competition in our society in every sphere of life almost inevitably leads to occasional failure by seting an unrealistically high goal or by undertaking new ventures without adequate preparation.

(*ii*) *Losses* : There are several losses that people inevitably experience—losses involving objects or individuals with whom they strongly identify. Loss of money, and social status tend to devalue an individual in his own eyes as well as in the eyes of others.

(*iii*) Personal limitations and lack of resources. Poverty is the root of all evils and is a powerful source of frustration. Physical handicaps and other personal limitations that restrict one's activities and attractiveness to members of the opposite sex can be highly stressful. Comparing oneself with others who are favourably endowed can unnecessarily increase frustration and self-devaluation.

(*iv*) *Guilt*: Behaving in ways that one considers immoral leads to both self-devaluation and apprehension. Guilt is more stressful if it seems that nothing can be done to rectify one's misdeeds.

(*v*) *Loneliness* : Some people experience painful feelings of loneliness and isolation at some time in their lives. Being unloved and lonely cause great frustation and anxiety in some people.

(vi) Value Conflicts : There are some core value conflicts that frequently lead to tension and inner turmoil that impair seriously the adjustive capacities.

(vii) Conformity Vs. Non-Conformity. Members generally under social pressure or discipline conform to the norms of groups. A problem which often proves deeply disturbing is when to conform or not to conform to gronp expectations and pressures. Blind conformity or pon-conformity is considered maladaptive.

(viii) Avoiding Vs. Facing Reality: People in modern society try to avoid facing reality. They live in a fool's paradise and thus deceive themselves.

Pressures of Modern Living

Following are the common pressures of modern life :

(i) Competition : There is cut-throat competition in all walks of life such as grades, sports, jobs, marital partners. In this competitive struggle we are encouraged to surpass others. This constant struggle to get success creates tension and anxiety.

(ii) Educational, Vocational and Family Demands : The long hours of study, the tension of examination and the sustained concentration of effort over many years results in considerable stress for many students. Occupational demands can also be highly stressful. Many jobs makes severe demands in terms of responsibility, time and performance. Marriage and family make demands on both partners, demands that may be especially stressful if either partner is immature and poorly perpared for the responsibilities involved.

(iii) Complexity and Pace of Modern Living : The mere complexity and rapid pace of modern living tend to overload the human organism. The stress of liviug under such highly complicated and demanding conditions can play havoc on both biological and psychological levels.

C. SOCIO-CULTURAL FACTORS

In addition to the above biological and psychosocial factors that have been listed, there are other conditions which affect mental health.

D. WAR AND VIOLENCE

War and violence have been the unavoidable evils of Indian society from time immemoral. The conditions of war and violence have place great stress on a large number of people. Privation, mutilation, death, grief and social disorganization have been inevitable accompaniments of war and violence.

Today we live in the shadow of the new and incredibly destructive nuclear instruments of modern war-fare which are becoming available to an increasing number of nations. It creates constant fear in the minds of people.

The partition of India and subsequent violence in the country created fear and anxiety in people.

Hindu-Muslim riots create a constant fear in people of both the communities. The Hindu-Sikh conflict of 1983-84 is bound to leave permanent scars on the minds of the people. The people of Punjab have been put under great stress and strain due to the state-wide movement by terrorists and extremists.

E. GROUP PREJUDICE AND DISCRIMINATION

One of the most destructive forms of group prejudice is that of communal feelings and discrimination on the basis of caste, creed and region. While this is loudly decried in our society, it seems to be among our most ingrained cultural habits. The whole of our society suffers as a result of this prejudice, but the victims lose most by it. Racial discrimination, poverty and social disorganization tend to debase and confuse human beings. Children reared in such a setting have the almost impossible task of trying to learn what is predictable and possible, of striving to develop healthy motives and values and of attempting to achieve educational and other competencies essential for effective participation in our society.

F. ECONOMIC AND EMPLOYMENT PROBLEMS

Inflation, unemployment and job dissatisfaction are sources of mental stress for many people in our society. Unemployment has placed a burden on a sizeable segment of our population bringing with it financial hardship and self-devaluation of educated young people. Depression, sucide, and crime increase due to unemployment.

Job dissatisfaction for those who are employed creates stress and anxiety, tention and a wide range of psycholosomatic disorders.

Accelerating technological and social changes have also placed new responsibilities to which adjustment is becoming a bit difficult for a society which is tradition and conservative in its outlook to change.

QUESTIONS FOR DISCUSSION

1. What are the hereditary factors that affect the mental health ?
2. Describe in brief the psychosocial factors which affect mental health ?
3. What are the major stresses of modern life ?
4. List the various factors that may cause frustration ?
5. What are the pressures of modern life ? Describe them.
6. What are the adverse relationship within the family that may affect the mental health of children ?

SUGGESTED READINGS

1. Achenbach, T. M. . Development Psychopathology, John Willey and Sons, NY, 1982.

2. Beck, Robert C. : Applying Psychology : Understanding People Prentice Hall, INC NY, 1982.

3. Cameron, N. : The Psychology of Abnormal Disorders, Hougliton Mifflin, NY, 1987.

4. Coleman, James, C. : Abnormal Psychology and Modern life, D. B. Taraporevala and Sons, Bombay, 1982.

5. White, R. W. et. al. : The Abnormal Personality, 5th ed., John Wiley and Sons, NY, 1981.

CHAPTER 4

Adjustment and Adjustment Problems

Observe the behaviour of any person from morning till evening and you will find that most of his behaviour represents attempts to fulfil his needs which may be either physical, psychological or social. The process of needs arousal continues through out the life of human beings. This process of needs arousal and their satisfaction is, in a broad sense, adjustment.

Psychology is the science of behaviour, Adjustment constitutes an important part of this science. Psychology attempts to understand, to control and to explain the dynamics of complex interprersonal hnman behaviour. It álso enables us to improve our understanding of the ways in which the people meet the changes of daily life.

Historically, the concept of adjustment was biological and was the corner stone of Darwin's theory of evoluation who maintianed that only those organisms that are fitted to adapt to the hazards of the ever-changing physical environment, survive. He propounded the theory of "Survival of the Fittest" in the continuous struggle going on among different living beings. The behaviour of organism can rightly be described as reactions to a variety of demands or pressures that are brought to bear upon them in their environment. A great deal of human behaviour can be explained in terms of human actions as adaptation to various kinds of physical demands. Just as a person adapts to physical demands, he also adjusts to psychosocial demands that emerge in the interactional processes with other persons in society. The biologically originated concept of adaptation was borrowed by psychologists and renamed as adjustment because they are primarily more concerned with psychological adjustment than physical adaptation of human beings in society.

Human behaviour is interpreted as adjustment to demands which are basically psychosocial and influence the personality development of human beings to a great extent. The psychological demands to which a person makes adjustment may be external or internal. There is a large number of internal and external demands that arise in the course of life and require adjustment to the conditions of the environment.

From the psychological point of view, however, those demands and pressures which arise out of our existence as social beings are of greater importance. The demands in early childhood are simple, mostly physiological, such as food, water, and oxygen etc., but become more subtle and complex during adolsescence and adulthood when the individual's socialization is completed. The compliance of the demands leads to approval and positive consequences. On the other hand non-compliance of demands of any type leads to disapproval and negative consequences.

Human beings are born with a number of internal needs for example need for food, water, oxygen, and elimination, etc., the frustration of which leads to discomfort and sometimes to death. Many of these are physiological needs and in the course of development additional internal needs emerge, which are primarily social rather than physiological in nature.

Adjustment has been interpreted in two ways i.e.. adjustment as achievement, and adjustment as a process. Adjustment may be defined as, "A state of life when the individual is more or less in harmony with personal, biological, social and psychological needs and with demands of the physical environment."

Another definition of adjustment has been given in the Dictionary of Behavioural Sciences by Wolman : "Adjustment is harmonious relationship with the environment involving the ability to satisfy most of one's needs and meet most of the demands, both physical and social that are put upon one."

According to White, "Adjustment represents a compromise between the needs of the individual and demands of the society in which he lives. Individual tendencies must be restricted and channelled in certain directions if the person is to function as a member of the social organism......"

In brief we can say that adjustment is perfect relationship with the environment involving the satisfaction of all types of needs of the individuals and meeting satisfactorily most of the demands that are put upon them.

In the next para we will examine the various views on the concept of adjustment.

VIEWS ON ADJUSTMENT

To develop an adequate understanding of the psychological concept of adjustment, it is necessary to adopt some more or less consistent view point concerning basic human nature. Here we will describe human nature under three headings : the moral view, the phenomenological and behavioural or social learning view.

The Moral View

Every society in the course of its development evolves certain moral values which are transmitted to the next generations. These moral values provide guidelines for human behaviour and a criteria for evaluating the quality of one's adjustment in society. Now let us first examine the views of western philosophers as regards the basic moral view point. Popular Christian thought has considered human beings basically evil. It has defined the goal of human life as return to the state of grace from which they (Adam and Eve) fell. This is done by following a prescribed set of moral rules which comprehensively cover all behaviours and even the thoughts and feelings of individuals. Transgressions of the moral code by individuals are reported either to God or to his representative on earth. It is worth mentioning, however, that Protestants (a sect of Christians) have emphasized human capacity for change, implying that our ability to adapt to the demands of life is to a large degree within our own control.

Freud, one of the most influential psycho-analysts in the study of human adjustment took the view that people are governed by instinctive or biologically based forces of the negative type. One of his most important constributions was his adaptation of the theologically based notion of human beings, as evil to the psychologically based notion of 'bad motives'. In the process of socialization one learns socially acceptable ways to discharge his energies.

Neo-Freudians place much less emphasis on the biological or innate components of basic human needs. They are concerned more with needs produced by the demands of the interpersonal and social environment. Another group of psychologists who are referred to as ego-psychologists have disputed Freud's view that human nature is innately evil. They have emphasized the importance of the adaptive and rational capacities of human beings.

Contemporary investigators have offered another alternative to Freud's position on human moral nature. In the humanistic view people are seen not as innately evil but as good. According to Maslow, "The best of most well-adjusted people are those who have developed successfully through their formative stages and have reached the highest stage—self-actualization in which their basic potentials are expressed most fully and completely".

The Phenomenological View

Phenomenologists argue that the behaviour of human beings can only be understood through the internal frame of reference of the behaviour.

According to them it is not possible to decide for another person which behaviours are adjustive and which are not. Only the behaving individual can evaluate the adequacy of his behaviour, using his own unique frame of reference. Moral absolutes differ from culture to culture and hence cannot be generalised from individual to individual.

This view emphasizes that individuals see the world through the selective filter of their own unique view points and their own phenomental fields. In order to predict an individual's behaviour, it is thus necessary to have a knowledge of his phenomenal fields. Each person's phenomenal field is constantly being restructured according to changing needs. Parts of it, however, include relatively stable self-perceptions which form the self-concept.

The fundamental force motivating all behaviour is to preserve and enhance the phenomenal self. In other words we can say that behaviour is adaptive if it meets the needs of the individual as perceived by him. A specific phenomenological position regarding adjustment is offered by Existentialists who argue that we are each individually and uniquely responsible for our own destiny. Man is the master of his destiny. Each person decides upon a particular path of action. Life is a constant series of decisions, some of which may appear trival. It is the pattern of these decisions and their consequences that really determines the quality of the individual's adjustment to his environment. In making these decisions, the individual's free will is empbasized above environmental influences. Past experiences or internal psychological or biological state also play an important role. Each person decides his own fate and is responsible for the consequences of the decisions that are made by him.

The Social Learning View

Social learning approaches the study of human adjustment as the study of problem solving or coping behaviour. By coping we mean the degree to which individuals are able to meet and master at least three challenges to their existence (a) direct challenges from the physical environment (b) challenges stemming from their limitations and (c) interpersonal challenges from the environment.

Direct challanges include the adequacy or skill with which the individual copes with physical realities of the environment. The second type of challenges involve responess to their own physical and intellectual limitations such as physical weakness, defective vision and hearing etc and limited capacity for problem solving. The third group of challenges includes those posed by the interpersonal environment: How adequately they interact with others to satisfy their personal needs and how they cope with psychological demands made by others.

In brief we can say the social-learning view of adjustment regards an individual's adjustive capacity as the ability to meet and cope with stresses and problems with a minimum of disruption to the on-going process of life considering both the immediate and long term consequences of the behaviour.

The social learning view analyses behaviour in terms of the needs which precede the behaviour and the consequences of satisfying these needs. In general, the social learning view offers a comprehenensive yet theoretically simple approach to the understanding of human behaviour. Before we discuss adjustment as process and adjustment as achievement let us in brief examine the need to study adjustment.

The greatest need to study adjustment, in a fast changing society, is to prepare the individuals by providing guidance and counselling to cope with the ever increasing problems in society. The second need which has been felt due to the revolutionary changes brought about by socio-economic conditions, unprecedented growth in population and scientific advancement is to study the nature of the problems and to develop appropriate strategies to prevent the mushroom growth of adjustment problems in society and to enhance the resistance of the individuals to maintain their adjustment.

(a) Adjustment as Achievement

There are two aspects of adjustment. The first has to do with quality or efficiency. Adjustment is regarded as an achievement, which is accomplished either badly or well. It makes possible the comparison of individuals in terms of their adjustive adequacy in society. This makes sense to businessmen, to military leaders and to educators who deal with human beings.

Critreia of Good Adjustment

Certain criteria have been evolved to assess the adequacy of adjustment of an individual to his environment. For example, the following characteristics are important to assesss adjustment as achievement.

(i) Psychological Comfort

One of the most compelling signs of adjustive failure is that a person is psychologically uncomfortable in someway. Discomfort may include states of depression, acute anxiety, obsessive, thoughts of guilt or fear of illness etc. Experiencing discomfort often implies some inadequacy in psychological adjustment. A person who is free from all types of psychological disorders may be termed as having good adjustment.

(ii) Work efficiency

Another sign of adjustive difficulties is impaired ability to make full use of social capacities. Therefore, it is implied that a person must have full work efficiency for normal adjustment.

(iii) Physical symptoms

Sometimes, the only evidence of inadequate adjustment appears in the form of damage to body tissues. A normal and well-adjusted person must not suffer from any physical symptoms.

(iv) Social Acceptance

Some kind of adjustments are socially acceptable—that is, they are what other persons want.

Norman Tallen: has suggested the following criteria for good adjustment.

(*a*) *Good Subjective Feelings*

A well-adjusted person must be free from neurotic fears and anxiety and must feel psychologically comfortable. The individual sees a meaning in his life.

(*b*) *Personal and Social Achievement* :

The individual should be able to develop his potentialities to the maximum for his own benefit and for the welfare of society. He should be able to achieve self-actualization, the ultimate goal of life. He should establish good relations in society in conformity with the norms of the society. But R. D. Laing says about conformity, "Some degree of conformity is, of course, necessary in any organized society, and it is over-conformity that is likely to be seen as "dehumanizing and psychological sickness "

(*c*) *Ability to work*

Adjustment refers to the performance of physical and mental work satisfactorily in accordance with one's capacities.

(B) Adjustment as process

The process of adjustment starts from the birth of the child and continues throughout life. The nature of the adjustment of an individual is governed by biological factors as well as the social experiences which he receives in his environment.

The broad types of adujstive process

When a conflict occurs between an individual's internal needs and external demands, two broad clauses of adjustment patterns seem to be possible. The individual can modify or inhibit the internal impulse or he can attempt to alter the environmental demand in some way so as to eliminate the conflict. With respect to biological adaptation the organism can modify his own state in some way or attempt to alter the environment.

The two general adjustive modes which people use have also been recognized by psychologists. For example, Piaget who has been greatly concerned with the adjustive process has used the terms accommodation and assimilation to represent the alternation of oneself or the environment respectively as means of adjustment. Both accommodation and assimilation produce resolution of conflicts. It is interesting that as we move up the phylogentic scale from the lower animals to human beings we find an increase in the availability of means of assimilating. For examples, lower organisms such as insects and worms, mushtroomed in the rainy season, die as soon as winter starts because they do not possess the capacity to adapt to changing conditions of the winter season in comparison to human beings.

Adjustment as process is a dynamic, complex and continuing process through which individuals respond to their ever changing needs and desires with a variety of behaviour in order to adjust adequately in their social environment.

The process of adjustment involves two important facrors (a) the individual, his characteristics including needs and desires as well as the competencies and skills to fulfil those needs (b) the situation in which individuals find themselves and the demands placed upon them by that situation.

Now let us explain the dynamics of the adjustment process with the help of an explaint a child at birth has some biological needs and a repertoire of behaviours by which these needs can be satisfied. This hungry infant can cry to signal its hunger and can consume and digest the food which is offered to him. As socicalization progresses, a variety of other needs emerge with the responses for their gratification. Thus gradually in the process of social interaction, the child learns to need or desire the approval of its parents and peers and also comes to learn the skills for becoming a useful member of society. Both the learning of new needs and learning of the skills and competencies to gratify those needs are dependent on the previous learning experiences of the individual so that the process of adjustment can be seen as a continuous one, best understood in a developmental context as the individual progresses through life. Whenever people encounter a new situation, they bring to in their own unique developmental history of experienced needs and need gratifications plus the experiences and skills which they may be able to exercise in this new situation. They respond to the new situation not as passive observers but as active participants. For example, students entering a university come with some psycholgical needs that are a result of their previous social learning. They know how these needs have been satisfied in the past and how they might be satisfied in the new situation. It will depend on the past experiences of the students as to how adequately they adjust in the new environment. People who have a reasonable idea of the nature of their own needs and the best ways of meeting them, experience no difficulty in the process of adjustment. But there are times, however, when we are faced with situations in which the demands are high and we lack the competence to deal effectively with them. These situations often involve new and unusual demands such as accidents, death of a family member, failure of business, natural calamities, and war, etc., for which coping skills have simply not been developed in previous circumstances. Such situations are called psychological crises. Since psychological crises are rare events it is difficult to predict how any given individual will respond to them in a satisfactory manner.

At any moment, an individual with needs and modes of gratifying them will find that the environment is also making demands. The effectiveness with which people continue to meet their own needs and also respond to the demands of the situation provides one important index of the affectiveness of their psychological adjustment. When the demands of the situation are congruent with the person's needs, there is no problem. However, when there is conflict between the person's needs and the demands of the situation, the effectiveness of their adjustment is put to test.

The effectively adjusted individuals will carefully evaluate both sides – the situation and its demands and their own needs and resources to meet them. Since adjustment is a continuous process, people's needs at any moment of time, there level of need gratification, resources to meet new situations and perception of new situations are all determined by what has gone before.

Now we will list the major and common adjustment problems of childhood, adolescence and adulthood.

ADJUSTMENT PROBLEMS

According to psychologists, the foundation of human behaviour is laid down in early childhood which sets the personality pattern for later stages of development. The early interaction of the child within the family plays a crucial role in the adjustment process. A child who feels insecure and inadequate in his family due to faulty attitudes and behaviour of parents or significant others may develop emotional problems which may lead to maladjustment. This part of the chapter deals with adjustment problems of children and adolescents. The reader should keep in mind that here only common problems of the two stages have been listed.

CHILDHOOD PROBLEMS

1. Eating Problems

It has been observed that many children develop eating problems such as loss of appetite, overeating, etc. These problems are caused by emotional or other psychological factors. There is a great need to study carefully the eating problem of children to find their solution.

2. Sleeping Problems

Some children develop sleeping problems, for example, bed-time patterns, restless and disturbed sleep and sleep-walking (somnambulism). These problems are created by emoti onal disturbances and feelings of insecurity and anxiety in children.

3. Elimination Problem

One of the earliest problems which results from improper handling of children by parents is elimination problem. This problem is created by parental attitude and emotiona disturbances.

4. Tension Problem

Bad-habit patterns which are manifested in children's behaviour are the symptoms of deep emotional disturbances. Through these bad habits children release their deep rooted tension. The major tension problems of children are.

1. Excessive crying, enuresis, nightmares, schoolphobia.
2. Thumb sucking
3. Nail biting
4. Temper-tantrums, overdependence on parents
5. Tics
6. Stammering and stuttering, stealing, delinquency.
7. Aggression and destructiveness, social isolation.
8. Showing off
9. Timidity
10. Hyperactivity, low frustration tolerance
11. Learnining difficulties etc.

The above mentioned problems are major. There may be great variations in the problems of individuals.

PROBLEMS OF ADOLESCENTS

Adolescence is a period of rapid changes in all dimensions of development. Changes in behaviour are accompained by problems and potential difficulties. Increased complexity of our social and economic developments due to the use of modern technology have created many adjustment problems that did not exist in the past.

Classification of Problems

Laycock grouped all problems of adolescents as under :

1. Problems of adjustment to changing physical growth and physiological development.
2. Becoming emancipated from family and free from emotional dependence on parents.
3. Accepting own characteristic sex-role and making adjustment to the opposite sex.
4. Finding and ensuring a suitable vocation; and
5. Developing some sort of philosophy which will give meaning and purpose to life.

Charlotte Pope studied the problems of adolescents by means of essays written by about 2000 adolescents. She grouped the problems as under :

1. Studying learning relationship
2. Occupational adjustment
3. Personal adjustment
4. Home life relationship
5. Social adjustment
6. Health problems.

Purdue University conducted an opinion poll on 15000 teen agrees and classified problems as :

1. Health and physical development.

2. Finances. living conditions and employment.
3. Social and recreational activities.
4. Sex and marriage.
5. Social, psychological relations.
6. Personal psychological relations.
7. Morals and religion.
8. Home and family.
9. Future educational and vocational problems.
10. Adjustment to school work.
11. Curriculum and teaching procedures.

PROBLEMS FREQUENTLY REPORTED

The following problems have been reported more frequently by adolescents.

1 Educational adjustment

It has been reported by various studies that about 50 per cent of adolescent problems in high schools pertain to education. The specific problems are : (i) Dislike for study, (ii) Fear of failure, (iii) Restlessness in class, (iv) Low grade in the examination, (v) Fear of speaking in the class, (vi) Too much work, (vii) Dislike for school, (viii) Partial behaviour of teachers, (ix) Groupism on the basis of caste, creed and religion.

2. Home Adjustment

Development in socio-economic conditions due to the introduction of technology have created a number of problems for the new generation of youth in home and society. Indian parents have not changed their traditionala ttitudes towards their adolescent sons and daughters. In the majority of cases parents are responsible for the problems. Four types of problems are reported as under :

1. Involving restriction on their freedom.

2. Problems due to lack of understanding between parents and adolescents.

3. Problems involving money.

4. Home atomosphere.

The most acute problems are being treated as a small child by parents, no fun with parents, keeping secrets from the adolescent, parents working too hard for livelihood and poverty,

3. Financial Problems

Financial problems include :

1. Wanting to earn money.

2. Learning to spend money.

3. Asking for money.

4. Learning how to save money.

5. Having no regular allowance.

6. Less money than needed (poverty of parents).

7. Too few nice clothes.

4. Health Adjustment

Boys are more curious about practising good health than girls. Girls manifest more concern over sex guidance. The frequently checked problems are: (a) weak eyes (b) lack of physical strength (c) frequent headache (d) underweight (e) poor teeth (f) lack of height (g) poor complexion (h) frequent colds (i) fatigue.

5. Vocational Adjustment

Adolescents are very much concerned about their future vocation. The problems are selection of vocational preference, and preparation for a vocation.

6. Personal-social problems

1. Worry
2. Daydreaming
3. Nervousness
4. Feeling of guilt
5. Ill-behaviour by others.

7. Hetrosexuality

Many problems involve boy-girl relationship during adolescence.

1. Boys do not have a girl friend, bashful to ask for date; do not know how to keep girls interested in them.
2. Girls do not have a boy friend; feel as if they are not popular; do not know how to keep boys interested.

As we know our society is a traditional and closed one. So we do not allow our adolescent boys and girls to mix freely but the fact remains that boys and girls are attracted to each other and are curious to know more about the member of the opposite sex.

8. Philosophy of life

Growth through adolescence is accompanied by wider social contacts, increased mental ability and understanding as a changed physiological self. Thus, moral, religious, social problems, economic problems future aspirations and the standpoints from which they were earlier viewed undergo dramatic changes during adolscence.

An investigation into the adjustment problems of Adolescents in relation to their sex and age was conducted by J. P. Sharma (H. P. U. Simla). The conclusions of the study are :

— Boys and girls of age-group 14-15 seem to be better adjusted as compared to the boys and girls of age-group 16-17.

— Girls of age-group 14-15 are more adjusted as compared to girls of age-group 16-17.

— Boys and girls are equally adjusted in the same are group; 16-17.

Another study of social-emotional and educational adjustment among academically high and low achievers was conducted by M. L. Dutt (1978). The main conclusions of the study are :

— Boys and girls are equally adjusted in their social environment irrespective of their academic achievement.

— Academic achievement has no relevance to the social environment.

— In the field of emotional adjustment the study revealed that boys and girls are equally adjusted.

— There is significant effect of sex on educational adjustment.

— High achiever boys and girls are better adjusted.

Girls are better adjusted educationally as compared to boys. There is positive effect of academic achievement upon educational adjustment.

QUESTIONS FOR DISCUSSION

1. Define adjustment. What are the different views of adjustment
2. What are the criteria of good adjustment ?
3. What are the adjustment problems of adolescents ?
4. Write a brief essay on the adjustment problems of children ?

SUGGESTED READINGS

Atwater, Eastwood: Psychology of Adjustment; Prentice-Hall, NY, 1979.

Shaffer, L.F. : The Psychology of adjustment; Harper, London, 1935.

Tallent, Norman: Psychology of Adjustment; D. Van Nostrand, NY, 1979.

Lazaraus, R. S. : Patterns of Adjustment, McGraw Hill, 1976.

Vander & Zenden, James W. : Human Development; Alfred A. Knoph. NY., 1978.

CHAPTER 5

Adjustive Demand (Stresses)

There would be no problem of adjustment of one's needs were automatically gratified in society without resistence. But life is not so simple. Modern society is plagued with a number of problems in all walks of life. Obstacles and barries come in the way of fulfilment of needs causing frustration and tension in the minds of people. Frustration may be casud either by personal factors operating within the individual or environmental factors or by their interplay.

Adjustive demands (stresses) may be caused by a number of factors which may affect the mental health of people and if stress continues for a long period it may lead to maladjustment. This chapter deals with types of stresses and their causes.

Definition of stress

It is very difficult to define precisely the term stress because it has been differently used in psychological literature and no two psychologists agree on a single definition of the term. Stress is something external, like the pressure to compete on athletes. There is no doubt that much of our stress comes from expectations and demands of others but a great deal of it also comes from the way we react to these demands. Just think of the inner feelings of frustration, conflict and anxiety that complicate our responses to others ! Dr. Selye, who devoted much of his research to the study of stress, points out that whenever our bodies respond to any specific demand like an injury, there is also an increased non-specific demand for adaptation made on us as well. He defines stress as, "the rate of wear and tear on the body." Stress is defined by Dr. Peter in his book. "*How to Cope with Stress*", (1983) as; the reaction of mind and body to change".

Another way that stress may be defined is by combining stimulus and response. It is defined as any adjustive demand that requires an adaptive response from us. Alternatively stress is : "The non-specifie result of any demand upon the body". Stress is an inevitable part of modern life where at every step the individual has to face cut-throat competition in the society.

Stress may be of two types; positive and negative. Positive stress is not harmful whereas negative stress is injurious to the mental health of the individual.

Stressful events, according to Bowers and Kelly, are characterized by (a) a loss of control over events felt by people in their lives, (b) there is an anticipation or occurrence of physical or psychological pain. For example, the individual fears being injured or killed or is threated with a loss of self-esteem (c) there is loss of social or emotional support. In a disaster, friends or relatives may be missing or killed. Less dramatic events such as divorce, jobless, or marriage may separate indivlduals from family members and old friends (d) the event or some aspects of it is perceived as unplesant and aversive and the individual tries to avoid it.

Effects of Stress

Stress whether positive or negative has a deep influence on the development of the personality of the individual. The following are some of the effects of stress on human beings.

(1) Predisposition to illness

There is sufficient empirical support that continuous stress makes an individual more vulnerable to physical and mental illness. Continued stress may cause cancer and other fatal diseases. The stress may caused by socially undesirable events such as divorce, change of job, death of one's spouse, etc. Prolonged stress may cause mental disorders of severe type resulting in complete isolation of the person from society.

(2) Lowering of adaptive efficiency

Severe continued stress may alter the body's ability to fight with invading viruses. Adaptive efficiency may also be affected by the intense emotion that commonly accompanies severe stress.

Individual factors also affect one's experience of psychological stress. According to one study men with personality characteristics of intense drive, aggressiveness, ambition, competitiveness and the pressure for getting things done are three times more likely to have heart attacks in middle age than those who are equally but are easy going.

(3) Self-esteem

People with low self-esteem may find moderate criticism of their work highly threatening while people with high self-esteem find the same criticism helpful in improving their skills.

(4) Perception of work

Tolerance of stress varies from person to person depending on their personality characteristics. A high level of chronic anxiety or poor physical health predisposes one to low stress tolerance.

(5) Depression

In a stressful situation, the individual may experience depression.

(6) Sleep disturbances and tension

Stress may cause sleep disturbances in the individual. Tension and headache, are also caused.

(7) Anxiety

Stressful events create feelings of anxiety in people and children become more nervous and excited.

(8) Loss of appetite

The individual under stress experiences a loss of appetite.

Types of psychological stress

Human beings react to a great number of stimulus situations in their day to day life. They react as a whole and therefore it is difficult to differentiate between different forms of stress. However, two categories of stress have been mentioned in psychological literature (a) biological and (b) psychological. Since the present book deals with mental hygiene we will describe only psychological stress which is caused by frustration, conflict, pressure and anxiety. A brief description of them is given below.

1. FRUSTRATION

Human beings and even animals have been victims of frustration since life on earth by not being able to attain the goals they have set for themselves. But in recent years the incidences of frustration have tremendously increased due to a number of variables, such as cut-throat competition, growth of population urbanization and change in socio-economic conditions in society This has created a feeling of anxiety in the minds of all thos who are concerned with the welfare of society.

The term frustration has been differently defined by psychologists. It is not possible here to reproduce all the definitions of frustration. Therefore a sample approach will be followed.

According to one psychologist, frustration is, "The denial or thwarting of motives by obstacles which lie between needs and goal."

"Frustration is the emotional state resulting from being blocked, thwarted or defeated."

"Frustration is that condition which exists when a goal response suffers interference."

Maier says "We prefer to limit the term frustration to designate the state where continued failure causes learning function to case-operating and other mechanisms of adjustment being operating."

Rosenzweig defined it saying "Frustration occurs whenever the organism meets more or less insurmountable obstacles or obstruction in its route to the satisfaction of any vital need." If we analyse the underlying idea of the above definitions of frustration, we find that all psychologists agree on its general nature. Human beings have three types of needs, namely biological, psychological and social which motivate them to reach a particular goal. When motivated behaviour is locked by an obstacle, tension is produced and it continues as long as a barrier is present. But frustration occurs only when the organism meets hindrances which are difficult or impossible to overcome. In other words when progress toward a motivated goal is blocked by an insurmountable barrier before the goal is achieved and the underlying tension unresolved, it results in frustration. The mechanism of frustration may be explained with the help of the following figure.

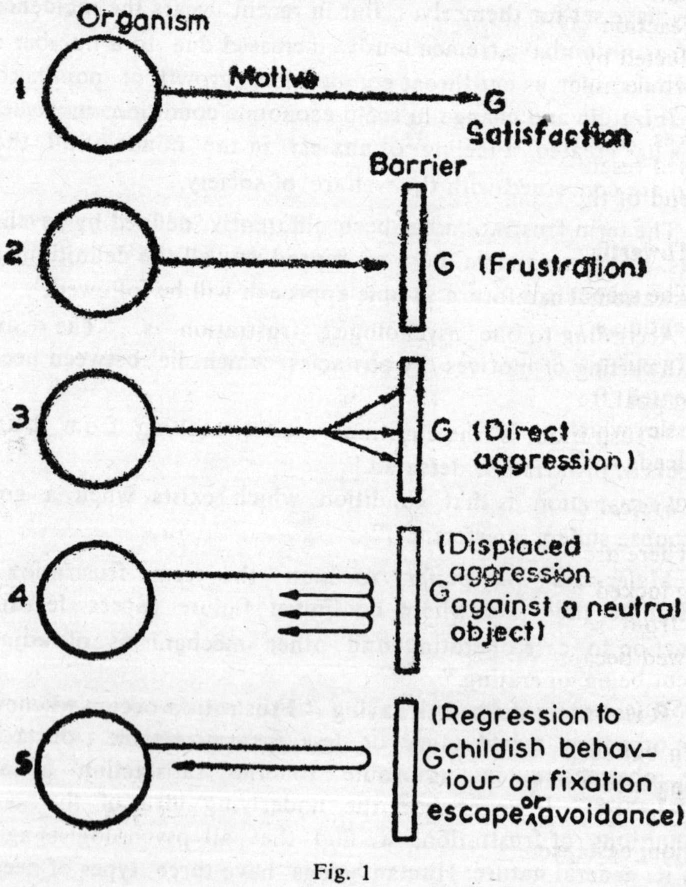

Fig. 1

Operations of Frustration

(a) Withholding reinforcement

The first operation of frustration refers to withholding of reinforcement that ordinarily occurs from an organism that has already been conditioned in a particular way. Frustration occurs when a response is regularly reinforced and then all of a sudden extinguished. This operation causes frustration by delay. The delay in reinforcement may vary from slight to an indefinite period of time. This operation of frustration has been experimentally studied by Seers and associates. An exp rime to know the reaction to frustration by withholding reinforcement was conducted by him. A group of college students was kept awake the whole night During this period the students were subjected to a series of futher frustrations such as being forbidden to smokes. Also, food was withheld from them. The students expressed resentment and aggression towards the experimenter at the end of the experiment.

(b) Thwarting

The second operation of frustration refers to mechanically preventing a response from occurring. It means that at point of an organism's activity, a barrier is introduced and behaviour is prevented from occurring. Following is the list of common obstacles which prevent the organis n from reaching its goal and leads to frustration.

(i) Physical Obstacles :

There are several types of physical obstacles such as a door being locked to prevent entry into a room, a guard preventing one from seeing an officer, a lower prevented from seeing belowed because of restrictions imposed.

(ii) Socio-economic barriers :

In our society wide gaps in sncio-economic conditions exist. Young men and women are preventen from reaching their goals because of these barriers Marriages are prevented because of religion, caste, socio-economic status and educational barriers.

(*iii*) *Sources from the self* :

The source of thwarting may also come from the person himself. His physical handicap, low intellectual abilities and undesirable personality etc. may thwart the fulfilment of his needs and may cause frustration.

(*iv*) *Authority* :

The behaviour of other person may operate as a source of constant frustration. Parents' negative attitude towards their children may create frustration, Sometimes people in authority are authcratic and unfair with their juniors and may create frustration in their minds.

(*v*) *Minority Groups* :

India is a country with a population of 700 millions consist of hundreds of minority groups. Members of particular minority group when discriminated against and made to feel inadequate and unwanted experience a high degree of frustration which may result in maladjustment.

(*vi* *Natural calamities*

Natural calamities such as floods, partition, drought, epidemics, earthquakes and wars etc. may prevent the fulfilment of needs and cause frustration.

2. CONFLICTS

Human beings have to achieve several motives in their lives. Sometimes it so happens that two motives of equal violence. conflict with each other and the achievement of one of the motives leads to the blocking of the other. It becomes difficult for the individual to choose one of the motives when each motive offers values that the other does not and the choice is an important one.

The conflicts with which every one has to cope with may be classified as follows :

(a) Approach-approach conflict

This type of conflict involves competition betweecn two

desirable goals. The individual experiences a conflicting situation in which he fails to make an immediate decision. For example a boy who is selected for both the IPS and the IAS may be involved in an approach-approach conflict and decision-making becomes stressful The approach-approach conflict situation moy also be illustrated by widely known fable of Aesop's ass when he saw bundles of hay at equal distance on his right and left sides. It said that the ass died in conflict.

(i) G ←—————— C ——————→ G
+ +

(b) Approach-avoidance conflict

It involves the strong tendency both to approach and to avoid the same goal. For example, a woman may want to marry for sexual, social and security reasons but at the sametime wants to avoid the responsibilities of married life.

(ii) C ←——————→ G
±

(c) Avoidance-avoidance conflict

It refers to the situation when two unattractive alternatives operate simultaneously, and the individual attempts to avoid the situation. A boy who is weak in studies is reluctant to attend school but at the same time if he stays at home, he is rebuked by his parents.

(iii) G ←—————— C ——————→ G
— —

Conflicts can be resolved with the help of several techniques, such as understanding, use of minor tranquilizers, psychotherapy and yoga therapy which will be discussed in subsequent section.

3. PRESSURE

Stress may stem not only from frustration and conflicts, but also from pressure to achieve a particular goal or to behave in a particular way. Pressure may be external or internal. For example, a college student may feel under severe pressure to achieve good grade because his parents demand it. Internal pressure generally originates from our ambitious and goals which we set for ourselves. For example, a boy wants to become an

IAS officer. To achieve his goal he remains under constant pressure All of us experience pressure from the 'shoulds' and 'oughts' of our ideal-self or conscience at one time or another. It has been seen that sometimes a pressure motivates us to do our best or to change the direction of our goal oriented behaviour. Pressures are generelly handled without much difficulty in our daily life but if they become excessive they may lead to break-down of organized behaviour.

4. ANXIETY

Anxiety is an old concept which has been the subject of debote among philosophers from the dawn of civilization Here we need not trace the philosophical history of the term anxiety since we are primarily concerned with the psychological concept of the term. Freud was the first psychologist who developed a scientific theory of anxiety in 1917.

Every human being experiences anxiety in his day to day life For example, students face anxiety when they appear at the examination; a candidate experiences anxiety when he is called for an interview.

The term anxiety has been used in different situations with different interpretation. It is very difficult to provide a undersally acceptable definition of anxiety. However, an effort will be mace to develop an objective definition by examining various studies conducted in the field.

Modern civilization with its highly developed technology has rightly been termed the age of anxiety. There is hardly an individual who has not experienced moments of anxiety in his life. Some examplas will clarify the concept more clearly.

Students are very anxious about their results candidates are anxious about getting a job; parents are anxious about the future of their sons and daughters, so on add so forth.

Anxiety has boen explained by some psychologists as a basic human emotion which cannot be avoided entirely in modern society. It may be termed as a disturbing feeling that arises as a result of one's own, or of the possibility of failing to meet, some preceived external standard.

Definitions

Sattre has defined anxiety as, "A fear of failure to meet a standard or fear that one does not hold the appropriate standard".

Madler and Watson : "Anxiety occurs when an individual is interrupted in the course of executing a desired behaviour sequence and has not an alternative course of action available. The result of interruption is an emotion of helplessness and disorganization which we call anxiety".

Sullivan: "Anxiety is a state of tension existing when one apprehends an unfavourable estimate bo a significant person".

May defines anxiety as, "The apprehension cued off by threat to some value which the individual holds essential to his existence as a personality."

Natrajan defined anxiety as, "An exaggerated fear state" Beck defined anxiety as an "unpleasant emotion that is accompanied by automatic discharge and subjectively experienced as tension or nervousness.

Components of Anxiety

The unanimity has not so far been achieved as regard the meaning of the term anxiety. There are certain terms which are used interchangeably with anxiety. We will consider each of these terms in turn to bring out differences among them.

Anxiety and fear

Anxiety and fear both appear to be the same but there are differences between the two. Sattre distinguishes between anxiety and fear as anxiety has an internal object whersas fear has an external object. Fear is an avoidance reaction directly related to a specific object, event or object whereas anxiety is not, It is a rather value and diffuse apprehension not directly related to any object or situation. Goldstein distinguishes fear from anxiety, as, "In fear there is an appropriate defense reaction, a bodily expression of tension and of extreme attention to a certain part of the environment. In anxiety, on the other hand, we find meaningl ss frenzy, with rigid or distorted expression accompanied by withdrawal from the world, a shut-off affectively, in the light of which the world appears irrelevant and any reference to the world, any useful perception and action suspended",

Another important distinction between fear and anxiety is that in fear the individual reacts to therats in the immediate si'auation whereas in anxiety the emotional reaction manifests itself as a dread of some future danger. This pattern of anticipating trouble is sometimes referred to as worry.

Horney, a Neo-Freudian psychoanalyst distinguishes between fear and anxiety by saying that the later entails feelings of diffuseness and an admission of helplessness in the face of a dangerous situation. She makes clear the difference between fear and enxiety with the help of a story : "A mother and her young daughter were living together in a house. One night both of them work up to the sounds of burglars breaking into the living room. The mother got frightened and went into her daughter's room. Meanwhile the daughter who also got up was also afraid but decided to go into the living room to look up. By going up to the living room and by the process of opening the door she was able to make the thieves understand that some one was around to catch them or chase them out. So they fled from the house " According to Norney, the daughter experienced fear while her mother experienced anxiety."

Phobia

A phobia is an irrational and unwarranted fear of some object or situation where the actual possible of harm to the individual is rather slight. Phobia in the majority of cases, is acquired in early childhood and continues throughout life until and unless properly deconditioned.

Worry

Worry is a vague and poorly defined term in psyholoaical literature. Worry may be defined as anxiety experienced by an individual thinking about a difficult personal problem who can see no immediate solution to the problem. Worry often attaches to events that are unpredictable—an unforeseeable accident which may be-fall the individual or significant others and may cause worry. Worry can interfere with the normal functioning of the individual and can pose serious mental health problems, if it continues for a long period.

Tension

Tension is also vaguely and poorly defined in books. It is, of course, closely related to anxiety. Tension is referred to as increase in muscle touns as part of physiological changes involved in anxiety.

Stress

Stress and anviety are also termed as synonymus with each other. Stress may refer to (1) certain characteristics of the environment such as taking an examination (a) reactions of the individual (3) characteristics of the individual situation and response of the persons (4) characteristics of individuals the account for their behaviour.

A stresssful situation is one where it is expected that anxiety will be aroused. In other words we may say that situations that are stressful are anxiety-arousing and stress reactions are anxiety reactions.

Shame and Guilt

Both are similar in some respects as both refer to the anxiety aroused by violating a cultural normal norm or taboo. However, there is also difference between the two. The behavioural pattern of shame is accompanied by the lowering of the head and eyes and blushing while guilt does not have a single, readily identifiable behavioural pattern response.

Shame refers to the anxiety that is experienced when an individual feels that other people will disapprove of his behaviour whereas guilt is the anxiety experienced when one disapproves of his own behaviour.

Psychotogists on the basis of the analysis of introspective

reports of persons have listed the following three characteristics of the phenomenon of anxiety.

(a) A consious feeling of fear or apprehension in the absencelof any immediate objective threat or danger(b) a pattern of physiological arousal and physical distress that usually includes physical complaints and (c) some disorganization of and interference with effective thinking and problem solving.

Types of anxiety

Anxiety has been broadly described as of two types: normal and neurotic. Normal anxiety is a fear reaction to threats to personal values that the individual consiners very essential to his existence as a personality. In normal anxiety the reaction is proporttonate to the threat. It is normal anxiety if the danger can be coped with on a conscious level and the anxiety relieved when the actual situation is changed. Normal anxiety is temporary and can be successfully handled. Neurotic anxiety is highly disproportionate to the actual threat. It manifests itself on an unconscious level and is rooted in early childhood experiences.

Scientific Conception

Scientifically the concept of anxiety may be traced to the writings of Darwin and Freud who established anxiety as a subject of scientific study. Subsequent, Hull, Spence, Taylor, Sarason, Spielberger and their associates transformed the concept of anxiety into a measurable and useful pscyhological construct.

Darwin in his famous book. *Evolution of the Species* placed the study of the Homospiens squarely in the realm of natural science by emphasizing the continuity with other species. He made anxiety and fear the subjects of scientific inquiry by describing and documenting their manifestations in ng and animals. He pointed out that these manifestations amothehgher mammals (rapid heart beat, perspiration dilation of ipmenupils, dryness of mouth, change in voice, trembling and so on) are so clearly established that one can readildy recognize teese emotions in species other than one's own. Darwin argues that the reason this pattern of expression is universally found in men and animals is that it is highly adaptive—only those having envolved this mechanism are able to fiight with or fly from sources of danger as required for survival.

Freud streessed the distinction between anxiety and fear. He proposed that there is an objective anxiety and a neurotic anxiety. Objective anxiety is somewhat more complex than fear, involving in addition a sense of helplessness and general malaise and results from some source of danger in the external environment. It is based on a substantial history of learning about that danger. Neurotic anxiety is a complex internal reaction to some verceived danger and has no source in the external world. it prepares the individual to flee from or cope with the impending threat. However, it differs from fear in that it is based not on external danger. but on the individual's own history of traumatic experiences such as biath, loss of a loved one or punishment of socially disapproved urges. Its source is some impulse to act, acquired sometimes in the individual's past that cannot now be perceived because it was balanced and repressed from memory.

According to Freudian theory, the way to reduce neurotic anxiety is to engage in psychoanalytic therapy which will bring the repressed material back to consciousness. Only when the individual is able to verbalize the danger cures and the fear they evoke. He can again control over his anxiety.

Psychoanalytically the development of anxiety can be explained as the prevention of the organism from carrying out an instinctively motivated act whether through repression or through prevention of gratification.

Otto Rank. a Neo-Freudian. emphasizes the importance of the birth trauma as the source of anxiety.

Horney explains the concept of basic anxiety as the feeling a child has of being isolated and helpless in a potentially hostile world. The emphasis is on the disturbances in inter-personal relations between the child and significant adults.

Sullivan relates anxiety to parental disapproval of the child.

Hull (1943) and his associate Spence (1958) proposed an explaination of anxiety that was built on Hull's learning theory and ultimately led to the development of Taylor's anxiety scale.

The Hull-Spence conception of anxiety represents a radical depenture from its predecessors. A brief description of Hulls' learning theory is given to explain his concept of anxiety. Hulls' explaination of learning consists of relationships between hypothetical variables which can be operationally defined in hypothetical variables which can be operationally defined in behavioural terms. It does not deal with mental events such as repression. The purpose of Hull's theory is to explain and predict the learning of response' Hull set out to accouut for the factors that affect the probability that the learning response will occur on any given occasion when the stimulus is presented. Hull's formutation regarding the basic variables among others affecting the occurrence of a response is

$E = (H \times D)$

E = Excitory Potential

H = Strength of a larned habit

D = Drive state.

The excitatory potential (E) is the multipliative function of the strength of the learned habit (H) and strength of the persons' drive state (D).

Within the formulation of $E = (H \times D)$ many substieties of learning and performance may be dealt with. For example H, in turn is affected by the number of learning trials that have occurred, and D is affected by such factors as the intensity of the srimulus and the emotional responsiveness of the individual. Emotional responsiveness is the important variable for our purpose, since it is Hull's term for what is otherwise known as anxiety. Emotional responsiveness is a personality voriable in the sense that there are consistent individual differences in the magnitude of reflex responses to a stimulus of intensity.

Another way of saying this is that highly emotional persons respond more strongly to stressful or aversive stimuli, have faster and more vigorous escape responses and express and demonstrates more extreme emotional responses to stressful situations

Taylor operationally defined this personality variable anxiety) by developing a self-report test which measures the extent to which persons admit manifest symptoms of emotionality.

5. TENSION

Tension is another important cause of stress in modern society. Every individual experiences tension in his daily life. Tension has become a universal phenomenon in modern society with its cut-throat competition in all walks of life. Constant tension in modern society creates feelings of insecurity, isolation frustration and worthlessness in human beings.

Definition

Tension has not been precisely defined in psychological literature. Some psychologists have defined tension as a tendency to become active in a certain way. In social and political thinking tension means an attitude of hostility among persons or groups towards each other, expressing itself in stained relationships which may break or rupture at any time. "Tension", according to Quincy Wright, "is the condition that arises out of inconsistencies and initiatives existing in the social structute. Decisions that regulate the employment of social energy are reached as a result of the resolution of such inconsistencies."

Causes of Tension

Several views have been advanced by psychologists regarding the causes of tension. All the views can be broadly put under two heads: namely those which relate to psychological factors and the others which attribute it to some environmental factors. A brief description of both is given below :

A. Psychological

According to McDugall, there is an instinct of pugnacity in man so that he is by nature aggressive. Tension and conflict are the manifestations of this innate pugnacity in man.

According to Freud, the founder of psychoanalysis, Thanatos, the instinct of death, and Eros, the instinct of love, are the two main human instincts. The imbalance between the instincts of love and death may result in tension.

The psycho-theological view is also very closely related to the above views. According to this view there is a typical fuse inherent in man's nature, which has been present for a long part of his biological inheritance and provokes him to be aggressive. Philosophers holding this view interpret this fuse as "human cusedness or even original sin." Since they explain it as an inherent tendency in man's nature, they conclude that though tension and conflict may be considerably reduced, it is impossible to eliminate them completely. There will always remain some sueh tendency of aggressiveness expressing itself occassiooally and that any effort to root it out will split up the individual's personality and prove disastrous.

The most common sources of frustration are: other persons and parents.

Stereotypes also create tension. Through the process of identification and attribution they led to false personifications and thereby create antagonistic tendencies among groups.

Aninrism consists in the universal tendency to attribute all events in the world to the deliberate aetivity of human or prehuman will. e. g. when the people of one nation ascribe economic depression, lack of national prestige and other frustrations to the hatred of the neihbouring states.

Repression is also held to be a cause of tension.

Due to the extreme repression of emotion, the aggressive drives of an individual may be channelized against an external object. Anxiety is held to be another source of tension – a feeling of isolation, helplessness and inrecurity. Keren Horney holds that anxiety is generated by a repressed hostility and. . . . it in turn generates prejudice which is also a cause of tension.

Oedipus complex

A bad father image and a good father image create a state of ambivalance in the child. It means coexistence of antithetic emotions or emotional attitudes toward a given object that creates tension. Rapid social changes in modern society is one of tne major sources of tension.

The root cause of all tensions may be attributed to man's not being aware of the existing social realities – that is, to his ignorance. Tension exists because man is ignorant of his own love self, of otherselves and of existing social realities.

Being unaware of their mutual relations, the individuals and the group feel isolated and confused and are thus led to dissociation which in turn breads repulsions hated and creates tension and conflicts.

How to deal with tension

Following are some suggestions for reducing tension.

1. *Talk it out* :
   Confide your worry to a close friend.

2. *Escape for a while* :

   Lose yourself in a movie, book or game or a brief trip for change. Forget your worries by engaging yourself in some useful activity.

3. *Forget your anger* :

   You should forget your anger by engaging yourself in physical activity.

4. *Give in occasionally* :

If you yield. you will find that others will yield too.

5. *Do Something for others* :

You should do something for the welfare of others.

6. Do one thing at a time.
7. *Go easy with your criticism* :

Do not take criticism of yourself too seriously.

8. Schedule your recreation.
9. Do some exercise (e.g. yoga)
10. Make youself available to other.

FACTORS AFFECTING STRESS

The severity of stress is measured by the degree of disruption in the human system that will occur if the individual fails to cope with the adjustive demand. For example, lack of food over a sustained period is regarded as a severe stress because it may cause serious disruption of both physiological and psychological functioning.

The actual degree of disruption depends partly on the adjustive demand, partly on the individual and partly on the cultural and situational context.

Characteristics of the Adjustive Demands

There are several factors that influence stress. The following are some of the important factors :

(*i*) *Duration and multiplicity of demands* :

It has been shown that certain stresses such as the death of a loved one, divorce, serious personal illness unemployment for a long period tend to be highly stressful for most people. Usually the longer a stress operates, the more severe it becomes.

Encountering a number of stress at the same time makes a difference too.

(ii) Strength and equality of conflicting Forces :

A conflict between weak motives involves minimal stress but a conflict between strong motives is likely to subject the individual to great stress.

(i) Imminence of anticipated stress :

The severity of stress increase as the anticipated stress approaches. For example when the date of the annual examination approaches, the stress becomes intense in the minds of the examinees.

(ii) Unfamiliarity or suddenness of the problem :

Sometimes it so happens that new adjustive demands that have not been anticipated and for which no ready made coping patterns are available, place an individual under severe stress. For example, an earthquake may cause severe stress.

Characteristics of the Individual

The severity of stress to a large extent depends on the personality characteristics of the individual. It has been observed that some persons are more prone to stress in comparision to others. Resistance to stress depends on a number of internal and external factors. Some of the common factors are given below :

1. Preception of the problems

One importent factor that is very crucial in determining the severity of the stress is how the individual perceives the situation in order to cope with it.

2. Degree of threat

Threat is the anticipation of harm. Stress situations that are perceived as potentially damnging/thnreatening to survival, such as being given a diagnosis of cancer, carry a high degree of threat, Loss of social status, failure in one's occupation also involve a strong element of threat.

3. Stress tolerance

Stress tolerance refers to one's ability to withstand stress without having integrated functioning seriously impaired. Individuals differ in their capacity for stress tolerance.

KEY STRESSES AND CIRSET

Continuing Stress : There are some key stresses which continue for a long period – such as a horing job. dicord in marriage, physical handicap etc. Unexpected and sudden death of a loved one may also have a lasting effect on a person's life.

2. *Crises* : The term crisis refers to a limited period in which an individual or group is exposed to threats or demands and are at or near the limits of their resources. A crisis may centre around a divorce, an episode, a suicide. The outcome of such crises has profund significanee for the person's subsequent adjustment.

QUESTIONS FOR DISCUSSIONS

1. Define stress Describe frustration in detail.
2. What are the different type of conflicts ? How do they causes stress ?
3. What are the causes of anxiety ? Describe in detail.
4. "Tension is related to the personality characteristic of the individual". Explain in detail.

SUGGESTED READINGS

1. **Chaitow, L : Relaxation and Meditation Techniques, Thomsons Publishers, 1983.**
2. **Lazarus, R.S. : Psychological Stress and the Coping Behaviour McGraw Hill, NY, 1966.**
3. **Mechanie, D. : Students under Stress, Free Press, NY, 1962.**
4. **Style, Hans : The Stress of Life. McGrow Hill, NY, 1956.**
5. **Selye, Hans : Selye's Guide to Stress Research Vol. I. (Ed.), Van. Nostrand Reinhold Co., NY, 1980.**
6. **Selye, Hans: The Stress of My Life : A Scientist's Memories, Van, Nostrand, NY, 1979.**
7. **Spielberger, C.: Understanding Stress and Anxiety, Harper and Row pub., NY, 1979.**

CHAPTER 6

Adjustment Mechanisms

In the previous chapter, we heve described in brief the various factors which cause frustration of motives which is the basic cause of anxiety that uuderlies all types of maladjustment. The frustrated person may react against the source of frustration in different ways. For instance, he may physically attack the source in order to reduce his mental tension and hostility (Aggression) or he may destruct the object of frustration. He may also use withdrawal, fantasy or stereotype etc. to maintain the balance of his personality.

There are some common ways which individual normally use to defend there ego or escape from conflicts and anxiety that are known as defense or adjustment mechanisms. An adjustment mechanism may be defined as "any habitual method of overcoming blocks, reaching goals, satisfying motives, relieving frustration and maintaining equilibrium". Every individual uses his own mechanisms to maintain the balance of his personality in society. The type and frequency of the mechanisms differ from individual to individual depending on his background and previous experiences. Psychologists have listed certain adjustment mechanisms which are used by the majority of people in the constant struggle for survival in the environment. In the present and subsequent two chapters we will describe the mechanisms which are used by normal, psychoneurotic and psychotic people.

Characteristics of Adjustment Mechanisms

1. Adjustment mechanisms are used by almost all people. They are constructs which are inferred from the behaviour of the individuals. They have protective orientation. All adjustment

mechanisms are used to protect or enhance the person's self-esteem against dangers. They defend the person against anxiety and frustration. They increase satisfaction and help in the process of adjustment if used within limits.

2. The danger is always within the person. He fears his own motives. The fear and danger are manifested in adjustment mechanisms.

3. Invariably in all adjustment mechanisms, the individual distorts reality in one way or the other because the method of protecting against dangerous inner impulses or escaping from anxiety involves some kind of distortion of the conscious representation of the person's impulses.

4. The overall effect of adjustment mechanisms is to cripple the individual's functioning and development through falsifying some aspects of his impulses so that he is deprived of accurate self-knowledge as a basis for action. There is self-deception underlying all adjustment mechanisms. We deny and disguise the real cause of our behaviour in order to maintain the balance of our personality.

5. Adjustment mechanisms are learned from the environment. They are designed to deal with anxiety, inner conflict and self-devaluatlon They operate on habitual and automatic levels.

Types of Reaction Patterns

There are broadly two categories of reaction patterns which are commonly used by people to cope with stress. Every person in a stressful situation is faced with two types of problems : (a) to meet the requirement of adjustive demand and (b) to protect the self from psychological damage or disorganization When a person in a stressful situation feels competent to handle the situation, his behaviour tends to be task-oriented. But when his feelings of adequacy are seriously threatened by the adjustive demand, his reaction tends to be defense-oriented, primarily aimed at protecting the self from hurt. The following figure depicts the operation of the ego defence mechanism.

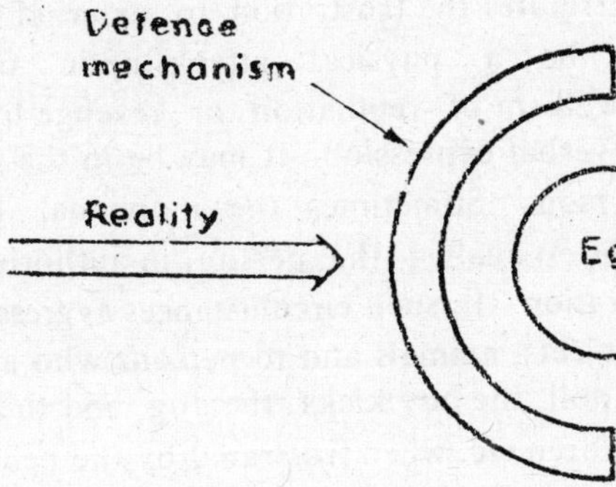

Fig. 2

ADJUSTMENT MECHANISMS

1. Simple Denial

The easiest way to manitain the balance of one's personality is to deny the facts which could create conflict in the mind. If parents call children when they are busy in play-activities. they will pretend that they have heard nothing. In fact what was said was not allowed to penetrate into their consciousness. In adults, the percentage of denial is higher than it is in children. Adults are not always prepared to admit frankly failures in their daily life. Denal helps to postpone facing a problem or a failure.

2. Aggression

The word aggression has been interpreted in several ways. For instance, we call a vigorous person aggressive. A person who tries to gain something from others by force is also called aggressive. The person who tries to dominate is also called aggressive. Aggression is a typical adjustment mechanism used as an attempt to hurt or destroy the source of frustration. It may be classified into two broad categories :

(i) Extrapunitive, (ii) Intropunitive.

(i) Extrapunitive

Exrapunitive responses are those in which the individual

agaressively attriuutes the frustration to external persons or things. It may be a physical attack upon the obsst acle. It may take the form of retaliation or revenge by the person in the form of verbal expression. It may be in the form of criticism of the person. Sometimes the individual fails to take any aggressive step against the person in authority who is the source of frustration. In such circumstances aggression is shifted to inanimate objects, animals and to persons who are weak. The child beats his doll, the boy kicks the dog and the house-wife rebukes her children etc. when frustrated by the behaviour of her husband against whom she cannot do anything. Aggression tends to generalize from the original object to similar objects in the environment. For example after the assassination (1984) of Mrs. Indira Gandhi, the late Prime Minister of India by a member of the Sikh community, the agression was generalised to all persons of Sikh community throughout India with great lose of life and property.

(ii) Intropunitive

Intropunitive responses are those in which the individual aggressively attributes frustration to himself. Sometimes the person feels that he himself is the source of frustration. He criticises himself and may inflict physical punishment on himself.

The release of pent-up feelings through aggression gives relief to the person. The teacher by his sympathy, fair treatment and by organising positive programmes for catharsis can reduce aggression among children.

3. Compensation

It is the tendency of every person to make-up deficiency in one trait or area by development in another area. When a person feels weak and fails in one area, he compensates his weakness in another field. He works hard to become strong and successful. Needs which are frustrated and unmet are gratified in order to release tension and conflict. The person may compensate in the areas of biological, psychological and social weakneses.

Students who do poorly in school work, compensate in non-academic activities. The boy who is weak in English, may compensate in Hindi. There are many interesting examples of compensation as Sandoz who was physically weak, worked so hard that he became the best in physique. Lord Byron compensated his physical weakness in verbal expression and became the best speaker of his times. Compensation is generally of the following types :

(i) Direct Compensation

It is the process when an individual removes his specific weakness and frustration in the same field by unusual effort. The boy who is weak in English compensates directly when he tries to become strong by hard labour in the same field. Demosthenes who was not able to speak effectively due to stuttering, later became a great orator.

(ii) Over-Compensation

It is the process when an individual moulds his outstanding weakness into an outstanding strength. Theodore Roosevelt, asthemic and often sick as a child, became a rough horse rider and a lion hunter in his later life.

(iii) Substitute Compensation

When an individual finds himself weak in one area and sees no scope for improvement in that area, he attempts to become outstanding in another area. An academically weak student may compensate by becoming an outstanding athlete.

(iv) Indirect Compensation

Most of the compensation is indirect. A boy may steal things to compensate for being humiliated by his parents. A weak student who is poor in academic achievement may compensate in games, The most common form of indirect compensation is that sought by parents through their children. The father who wanted to be an engineer but failed, enjoys his son's success as an engineer. This compensatory mechanism used by parents sometimes pushes children into unsuitable vocation.

(v) Neurotic Compensation

Neurotic compensation is used by an individual when normal compensatory mechanisms fail. The mentally weak person attempts to get a first division but he does not possess adequate mental abilities to achieve his target. Consequently he fails in his attempts again and again. In such circumstances, he develops neurotic compensation. He falls ill and develops physical as well as mental symptoms, stays at home and becomes the centre of attention.

4. Sublimation

A substitute reaction may be classified as compensation. Among all mental mechanisms of defense, sublimation is the most advanced, highly developed and constructive mechanism. Through the use of its operation, the energy of personally or socially intolerable impulses and drives is successfully directed into consciously acceptable channels. Their direction and aim thus become deflected and redirected toward substitute goals. It contributes to character and personality development and plays an important role in the prevention and resolution of emotional conflicts, anxiety and in the maintenance of emntional and mental health. Sublimation provides an outlet for blocked and intolerable drives.

Sublimation has been defined as a major mental mechanism operating outside and beyond conscious awareness, through which instinctual drives which are consciously unacceptable or blocked and unobtainable, are diverted so as to secure disguised external expression and utilization in channels of personal and social acceptability. In suceessful sublimation, the direction and aim of the repressed drives have been deflected into new pathways of creative endeavour. In sublimation, intrapsychic energy is usefully employed extrapsychically. The consequence is personal gain.

All port defines sublimation, as : "A device by which an individual's anti-social impulses are made socially acceptable."

Coleman defines sublimation as, "The gratification of sexual desires in non-sexual activities that serve as a substitute."

Sublimation plays a major role in moulding personality and in the development of specific character traits. Traits such as studiousness, research ability, curiosity and literary interest can be fostered by sublimation.

Sublimation is healthful. It is the mechanism in which all divisions of the psyche-the id, ego and the super-ego work in concert with each other.

Sublimation can be done through dancing, music, arts, crafts, etc.

5. Identification

Identification may be identified as a mental mechanism operating outside and beyond conscious awareness through which an individual, in varying degrees makes himself like some one else; he identifies himself with another person. This results in the unconscious taking-over and transfer to oneself of various elements of the other. Such elements may include thouhts, tasks, behaviour mechanisms, or character traits and emotional feelings. Adolescents identify themselves with some political leaders, youth leaders or actors and actresses and attempt to acquire their characteristics.

6. Projection

It is the most common adjustment mechanism which is used by people in daily life. Freud used projection as a process by which we ascribe to the external world the rejected impulses of the id. We defend ourselves against our repressed guilt feelings by projecting them into other things and people. It is a mechanism which relives frustration of the individual.

The range of projection in the classroom is very wide. Children who are doing poorly, are often, very critical of the teacher or other pupils. They frequently act as if they were expecting the teacher or another child to display toward them the hatred, love and contempt which they feel for themselves.

When projection is used too frequently, it indicates symptoms of mental ill-health. The most extreme from of projection is a central quality of the psychosis known as paranoia in which the patient experiences delusion of persecution.

Projection provides an unsatisfactory solution to frustration and can cause harm to the person because it involves distorting an important part of the world.

7. Rationalization

Rationalization has been defined as a mechanism by which the individual justifies his belief and actions by giving reasons other than those which activated or motivated him. Rationalisation i the most popular adjustment mechanism which is used by almos all persons in daily life. It is a response to reality that falsifies circumstances. The aim of rationalization is to lessen frustration by giving sound and worthy reasons for an action which frustrating. No one is ready to accept failure to reach his g l or accept that his behaviour falls short of what people ex t of him The child who fails in the examination blames the ptaper setter or lack of books etc. The stumbling child blames the chair. The boy who is rejected by a girl finds fault in the girl. In rationalization, we try to give socially acceptable reasons of our failures. It is a mild form of repression in which the facts are distorted rather than forgotten. There are two types of rationalization.

(*i*) *Sour grapes*

When the individual fails to attain his cherished goal after repeated efforts he starts blaming various factors in order to rationalize his failure. When the fox in Aesop's fable could not reach the grapes, out of sheer frustration she blamed the grapes for being sour. The boy who fails in his examination blames teachers, examiners or attributes his faliure to illness.

(ii) Sweet lemon

It is a form of rationalization when the individual is not satisfied with his achievement or the situation he is in. But in order to maintain the balance he accepts them as good. Most teachers in our country use this adjustment mechanism to maintain the balance of their personality. Let me explain it further. A teacher before entering the teaching profession tries his best to get a better job than teaching but when he fails, accepts teaching as a means of livelihood and rationalizse his failure by speaking very highly of the teaching profession.

8. Regression

Regression has been defined as an unconscious "back tracking" either in memory or in behaviour which might have been successful in the past. The adult who has been frustrated in fulfilling his needs may return to more primitive modes of behaviour. He may cry like a child, and have temper tantrums. He may attack his problems like a child in a simple. emotional and primitive manner. Sometimes psychologists call regression the process of fixation. The old man who always talks of his youth, shows regression. The old man, by this mechanism, is trying to live again in "the old days". Teachers encounter problems of regression in their classes, particularly when they reprimand a girl who starts crying like a baby. Regression explains manifestation of infantile behaviour in adolescents and youths.

Some regression is moral for maintaining mental balance in the social environment. Ability to regress is an asset to teachers and leaders of youth groups to enjoy youthful jokes and similar times of juvenile gaiety They can establish good rapport with youth by the mechanism of regression. But regression can pose a serious problem for those who use it habitually for all problems and in its extreme from may indicate severe form of mental ill health.

9. Repression

Repression is a fundamental and very important concept in the Freudian theory of personality. It has been defined as motivated forgetting. White (1964) defined repression as, "the forgetting or ejection from consciousness of memories of threat and, especially, the ejection from awareness of impulses in oneself that might have objectionable consequences." It is an attempt by the individual to push into the unconscious those experiences and thoughts which are in conflict with his moral standard or which are painful to contemplate. Repression is caused by forces active within ourselves. We try to forget what makes us feel inferior, ashamed. guilty and anxious.

Repression and suppression are differented by the mechanism used. In suppression we consciously decide and make an effort to exclude an idea from our thought, action and conversation whereas in repression painful and anxiety producing experiences are unconsciously and automatically excluded from the conscious thought process.

Sears, commenting upon the mechanism of repression, says that repression is difficult either to measure or to experiment upon because the process in unconscious. However, experiments conducted in clinics verify that it occurs.

Through the process of repression, the individual forgets sad and painful experiences to escape from his troubles and conflicts, There is constant struggle between the impulses of id and social taboos. The ego drags into the unconscious those impulses which are in coflict with social norms. In brief we can say that repression is a mental mechanism by which we keep out of consciousness dangerous anxiety—producing ideas.

10. Reaction Formation

Reaction formation is also called reversal formation. It is to substitute opposite reaction formation which causes anxiety. It is accompanied by behaviour and feelings exactly opposed to the repressed tendency. The boy frightened by a graveyard whistles happily; an extremely aggressive man, afraid of his own destructive impulses, acts humble. The man who is kind and idealistic can be diagnosed as either loving or hating mankind.

11. Negativism

Negativism is a mechanism by which an individual draws the attention of other persons. It is partly a defense and partly an escape meahanism. The person develops strong and irrational resistance to accepting the suggestions of others. The use of this mechanism is at peak at the age of two to three. The foundations of this mecnanisms are laid in early childhood and later on appear in adulthood. Most adults use negativism in milder forms in special situations. They do not oppose, but they do resist suggestions by others.

Students have some negative feelings toward their teachers. Negative feelings do not serve any useful pnrpose but they hinder the achievement of a goal.

12. Fantasy (Day dreaming)

It is a fact that. mostly, we hope to reduce tension by fantasy. It is a defensive reaction to anxiety. Our thoughts can be a realistic effort to remove the obstacles that make us anxious. They can also provide an escape from frustration by giving us imaginary satisfaction. A hungry man dreams of food; an unsucessful man dreams of success, Fantasy is a mechanism of wish fulfilling Fantasy is at its peak in adolescence. Adolescents may dream of their future success in life. Fantasy has powerful adjustive implications for people of various categories. Jones has noted that fantasy plays an important role in creativity and that to enhance creativity, the use of fantasy should be encouraged in the educational process. The use of fantasy in desenitization therapy and self-exploration exercises provides evidence of its importance in the process of adjustment. Critics of fantasy point out its non-adjustive implications. For example, it occupies time that could be spent in real accemplishments; it provides tension reduction without any accomplishment and sets urealistic expectations that cannot be met in real life. There are two types of daydreams the conquering hero and the suffering hero type. In the conquering heeo type the individual perceives himself as omnipotent and omnipresent. He is all powerful, all knowledge and present everywhere at the same time. He can do anything he wishes. He can be the greatest writer, poet, artist, scholar and athlete, etc. in the world. Such type of dreams completely eliminate competitors and rid the world of tension pressures and problems.

In the suffering hero type of dreams the person feels he has been wronged, hurt or persecuted. He may become self-critical, self-depreciating and guilty of his behaviour. If his thoughts become more depressive, he may commit suicide and if they continue for a prolonged period he may develop an obsession, a compulsion or a phobia.

13. Introjection

Identification and introjection are very closely related to each other. Introjection is identification with the aggressor. Introjection values the aggressor's beliefs as one's own even when they are contrary to one's previous beliefs. In Medieval India, when the Moghul Emperor Aurangzeb ruled and livied "Zajia" on Hiudus to harass and convert Hindus to Islam, many Hindus introjected Islamic values to protect themselves from the warth of the Emperor.

14. Undoing (atonement)

Undoing or atonement refers to the action of an individual to negate some disapproved thought, impulse or act. The common methods of undoing are apology for wrong act, repentance, penance of undergoing some punishment. Atonement develops out of early childhood training when the child learns that once he undergoes some atonement, his misdeed is negated and he can start with a clean slate and with renewed parental or societal approval. Here are two examples which make clear the concept of undoing. An adolescent in fury of anger kills a cat. The parents in order to atone the death of the cat ask the boy to keep fast for two days. Another example may be given of donating huge amounts of money in charity by unethical businessmen to atone for their corrupt practices.

Substitution

There is difference between sublimation and substitution. In sublimation, there is actually a change of goals. Sexual energy is rechanneled to some object that has no direct relation to sex whereas in substitution the goal, that is sexual satisfaction, remains the same However, rather than direct satisfaction of the sex drive, the person finds some substitute satisfaction. The rechanneling is marginally acceptable to society and in some cases it is totally unacceptable.

One marginal substitution is masturbation which is almost universally practised.

Another marginal substitution is the partial satisfaction of sex vicariously through magazines, books, movies and TV: etc.

Sexual deviation is a type of substitution which is unacceptable to a majority of people in India.

Fixation

In regress on, a person has to develop to a certain point and then returns to an earlier stage whereas in fixation he never progresses beyond a certain stage in various areas of psychological development. Fixation is defined as a stoppage in psychological growth caused by an overinvestment of psychic energy in an object, person or situation. For example, a person invests too much energy in his mother. We think of such a person as psychologically immature. According to Freud, fixation develops out of too much frustration or too much gratification.

Nomadism

Several types of defense mechanisms are used by all persons.

If they are used occassionally, the person has no problem but on the other hand their excessive use leads to psychoneurosis.

Nomadism is characterized by wandering from place to place and from job to job. The nomad stays in a place or a situation for a brief period. Thus tension begins to mount, interpersonal relationships become hampered and soon the problems are too severe and too frequent. The nomad deals with these problems by fleeing the scene. He tries to run away from the tension—producing situations,

Displacement

This is the mechanism by which psychic energy is channelized from one object, person or situation to another. Displacement may be of several types. For example, when aggression or hostility are involved, the displacement is called scapeating. This mechanism involves tracsferring hostility to sŏme one or something else. Let us understand it by an example. A husband and wife quarrel the wife is abused. She, instead of becoming aggressive, holds back the emotion and takes it out on the children who are not responsible for her pent-up emotion. But since they are non-threatening, they are the logical choice of the wife. Children should be provided with safe scapeating like destructible toys, and dolls, etc.

When aggressive emotions do not find any outlet, they can turn inward on the person and may produce psychosomatic disorders such as ulcers, headache and depressive reations, etc,

In conclusion we can say that all normal people use adjustment mechanism in order to adjust in their environment. But when the use of adjustment mechanisms becomes too much, it may lead to mental disorders.

QUESTIONS FOR DISCUSSION

1. Define adjustment. What is the importance of adjustment mechanisms ?

2. "Too much use of adjustment mechanisms leads to maladjustment." Comment.

3. Write notes on rationlization, projection, compensation, repression and atonement.

4. Write an eassy on the importance of fantasy.

SUGGESTED READINGS

1. Bruno, F.G. : Human Adjustment and Personal Growth, Wiley and Sons, NY, 1977.
2. Chauhan, S. S. : Advanced Educational Psychology (8th Ed). Vikas Publishers, New Delhi, 1985.
3. Lazarus, R. S. : Psychological Stress and the Coping Process McGraw Hill, NY, 1966.
4. Miller, D.R. et al : Inner Conflict and Defense, Holt, Rinehart, NY, 1960.

CHAPTER 7

Psychoneurotic Adjustment Mechanisms

Psychoneurosis or neurosis as it is generally called, is an emotional disorder which is basically rooted in anxiety and affects certain aspects of personality. Historically, the term psychoneurosis is attributed to W. Cullen, an Englishman who referred it to disordered sensations of the nervous system. The psychoneurotic attempts in his own way to maintain the balance of his personality for adequate adjustment in his environment. He remains in touch with reality but is seized with anxiety and threats of harm to his body. Psychoneurosis is a dysfunction of behaviour due to emotional stress caused by frustrations, conflicts, deprivation of personal insecurity and inadequacy of the individual to cope with his problems. It has been observed that the individual suffering from neurosis experiences great difficulty in satisfying his needs and desires as well as his social obligations. It has been reported by almost all psychotherapists that anxiety is the root cause of psychoneurosis.

Characteristics of Psychoneurosis

— It is a functional disorder which does not involve any damage to nervous tissues.

— Symptoms are unconsciously designed to protect the individual from threats or harm.

— The individual clings to his symptoms as long as external threats exist.

— Symptoms represent the best possible ego-defenses of the individual from external threats.

— Symptoms appear automatically and not at the will of the individual.

— The neurotic is characterized by insecurity, inadequacy and emotional immaturity.

— He is unhappy and lacks self-confidence. He looks for guidance to others whenever there is a problem.

- He develops a life style characterized by defensive and avoidance behaviours that enable him to escape from anxiety-arousing stressful situations in the environment.

TYPES OF NEUROTIC DISORDERS

1. Anxiety neurosis
2. Hysterical neurosis
3. Hypochondric neurosis
4. Phobic neurosis
5. Obsessive-compulsive neurosis
6. Fugue states
7. Neurosthenic neurosis
8. Traumatic neurosis

ANXIETY NEUROSIS

Anxiety neurosis is the most common of the various neurotic disorders listed above. It comprises 30% to 40% of all neurotic disorders. It is characterized by chronic anxiety and apprehensiveness which may be punctuated by recurring episodes of acute anxiety. According to Wolpe, the eliciting stimuli are obscure, complex and quite pervasive.

Symptoms

— *Inability to Concentrate* : The person suffering from anxiety neurosis fails to concentrate on any problem. His mind fluctuates very rapidly from one object to other.

- *Difficulty in Making Decision* : The person cannot make decisions on any problem facing him.
- *Excessive Sensitivity* : The person becomes excessively sensitive to what others say and feel about him.
- *Lack of Confidence* : The person lacks self-confidence and feels discouraged to start any work independently.
- *Sleep Disturbances* : He does not have sound sleep. He is often disturbed in his sleep by horrible dreams and does not enjoy full sleep.
- *Excessive sweating* : The individual suffering from anxiety neurosis sweats excessively in the presence of any problem.
- *Sustained Muscle Tension*: The individual experiences tension in his muscles.
- *Tires easily*: The individual suffering from anxiety neurosis tires easily and feels weakness.

Causal Factors:

It is impossible to isolate a single factor of anxiety neurosis because it is caused by an interaction of several factors. The following are some of the important factors which may cause anxiety neurosis.

1. Conditioning

According to Behaviourists, all behaviour is learned and thus anxiety is also learned in the environment. Early childhood training within the home is very crucial in the development of personality. A tense and anxious mother can transmit her anxiety to a very young infant. The interaction with a faulty parental model may also cause incalculable harm to the child in later life. The findings of Jenkins (1966) support the view that overanxious children tend to have neurotic mothers.

He also reported that neurotics often come from families

where parents have high expectations from their children and reject the actual accomplishment as standard.

2. Inability to handle dangerous impulses

The neurotic is likely to experience intense anxiety in situations that elicit dangerous feelings that is, feelings that would devalue his self-image or endanger his relationship with other people. The handling of hostility, for example, is difficult for the neurotic who feels forced to take a compliant subservient, self-suppressing attitude towards others as the price of security, love and acceptance.

Such repressed hostility reveals itself in indirect ways such as fantasies. Similarly, repressed sexual desires may threaten to break through existing defenses and elicit intense anxiety. For example, a man may attempt to repress his homosexual impulses that he considers highly immoral. For some time the repression projects him, but repression is rarely complete and the individual is likely to experience periodic flare-ups of anxiety neurosis.

3. Anxiety arousing decision

Neurotics have great difficulty in making decisions under certain conditions such as conflicts involving immoral values or possible loss of security and status, there may be acute anxiety and paralysing indecisions.

4. Reactivation of prior trauma

A stressful situation that parallels some earlier trauma may elicit intense anxiety in an individual who is basically insecure.

Concluding, we may say that neurotics develop inadequacy, over-sensitivity and low stress tolerance. It may be pointed out that often a neurotic puts up a good battle in view of his faulty evaluation of himself and his environment.

As Portoney (1959) has pointed out : "To the picture of an anxious individual apprehensively coping with life in the face of inner and outer dangers must also be added the picture of a human being with courage, able to endure this much anxiety without the more massive defense and character distortions, which characterize the other psychiatric syndromes."

Treatment

Anxiety neurotics may find some relief in mild tranquilizers but it is not possible to modify thair life style with them. Psychotherapy is used to cure anxiety neurosis which we will describe in the subsequent chapters on psychotherapy.

2. HYSTERICAL NEUROSIS

The term hysteria is derived from the Greek word meaning uterus. It was formerly thought to be the disease of women which was caused by sexual difficulties. But the old belief that hysteria is a disease of women, is not accepted in modern times. There are mainly two types of hysteria : conversion type and dissociative type. A brief description is given below :

(A) Conversion Type

The concept of relationship of sexual difficulties to hysteria was later advanced by Freud. He used the term conversion hysteria to indicate that the symptoms were an expression of repressed and deviated sexual energy—that is the psychosexual conflict is converted into a bodily disturbance.

In modern psychopathology hystericale reactions are no longer interpreted in Freudian terms. Rather the physical symptoms are now usually seen as serving a defensive function, enabling the individual to escape or avoid a stressful situation.

(*a*) *Sensory Symptoms* :

Any of the senses may be involved in sensory coversion reactions such as :

Anaesthesia—loss of sensitivity.

Hypesthesia—partial loss of sensitivity.

Hyperesthesia—Excessive sensitivity.

Analgesia—Loss of sensitivity to pain.

Paresthesia—Exceptional sensation.

Astasia —abasia—inability to speak.

(*b*) *Motor symptoms* :

Hysterical motor disorders cover a wide range of symptoms such as paralysis of arm, leg, trembling of fingers, facial paralysis, and tic etc. The most common hysterical disturbances of speech are aphonia in which the individual is able to talk only in a whisper, and mutism in which he cannot speak at all. Aphonia usually occurs after some emotional shock.

(*c*) *Viscereal symptoms* :

Hysterical viscereal symptoms also cover a wide range of distortions including, headache, "lump in the throat," coughing spells, choking sensations, difficulty in breathing, cold and clammy extremities, beleaching nausea and so on.

Causal Factors

The development of hysterical conversion follows a chain of events beginning with : (a) a desire to escape from some unpleasant situation (b) a fleeting wish to be sick in order to avoid the situation and (c) under additional or continued stress, the appearance of some physical ailment.

(a) Personality and role factors

The conversion hysteric is highly suggestible and dramatic; excitable but shallow in emotional responsiveness, prone to exaggeration: demanding and manipulative in interpersonal relationship. Female conversion hysterics have also been described as sexually seductive but often frigid in actual sexual relationship :

(*i*) The sick role of conversion hysteric is useful only in a culture that provides sympathy and support for sick persons and enables them to avoid normal responsibilities; (b) the role is enacted on the basis of information the individual has, concerning the physical ailment he is simulating; (c) the role tends to be self-perpetuating, since it is reinforced by anxiety reduction and other gains.

(*ii*) *Avoidance of or defense against threat* : The coversion pattern enables the individual to avoid or defend himself against a threatening stress situation.

Conversion reactions may also represent defenses against dangerous desires and impulses. A case has been cited of a middle aged male who suffered total paralysis of his legs after his wife left him for another man. Some time conversion reactions seem to stem from feelings of guilt and the necessity for self-punishment.

(*iii*) *Secondary gains stemming from actual illness or injury* : In some cases conversion sysmptoms develop following physical illness or an accident. Whatever specific causative factors may be involved, however, the basic dynamic pattern seems to be the avoidance or reduction of anxiety-arousing strees by getting sick—thus converting an intolerable emotional problem into a face-saving physical one. The initial learning of the reaction and its maintenance are reinforced both by anxiety reduction and by interpersonal gains in terms of sympathy and support that result from being sick.

(B) Hysterical Neurosis (Dissociative type)

The dissociative type of hysteria is also a way of avoiding stress while gratifying needs in a manner permitting the person to deny personal responsibilities for his inacceptable behaviour.

Dissociative patterns include amnesia, fugue states, somnambulistic state (sleep walking) and multiple personality.

Amnesia

Amnesia is partial or total inability to recall or identify past experiences. It is caused by brain pathology and involves an actual failure of retention—either the formation is not registered or does not enter memory storage or it is not retained in storage.

Psychogenic amnesia is usually limited to failure to recall; the forgotten material is still there beneath the consciousness as becomes apparent under hypnosis-narcosis interviews.

In the neurotic amnesia, the individual does not even remember his name, age and home and does not recongnize parents, friends, etc. yet his basic habit of readiug and talking remains intact and he appears quite normal.

Fugue state

Fugue literally means flight. It is a reaction to a defense by actual flight. The individual wanders away from home for weeks' months or some times for years and finds himself in a strange place, not knowing how he got there and with complete amnesia for the period of fugue.

Somnambulism

It refers to sleep walking. The patient suffering from somnambulism, gets up in his sleep and walks outside his home. He forgets his identity. It is common in childhood but it may also occur in some adults under stress from internal or external conflict. Somnambulism may be treated with psychotherapy.

Multiple personality

The multiple personality is the most interesting dissociative disorder and has been a subject of research in recent years. It refers to the condition in which an individual has two or more unique personalities coexisting in one body. Each personality has a relatively unique and stable identity with its own emotional structure and thought process. The individual may switch from personality to personality in a matter of minutes or hours and these personalities usually have no awareness of each other. The author had the opportunity to meet in Meerut Sri Kishan Dutt Brahmachari with three different identities. For instance in his walking state he is a simple and illiterate person but when he lies down in a specific posture, he shows two different personalities: one of 'Rishi Shrang' who lectures in Sanskrit and another of his disciple Mahanada who translates the lecture in to Hindi

Causal Factors

The pattern in psychogenic amnesia is essentially the same as in coversion reactions except that instead of avoiding some unpleasant situation by being sick, the person does it by avoiding thoughts about it. The process of amnesia is highly selective and involves only material that is basically intolerable and threatening to the self.

The psychogenic, is egocentric immature and highly suggestible when faced with an unpleasant situation from which he sees no escape and which he wants to repress.

3. HYPOCHONDRICAL NEUROSIS

Hypochondrical neurosis is relatively rare. It is hardly 5% present of the neurotic population. The individual is preoccupied with his state of health and with various presumed disorders or diseases of the bodily organs. According to Kenyon' this maladaptive of pattern behaviour appears to be common during later adulthood and is found more frequently among women and men.

Hypochondrics are characterized by their multiplicity of complaints about physical illness. They may complain of a peculiar sensation in the general area of stomach, chest, head or anywhere else in the body. Hypochondrics develop typical attitude towards diseases and consider themselves seriously ill. They read medical magazines and use a wide range of medicines. However, they do not show loss or distortion of sensory, motor, and viscereal functioning.

Causal Factors

1. Early experiences

Over-emphasis on body functions in early life is one of the causes of hypochondria. Early experiences are very important in the development of personality. Faulty parental model and over concern about the health of the child may be one factor which may cause hypochondria in later years. Actual illness or injury which focusses the attention of parents may also cause hypochondria.

2. Disappointing life situations

When an individual finds himself incapable of achieving he goal in life; evaluates life unfavourably and fails to achieve his hopes and dreams, the stage is set for hypochondrical reactions, to escape and avoid stressful life situations.

3. Reinforcement

Maintenance of the hypochondrical pattern by reinforcement is an important cause. The hypochodrical pattern of behaviour enables the individual to avoid the demands and stress of an unpleasant life situation while at the same time gaining sympathy and support from significant others plus some measure of control over their behaviour.

In general, the anxiety aroused by his stressful life situations—often including the failure to achieve important goals—is displaced by a concern and preoccupation with his body and its functioning.

We can summarize by saying that the hypochondric utilizes actual physical disability as a defense against feelings of a filure and as an escape from future striving.

4. PHOBIC NEUROSIS

The word phobia comes from the Greek "phobos" which means fear or dread. A phobia is a persistent irrational fear of some object or situation that presents no actual danger to the person or in which the danger is magnified out of all proportions of its actual seriousness. There is no limit to phobias. They can develop against persons, places, objects or situations. Here we give a list of common phobias which will give some idea of the variety of situations and events.

Agora Phobia	Fear of often places
Acrophobia	Fear of high places
Aichmophobia	Fear of sharp and pointed objects
Algophobia	Fear of pain
Anthrophobia	Fear of man
Astrophobia	Fear of thunder and lightening
Claustrophobia	Fear of closed places
Ereutophobia	Fear of blushing
Gynophobia	Fear of woman
Hematophobia	Fear of blood
Hydrophobia	Fear of water
Mysophobia	Fear of germs or contamination
Monophobia	Fear of being alone
Necrophobia	Fear of dead body
Nyctophobia	Fear of darkness
Ocholophobia	Fear of crowds
Pathophobia	Fear of disease
Pyrophobia	Fear of fire
Phiphobia	Fear of snakes

Syphilophobia	Fear of syphtis
Thanatophobia	Fear of death
Toxophobia	Fear of poison
Zoophobia	Fear of animals or some particular animal.

Most of us have minor irrational fears but in phobic reactions such fears are intense and interfere with every day activities. Neurotics usually admit that they have no real cause to be afraid of the object or situation but they cannot help themselves. Phobic neurotics show a wide range of symptoms in addition to their phobias such as tension, headache, back pain, stomach upsets, dizzy spells and fear of "cracking up". Phobics have serious difficulty in making decisions, a condition that Kaufman called Decidophobia.

Causal Factors

1. Conditioning and avoidance learning

The classical study of Watson on little Albert who was conditioned to fear of a white rat is an example of zoophobia. The child generalized his fear to all white objects. Such phobias are not easy to understand because most of us have mild phobias based on previous learnning. A child who has been chased and bitten by a dog may feel uneasy around a dog. A pervasive pattern of fear and avoidance behaviour can be learned in much the same way. For example, if a child's fumbling attempts to master new skills are ridiculed by his parents or if he is discouraged from becoming independent, he may never develop the confidence he needs to cope with new situations. In fact he learns that avoidance is the appropriate response.

2. Defense against threatening impulses

A phobia may represent a defensive reaction that protects the individual from situations in which his repressed aggressive or sexual impulses might become dangerous.

3. Displacement of of anxiety

A phobia may represent displacement of anxiety from some external threat that elicited it to some other object or situation. According to Freud a phobia represents displaced anxiety associated with the Oedipus complex. Presumably a small boy wants to possess his mother sexually and is jealous and hostile toward his father. He therefore fears his father and in particular dreads being castrated. The fear of the avenging father may then be displaced to some external and formerly innocuous object. He concluded that phobias in adults develop due to disturbed sexual relationships.

But later investigators have disagreed with Freud's interpretation of phobia and have pointed out that many kinds of stress situations may lead to phobic reactions through the mechanism of displacement.

The phobic condition of a person brings him two types of gains : Primary and secondary. Primary gain lies in the control and better management of the anxiety which is the central problem of neurosis and secondary gain consists in the sympathy of others excuse from work and providing of services by other members of the family.

5. OBSESSIVE—COMPULSIVE NEUROSIS

Obsessive and compulsive neuroses are different patterns of behaviou. Obsessive neurosis is a behaviour pattern in which the individual is compelled to think about something that he does not want to think about whereas in compulsive neurosis the individual is compelled to carry out some action against his will. The individual knows that his behaviour is irrational but he cannot control it.

(i) Obsessive doubt

An inclination not to believe that a completed task has been accomplished satisfactorily as locking the door, and switching off the heater, etc.

(ii) Obsessive thinking

To repeat the same idea again and again : For example, the mind of the patient may be full of thoughts of infection and disease.

(iii) Feelings of guilt

Feelings of guilt which haunt the mind of the individual may become obsessive.

It has been seen that most obsessive-compulsive persons are insecure, anxious about morality and unable to tolerate stress.

One the basis of an analysis of obsessive-compulsive activities it has been found that there are three mechanisms involved in it, guilt and punishment, substitute thoughts and rigid ordering of the future.

The famous case of lady Macebth's handwashing to control her guilt about king Duncan's murder is a well known example of compulsive-obsessive neurosis.

6. NEUROSTHENIA NEUROSIS

The term neurosthenia was coined in 1869. Its definition has changed many times since its conception and even varies from country to country.

Neurosthenia is defined as a condition with the following essential components :

(a) chronic weakness

(b) easy fatigability

(c) exhaustion

(d) genuine distress.

There may be other components but these components are not essential for the definition.

Neurosthenia differs from all other neuroses in which somatic symptoms predominate.

Causal Factors

1. Nervous exhausion

One of the important causes of neurosthenia is nervous exhaustion of the patient due to excessive mental work.

2. Prolonged conflict and overwork

Conflict and overwork for a long period may also cause neurosthenia.

3. Prolonged frustration, hopelessness and discouragement

If an individual suffers from repeated frustrations and in his work, loses all hopes of his success in study/work etc. are defeated he may also become the victim of neurosthenia.

7. TRAUMATIC NEUROSIS

The concept of traumatic neurosis was developed during the two World Wars. It is a type of maladjustment which is referred as war neurosis. During the Second World War, one of the most common of maladjustments found among soldiers and officers was operational fatigue. It is described as a reactive state resulting from the physical and emotional stress of continued danger and hardship experienced in combat.

The most common symptoms of traumatic neurosis are :

— Deterioration of performance

— Inaccurate judgement

— Slow reactions

— Uncoordinated movements

— Lack of confidence

Causal Factors

Traumatic neurosis has its origin in an inhibitory process which is protective to the individual. The patient fears the world which appears threatening to him. In order to protect himself he inhibits certain physiological and psychological functions.

Because of certain traumatic experiences, the patient generalizes that the whole world is dangerous and threatening and attempts to void any type of contact with dangerous situations. The primary experiences in the traumatic neurotic physical injury and death.

Neurotic trauma can be cused by psychotherapy as well as chemotherapy.

QUESTIONS FOR DISCUSSION

1. What is psychoneurosis ? What are the common characteristics c. psychoneurotie patients ?
2. What are the various types of anxiety neurotic disorders ? Describe one of them.
3. "Phobias are learned." Explain the statement.
4. What is obsession ? Differentiate it form compulsion.
5. What are the ca ses of hypochondria ?
6. What are the symptom of hysterical neurosis ? Describe in brief its causes.

SUGGESTED READINGS

Angy A. Neurosis and Treatment, A Holisti : Theory, Willey NY , 1965.

Arietis Interpretation of Schizophrenia, Basic Books, NY, 196

Kleinmuntz, Benjamin, Essential of Abnormal Psychology. Harper an Row, [illegible]

Ullo[illegible] Psychological Approach to Abnormal Behav[illegible] [illegible] Cliffs, NY, 1975.

CHAPTER 8

Psychotic Adjustment Mechanisms

This chapter deals with major functional psychotic disorders in which the patient is completely cut-off from reality. A psychosis is a major disorder which involves the total personality of the patient. The patient is so much disturbed thathe cannot participate in routine activities. What he perceives and believes seems to be true to him. He tries to adjust toh is environment in his own way. His sense impressions cannot be verified. The personality of the patient is completely disorganized under severe adjustive stress. The patient becomes incapable of living in accordance with social norms. He becomes a liability to the society.

Characreristics of Psychotics

Following are the common symptoms of psychotics :

Disturbed mental functions:

The mental functions of a psychotic are disturbed to such an extent that he is incapable of carrying on his daily routine. For example, he cannot communicate with others and is unable to take care of his personal cleanliness.

Severe mental Symptom

The psychotic develops delusion, hallucination, incoherence in speech and violence which cut him off from environmental realities.

Injurious to society

The psychotic may be injurious to himself and to others.

Therefore he is usually placed in confinement where he is looked after by others.

Lack of insight :

The psychotic usually does not appreciate or realize the nature of his symptoms and disabilities. Here we will describe in detail two common symptoms of psychotics namely: delusion and hallucination.

Delusion

A delusion is a false belief, an idea which is without any basis and out of harmony with the facts of the patient's surroundings. For example, a psychotic may have the delusion of grandeur as if he possesses tremendous power and influence on others. Some psychotics may have the delusion of persecution as if they are being harmed by others. The psychotics believe their delusions to be true and defend them despite factual evidence to the contrary.

Hallucination

It refers to the preception of things and events that are wholly imaginary in nature. The most common hallucinations are visual and auditory. The psychotic may hear or see strange things in the void. For example, the patients see God in the void or hear the sound of ghosts etc. It has also been observed that some psychotics suffer from illusions in which the patient misinterprets or falsely perceives external stimuli. For example, a psychotic may believe that the bus driver is a detective who is watching his activities. Thus we see that a psychotic is much more severely disturbed and disorganized than a neurotic.

Types of psychotic Disorders

There are two major types of psychotic disorders : namely functional and organic brain disorders. Functional disorders are those that develop without damage to or disturbance in the brain. They are generally caused by emotional frustrations whereas organic disorders are caused by some structural alteration of the brain by injury or diseases.

A—FUNCTIONAL PSYCHOSES

Functional psychoses are classified as below :

1. Schizophrenia
2. Paranoia
3. Manic-depressive psychosis.

B—ORGANIC DISORDERS

Organic mental disorders refers to a great variety of mental diseases or behaviours which are caused by organic damage. They are grouped under the following seven categories.

1. Disorders of orientation

The individual may be confused about his location in time and space.

2. Disorders of memory

All types of memory disorders are caused by organic brain injury as loss of memory.

3. Disorders of communication

These speech disorders are called aphasia—difficulty in finding the words to explain one's ideas.

4. Disorders of perception

Many perceptional problems may be caused by brain disorders in which the individual may misinterpret the sensory input.

5. Disorders of motor behaviour

Disturbances in movements of the voluntary musculature in organic mental disorders may range from mild defects in motor coordination to total paralysis. Aproxia is a mild disorder of voluntary movements, in which the individual fails to carry out-sequential acts.

6. Disorders of intellect

Intellectual impairment like dementia.

7. Directors of emotions

Organic damage to the brain structure or changes in function of brain tissues may cause disorders of emotions. Here we will describe only functional disorders.

1. SCHIZOPHRENIA

Schizophrenia also called dementia, is the most common and the severest psychotic disorder which has drawn the attention of professional workers in recent years due to its high percentage of occurrence in society. Thorpe and his associates describing its seriousness said : "It accounts for approximately one fifth of all patients admitted to mental hospitals each year. It afflicts over 50 per cent of those hospitalized in mental institutions; it takes its toll principally between adolescence and early adulthood, between the ages 15 to 30."

The figures for schizophrenia in India are not exactly known but there is every possibility that problem is alarming.

Symptoms of schizophrenia

Some of the common symptoms of schizophrenia are given below :

(*a*) *Disorganized thinking and feeling* :

The behaviour of the schizophrenic is marked by disorganized thinktng and feeling. There is no reason or logc in what he says. His speech is incoherent.

(*b*) *Apathy* :

The patient develops apathy of feeling and emotions to situations.

(*c*) *Bizarre action* :

It refers to absurd, inappropriate, eccentric phrases and actions.

(*d*) *Seclusiveness* :

The patient withdraws himself from social situations and remains preoccupied with inward rumination.

(*e*) *Incoherence* :

The patient develops disorganized patterns of speech marked by irrelevance and repetition of the same idea.

(*f*) *Delusion* :

He sees delusions either of persecution or of grandeur.

(*g*) *Hallucinatory behaviour* :

The patient perceives objects when there is no appropriate basis for them in the external world.

(*h*) *Neglect of conduct and personal habits* :

The patient does not care for his clothes and does not care to charge his dress for weeks together. Generally he is looked after by others.

Arieti characterized schizophrenic as : "It must be repeated here that the schizophrenic does not mingle freely, that he prefers to be by himself...It is often said that a schizophrenic lives in a shell, that an autistic barrier separates him from others...There is an impairment of the ability to socialize, that is to communicate with others and to share experience with others."

Types of Schizophrenia

There are four types of schizophrenia which are described below :

1. Simple Schizophrenia

A person suffering from simple schizophrenia retreats from

society. He does not take interest in his work and becomes apathetic towards his family and friends. He becomes increasingly inattentive moody and highly irritable.

He does not participate in games or social functions. He has daydreams. He gives the impression of being stupid and mentally retarded. A person suffering from simple schizophrenia does not have delusions and hallucination and retains contact with reality.

2. Hebephrenic schizophrenia

A person suffering from Hebephrenic schizophrenia appears to be the most disorganized of all. He is characterized by giggling, screaming, masturbating in public, playing with his own excrement. He conforms most closely to the popular stereotype of the raving lunatic. The patient hallucinates and converses with people who are not actually present. He is incoherent in his speech. It represents a more severe disintegration of the personality than the other types of schizophrenia. The patient is more occupied with his fantasies and becomes seclusive.

As the disorder progresses, the individual becomes emotionally indifferent and infantile in his reactions, to others.

3. Catatonic schizophrenia

The common symptoms of catatonic schizophrenia are quite different from the above referred types of schizophrenia. Patients may appear agitated, a condition which is called "catatonic furor". After excitement, they become completely immobilized. They may remain in the same posture for long periods, staring blankly into space, seemingly unaware of their surroundings.

Catatonic patients appear to be completely oblivious to the outside world but they are not. The author had an opportunity to observe the behaviour of a patient suffering from catatonic schizophrenia. The patient remained standing in a specific posture with a stone in his hand for hours together.

4. Paranoid schizophrenia

The main problem with the patients suffering from paranoid schizophrenia is their delusion ; otherwise they seem to be reasonably intact. They can be annoying, difficult and even menacing. They appear to be chaotic and confused. Their delusions are apt to be more fantastic and their speech may be rembling and odd sounding.

Causes of schizophrenia

A number of studies have been conducted in recent years to locate the causes of schizophrenia but precise factors have not yet been located. It has been established by experimental studies on schizophrenia that it is essentially caused by personality disturbances arising from the individual's inability to satisfy his ego-needs and to cope successfully with his environment.

(i) Organic Factors :

Kallman attributes the basic cause of schizophrenia to hereditary factors on the basis of his studies on twins. He concluded that schizophrenia appears often in certain families than in the general population. But his claim that heredity must be a causative factor was questioned by Rosanoff who concluded on the basis of the study of identical twins that "hereditary factors in themselves are inadequate for the manifestation of a mental disorder—hereditary factors are not essential in the etiology of these mental disorders, since they are not always present."

Jackson concluded that the inheritance of schizophrenia is very much open to question.

(ii) Psychological Factors :

Most researchers in the field of schizophrenic disorders hold the view that psychological factors in the nature of frustration and conflicts are the primary causes in the development of schizophrenia.

Arieti has evaluated several articles on schizophrenia and concluded that organic and psychological factors both play their role in the manifestation of schizophrenia.

Meyer advanced his point of view by suggesting that unhealthy and inadequate habits of thought, feeling and action play an important role in the development of schizophrenia. He regarded schizophrenic behaviour as resulting from the inability of the individual to make satisfactory adjustment to his environment. Cameron supports Meyer and writes : "Schizophrenic disorganization and dissocialization involve principally the withdrawal and escape techniques but to certain extent they usually serve also as aggression and defuse."

Arieti states : "The psychosis may be viewed as the ultimate attempt on the part of the patient to solve his difficulties." The schizophrenic as the child was rejected, anxious and hostile and did not receive proper love and affection from either of the parents. Studies reveal that schizophrenic child is brought up in a cold, hostile and rejecting home environment. The unfavourable home environment in early childhood causes overwhelming feelings of anxiety and hostility in later stages of development.

Treatmemt

Schizophrenia is the most severe of all the personality disorders and the outlook for complete recovery is not good. It has admittedly been the most difficult mental disorder to treat. However, with the development of new methods of treatment, it has been possible to treat it successfully.

Arieti writes : "Generally after shock therapy, the patient is able to return to society ; he will no longer be a public charge, and although his functions may be curtailed he may be able to live some kind of limited life." Psychotherapy can only be made available to a very small percentage of schizophrenics. This is due to the fact that the therapist is unable to communicate with the patient. Psychotherapy thus becomes ineffectual in most cases.

Prevention

It is better to prevent the occurrence of mental disorders by providing a conducive environment to children right from early childhood where they can develop desirable habits for proper adjustment in their social environment. Children should develop a sense of security and personal adequacy. The role of mother is very crucial in maintaining a warm relationship with the child. She should not reject the child either by obvious or subtle means.

Parents should be aware of the damaging effect of harsh discipline, unfavourable comparison, scoldings, criticism and insufficient affection for the child. Parents should maintain a good relationship with each other. It has been reported that homes marred by marital discord, divorce, separation and frequent quarrels cause severe emotional damage to the child.

2. PARANOIA

Paranoia has been used by Greeks indiscriminately for all types of mental disorders but Krapeline has recently reserved the term paranoia to cases showing delusions and impaired contact with reality without severe personality disorganization The patient's delusional system is logical and systematized. He possesses adequate general comprehension.

Symptoms

—Well organized and logical delusions : The paranoic delusions are of a fixed type and of locally constructed nature.

—Judgement impaired : The patient of paranoia fails to pass judgement on any problems which confront him.

—Orientation correct : His orientation toward life is normal.

—Emotional responses adequate. His emotional reactions in social interactions are quite adequate.

—Hallucinations rate. He has no hallucinatory experiences

—He has average or superior intelligence and is suspicious of the behaviour of others. He is very sensitive.

Causes

(*i*) *Prolonged frustration and conflicts* :

Prolonged frustration and conflicts in childhood and adolescence resulting in marked feelings of inadequacy and insecurity are the basic factors which cause paranoia.

(*ii*) *Disturbed emotional relationship* :

If the relationship with parents in early childhood is disturbed, the child begins to feel insecure, unwanted, uncared for and unappreciated.

Parents who abuse each other, make false promises, threaten, scold, nag, condemn and punish excessively, create defects in the child's emotional relationship According to Freud, paranoia develops on the basis of repressed homosexuality. He held that the patient as a result of his homosexual tendencies feels inadequate, unworthy and guilty of his behaviour. He escapes from the intolerable pain associated with these feelings by projecting them upon others.

Treatment and Prevention

It has been reported that psychotherapy with paranoic patients proves difficult because of the lack of insight on the part of patient.

Cameron writes, "What the patient needs in therapy is not, of course, merely a chance to talk, to express himself and ventilate his feelings. He needs to break out of his isolation and share his frightening experiences with some one who does not take sides...The therapeutic aim at this level is to replace a generalized suspicion with a specific trust...trust in the neutral therapist which can become a base for further explorations." Prevention of paranoia depends on early childhood training and development of feelings of security and adequacy in children by parents.

3. MANIC-DEPRESSIVE PSYCHOSIS

Manic-depressive psychosis, as the name suggests is a mental disorder characterized by periodic attacks often alternating in nature between marked elation and depression.

Characteristics

The periods of depression or elation appear alternately. It is not neces ary that periods of elation and depression must occur in every patient. Patients may show either of the two.

Attacks of elation/depression vary in duration from days to years.

Normal periods appear between the attacks. It may also vary from patient to patient and in the same patient.

The disturbance is basically emotional in nature. But intellectual processes are impaired. Now we will describe different types of manias and depressions.

1. Mania

This period is marked by feelings of elation in which the patient is unduly boastful, enthusiastic and hyperactive. He is irritable and intolerable of personal criticism. Following are the important types of mania.

(*a*) *Hypomania* :

The hypomanic is usually very talkative, boastful and distractible. He is humorous, amusing and entertaining. He is sensitive to criticism and irritable. His speech is loud and rapid and frequently accompanied by gestures. The patient has no insight into his conditions.

(*b*) *Acute mania* :

The speech of the actue manic is confused. He suffers from flights of ideas. He shifts from subject to subject without any attempt to connect them. He becomes destructive and may break furniture, or may strike those near him. He is overactive.

Hallucination and illusions are frequent. Memory is not affected. Insight is seldom present in him.

(*c*) *Hypermania* :

The patient suffering from hypermania manifests pronounced symptoms of mania such as extreme motor activity with marked tendencies toward violence and destructiveness. The patient is extremely combative and under seizure of mania may attack people and destroy furniture and tear off his clothes. He is confused and incoherent in his behaviour. He is vulgar in his behaviour. Sometimes he urinates on the floor. Sometimes he makes noise, cries, yells, sings and dances. Hallucination and illusion are sometimes not present.

(*d*) *Delusional Mania* :

The patient suffers from delusions of grandeur of unsystematic and illogical types. The patient believes himself to be a great leader, a saint or even God. There is flight of ideas. Hallucination, illusions and much motor excitement are the common symptoms of delusional mania.

2. Depressive Psychosis

The patient suffering from depressive psychosis is characterized by extremely sad and pessimistic mood. He feels unworthy and lacks confidence to do anything. The patient is indifferent to his environmental stimuli and maintains silence. He experiences hallucination, illusions and delusions. Following types of depressions have been reported.

(*a*) *Simple depression* :

The patient shows general slowing down of physical and mental activities. He is gloomy dejected and sad. His attitude is of uncertainty and doubt. He feels unworthy and incompetent to do anything. He entertains thoughts of suicide. He neither eats nor sleeps well.

(*b*) *Marked depression* :

The patient feels himself completely helpless and unworthy

to do anything. His speech is slow and monotonous. Sometimes patient refusese to take food.

Delusions of sin and guilt are common.

(*c*) *Stuporous depression* :

Stuporous depression is marked by morbidity, dearth of ideas, stupor and clouding of consciousness. The patient is mute and negativistic. He neither speaks nor responds to others. He is looked after by others for all his needs. The patient is completely inactive. He may sit in the same posture hours together until disturbed.

(*d*) *Delusional depression* :

The patient develops delusions of persecution which are illogical and unsystematized. He may develop hypochondrical ideas, ideas of ruin, ideas of humility and ideas of guilt. Delusions are accompanied by hallucinations and illusions.

3. Mixed types

All patients who suffer from manic-depressive psychosis cannot either be manic or depreseed types. There are patients who possess the symptoms of both the phases and are thus called mixed types. A patient may be talkative and excited and yet be severely depressed or may be active at the same time.

(*a*) *Agitated depression* :

In agitated depression the patient is irritable and overactive. He exhibits restlessness in his activities by roaming here and there. The patient does not eat and sleep and thus loses weight. He often commits suicide.

(*b*) *Manic Stupor* :

The patient suffers from elation, dearth of ideas and clouding of consciousness. He shows retarded motor activity. He experiences great difficulty in thinking.

Hallucinations and illusions are sometimes experienced. The patients sometimes exhibit high motor activity and may tear off their clothes and throw food on the floor.

Comparison of Schizophrenia and Manic-Depressive psychosis

Schizophrenia	*Manic-Depressive*
1. Personality is seclusive and a social	1. Personality is energetic and social
2. Emotions and thought are incongruous	2. Emotions are related to thought
3. Emotions are blunted	3. Emotions are exaggerated
4. General behaviour is odd and silly	4. General behaviour includes period of excitement and depression
5. Excitement is purposeless and unrelated	5. Excitement is purposeful and related
6. Insight is rarely present	6. Insight is frequently present
7. Hallucinations are frequent	7. Hallucinations are rare.

Causal Factors

Manic-depressive psychosis is a defense mechanism through which the patient attempts to cope with his frustrations, conflicts and environmental difficulties. The patient is basically highly insecure, inadequate and full of feelings of guilt.

Richman stressed this fact: "When we study the life reactions of our manic-depressive patients and go into their childhood histories we often find an overactive extraverted child, placed in a situation of emotional frustration. There is friction between the parents, a broken home, a dominating mother or a drunken father; a home in which a child feels no security and received little help in handling the problems of his own personality development."

Arieti emphasizes the dynamic factor displacement by the younger sibling and role of the mother in rejection of the child. He says: "It is only by complying, obeying and working hard that he will recapture the love or state of bliss which he used to have as a baby or will at least maintain that moderate love which he is receiving. Love is still available but not as a steady flow. The flow is intermittent, conditioned and therefore does not confer security. The child feels that if he does not do what he is supposed to, he will be punished; mother may withdraw her love totally. At the same that the anxiety of losing mother's love or to recapture it if and when it is lost.... The anxiety about being unable to fulfil parental expectations changes into guilt feelings. If affection or forgiveness is not forthcoming, the child feels that is his own fault; he has not lived upto what was expected of him and he feels guilty."

Hutt and Gibby also stressed the role of the mother in causing manic-depressive psychosis. They say that "In the manic-depressive psychosis, the major anxiety provoking situation occur when the closeness of identification with the mother begins to disappear, but the mature relationship based on recognition of others has not yet been adequately developed.

Maslow discussing the psychodynamics of depressive-reactions says, "Depressed patients are unable to turn away from the people who hurt them because of their emotional dependence on them. The profound feeling of worthlessness is caused by their self-condemnation and their expectation of disapproval resulting from their hostility, toward these indispensable individuals. Such a patient then feels not only disapproved of by this individual but also abandoned and rejected."

Klien contends that manic-depressive psychosis is related to frustrations involving ambitions and the striving for personal prestige.

Cohen and associates on the basis of an intensive study of manic-depressive psychosis found that there was a lack of consistent authority on the part of the parents as to what outsiders thought of the family position. Kallman and associates postulated that hereditary factors are the primary cause of manic-depressive psychosis. But Rosanoff contradicted their claim and concluded that hereditary factors per se are not responsible. They do not suffice to produce manic-depressive psychosis."

Treatment and Prevention

The treatment depends on the severity of the attack. Mild attacks may be treated by psychotherapy and severe attacks by shock therapy. Psychotherapy has been found very effective in all types of mild manic-depressive states but psychotherapy should continue for a pretty long time to give lasting improvement. Psychotherapy should be directed to enable the patient to learn new patterns of living and a more realistic regard for himself.

Physical treatment in the form of electric shock has been found especially effective with the depressed patients.

Patients in manic phase are some times treated by the method of prolonged narcosis which induces sleep. As regards the prevention of manic-depressive psychosis, the methods which are applied in the prevention of other emotional disturbances are generally used. Improved marital relations, positive attitudes good handling of children are basic to the prevention of this mental disorder.

QUESTIONS FOR DISCUSSIONS

1. What are the characteristics of psychotics? Describe them.

4. Define schizophrenia. What are its causes ?

3. What is manic-depressive psychosis ? Describe its causes,

4. Compare schizophrenia and manic-depressive psychosis.
5. What are the causes of manic-depressive psychosis.

SUGGESTED READINGS

1. Broen, W.E.G. Schizophrenia: Research and Theory; Academic Press, NY, 1968.

2. Butcher. J.N: Abnormal Psychology; Elmont. Calif, Wadsworth, 1971.

3. Eysenck, H.J. (Ed.): Handbook of Abnormal Psychology; Pitman, London, 1966.

4. Goldenberg. H.: Abnormal Psychology; Brooks/Cole Montechery, 1977.

5. Mehar, Joseph; Abnormal Psychology: Holt Rinehalt. NY., 1983.

CHAPTER 9

Neurotic Character Disorders

Neurotic character disorders represent conditions of acting out of conflicts and frustrations through activities which are not socially approved and violate social norms. Acting out, psychologically, means the occurrence of behaviour that is symbolic of the individual's earlier conflict and that is repressive in nature and is likely to be condemned by the society to which he belongs. The individual, through neurotic character disorders, freely acts out his repressed childish impulses without any inhibition and restraint.

This chapter briefly deals only with four neurotic character disorders namely: delinquency, sexual dysfunctions, alcoholism and use of drugs.

A. DELINQUENCY

It is universally acknowledged that children are that greatest national asset on whom depends the future development and prosperity of a nation. It is, therefore, very essential that children should be physically, mentally and emotionally healthy so that they may develop their potentialities to the maximum for the benefit of the nation.

In the last two decades there has been sufficient evidence of increase in the rapid juvenile delinquency both in terms of absolute number of offences and in the rate of delinquent behaviour. We read daily in newspapers reports of cases of delinquency of different types such as theft, truancy, rape, etc. This increasing trend in the percentage of delinquency has caused great concern to all those who are closely associated with the social and economic welfare of the society. Ours is a developing country, so we are more conscious of the problems of our adolescent boys and girls who are an asset to the nation.

Meaning of Delinquency

The term juvenile delinquency has existed in our literature since Manu developed a code of conduct for the society and prescribed punishment for various types of crimes ranging from petty thefts to murders. The term has undergone radical changes according to the socio-economic and other developments in society from time to time.

Definition of Juvenile Delinquency

There is no general agreement as regards the definition of the term because researchers in the field define the term from different angles. Here we will give a few selected definitions of juvenile delinquency. According to clinical psychologists who deal with the treatment of delinquents, "delinquency is super-ego deficiency." This means that the delinquent fails to incorporate primitive taboos of the society and fails to internalize the moral values of his family. He seeks pleasure and gratification of his needs by sacrificing the principles of reality and morality. The super-ego of delinquents is weak and improperly developed. The anti-social behaviour is not checked by the super-ego. Adolescents who have weak super-egos may develop anti-social behaviour.

Learning theorists explain delinquency from another point of view and define it as: "Delinquent behaviour reflects the moral deficiency of the individual which is caused by improper training in early childhood." They emphasize the importance of early childhood learning. If early childhood training fails to develop proper moral values in children, they may become delinquents.

Bandura and Walter explain delinquency as aggression which is developed by frustration of dependency needs of the child.

Criminologists who believe that criminal behaviour is inherited explain delinquency in terms of the underactivity of the central nervous system. According to them, the central nervous system of delinquents is defective and does not function properly.

Robinson defines delinquency as "any behaviour which a given community at a given time considers in conflict with its best interests, whether or not the offender has been brought to Court."

Herbert Quay defines: "The delinquent, then, would be a person whose behaviour is a relatively serious legal offence; who is inappropriate to his level of adjustment development; is not committed, is a result of extremely low intellect...; pathology or severe mental or metabolic dysfunction; and is alien to the culture in which he has been reared."

Richard, A. Cloward defines: "the delinquency act...is behaviour the violates norms of the society, and when officially known, it evokes a judgement by agents of criminal justice that such norms have been violated."

C. Burt defined delinquency as: "A child is to be regarded delinquent when his anti-social tendencies appear so grave that he becomes or ought to become the subject of an official action."

Summing up we can say that as regards the definition of delinquency, psychologists, clinicians and sociologists disagree to a great extent and present different explanations of delinquency. But all agree that delinquent behaviour is anti-social and in violation of the social norms of the society.

THEORIES OF DESINQUENCY

Several theories have been developed by psychologists, sociologists and educationists to explain the anti-social behaviour of children. Here we will discuss the major theories.

Biological Theories

Biological theories of delinquent and criminal behaviour assume that individuals vary in behaviour because their biological structures differ. Their belief in the biological inheritance of crime is viewed as a propensity, tendency or mental pre-disposition which is part of the physical environment.

In 1812 Benjamin Rush identified anti-social behaviour as a disease, labelling persons with no control over their impulses, as "morally deranged." According to him, this illness, led people to lie, steal and anti-social behaviour and arose from organic or functional pathology of the central nervous system.

Lambraso, an Italian, took another approach arguing that criminals have some characteristics physiological features which differentiate them from non-criminals. He advocated that criminals are the product of hereditary and social factors, some of them beyond their control. He believed that criminals could be recognised by their protruding ears, abundant hair, sparse beard enormous frontal sinuses, square jaws, protruding chin, broad cheekbones and so forth. He emphasized the importance of heredity in criminal behaviour.

Goring, an English criminologist, conducted research studies to test the reliability of Lombraso's claim of characteristic features of criminals. He found that anatomical differences did not distinguish criminals and non-criminals. He suggested some other factors, possible low intelligence, as being more responsible in developing criminal behaviour.

Sehlapp (1924) held that excessive glandular secretions were the cause of anti-social behaviour. He confirmed from his studies that one third of the criminals suffered from emotional instability caused by malfunctioning of gland cells and the central nervous system.

More recently, Sheldon (1940) categorized all human beings

into three body types. The endomorphic (round and fat), the mesomorphic (muscular) and the ectomorphic (lean). The Gluecks (1956) applied Sheldon's Typology to study delinquents and found that delinquents are in majority muscular and can be categorized as mesomorphics.

George B. Vold criticised the physical type theories by calling them, "a more or less sophisticated form of 'shadow-boxing with the constitutional factor in human behaviour." His varieties of delinquents do not differ significantly in somato types.

The simple question which arises is: can criminal behaviour be passed on genetically? The classic studies of "Jukes" by Dugdale (1877) revealed that an unusually large percentage of Jukes became criminals. The study of "Kallikaks" by Goddard also revealed that the descendants of Martin Kallikak from a feeble-minded bar maid had a long history of crime.

It is very difficult to say how much of these patterns of behaviour can be traced to genes and to bad environment. The question has not been conclusively solved as yet.

Psychological Theories

Psychological theories of delinguency attempt to link it with personality disturbances. Repeated delinquent behaviour may result from anti-social, psychopathic or sociopathic personalities. Psychologists believe that the anti-social acts of adolescents are the result of defective family relationship and defects in learning.

Green (1964) found 60% of psychopathic samples had lost a parent during childhood. In other cases a child may be deprived of parental affection. It has been established by studies that high incidence of parental neglect, emotional disturbance in family relations, and parental inconsistency in discipline are the main causes of delinquency.

Freud was the first psychoanalyst to advocate that behaviour is not always consciously motivated; the unconscious plays a major role in directing behaviour. Psychoanalytically defects in early parent-child relationship result in a failure to identify properly with parental figures. This results in faulty super-ego development with a resulting lack of feeling of guilt and inability to restrain the anti-social impulses of one's instincts.

Freud's contribution is largely based on his experience: The major conclusions are as follows:

1. Parents' reactions and early training of children is very important for the harmonious development of personality. Feelings of insecurity, frustration and constant anxiety will create a disturbed personality.

2. The parents' attitudes and the cultural environment play a crucial role in determining the reaction of the child to them and the environment.

3. The unconscious process and motives are very important factors shaping the personality.

Behaviourists explain delinquency from the learning point of view. According to them, all behaviour is learned. Delinquency is also learned from the environment.

Eysenck (1964) combines the biological and learning theory approaches. He suggests that some people may suffer from an excess of anxiety because they have inherited a nervous system that speeds up the acquisition of conditioned responses. Others have inherited a nervous system that leads to the under development of conditioned anxiety.

Numerous empirical studies have been conducted to link crime and delinquency to personality traits.

Stein, Sarbin, and Kulik (1968) find that delinquents have a poorer sense of future time perspective than non-delinquents.

Aichorn's Contribution

He attempted to apply Freud's theory to redirecting the behaviour of aggressive boys. According to him, delinquents are unable to accept either restraint or authority. They are unconcerned about the feelings of others and often show utter disregard for other people's property.

Eissler explained delinquent behaviour as a reaction to the value system of the individual. It involves a basic conflict with the value system of the society and is considered as aggressive behaviour which defies the established values in any given society.

Sociological Theories

Sociologists present a different explanation of anti-social behaviour. According to Durkheim, "serious economic or political stress can lead to a break-down of power in a social system, whereby cultural norms no longer have inhibiting influence over group and individual behaviour."

The first official study of delinquency in England (1916) blamed gangs, lack of education, improper presenting, broken homes, association with thieves, unemployment and failing in police and prison, as the major causes.

According to sociologists much crime is determined by factors operating outside the individual's choice such as urban ecology, local culture, social change and structure. These factors lead to conforming behaviour (CB). On the other hand, if the deviation factors (DF) predominate over the conforming factor (CF) then a deviation differentiation (DD) is created which leads to deviating behaviour (DB). The formula is as follows:

$$CF\,(1 \times E) - DF\,(1 \times E) = \begin{matrix} CD & CB \\ \text{or} & \text{or} \\ DD & DB \end{matrix}$$

Abrahamsen's Formula of Criminal Behaviour

$$C = \frac{T + S}{R}$$

C = Criminal act

T = Criminalistic tendency

S = Crime inducing situation

R = The person's mental and emotional resistance to temptation.

Sociologists see crime as a social event in all societies of the world having a predetermined function.

In 1930 with rapid urbanization, industrialization and immigration contributing to the disintegration of traditional communities, "The Chicago school" used the analogy of social biology for its image of the city.

According to them, "the city was an organism with its various parts in precarious balance. Foreign invasion (immigration), periodically disrupted the organisms' proper functioning and massive social disorganization such as crime or other social pathology resulted. Like the body, the city was divided into functional areas, with the business zone its heart. Pathology emerged primarily in zones of transition, between the centre where immigrants first settled and outer rings to which they moved to escape new invasions.

According to Shaw "contact with delinquent groups often marks the beginning of the boy's career in delinquency and his initial delinquencies are often identical with the traditions and established practices of the group. It is probable the participation in the activities of such group is one of the very significant contributing factors in cases of delinquency."

Characteristics of Delinquents

It is very difficult to pinpointedly list the characteristics of delinquents because children indulge in all types of delinquent acts. Sheldon and Gluceks in their study of delinquents listed the following characteristics :

(*i*) *Physical* : Mostly delinquents are mesomorphic in constitution. They are muscular and bold.

(*ii*) *Temperament* : Delinquents are aggressive, destructive, energetic, impulsive and extraverted.

(*iii*) *Attitude* : They are hostile, defiant, resentful, suspicious, unconventional and non-submissive to authority.

(*iv*) *Psychological* : Their behaviour, mostly operates on a concrete level rather than on symbolic, intellectual expression. They are less methodical in their approach to the problem.

(*v*) *Socio-cultural* : Lack of affections, instability and violation of social norms.

Types of Delinquent Acts

The types of act which can be termed as delinquent are difficult to list because of cultural variations in different countries of the world Socio-economic conditions also affect the definition of delinquency. For example, drinking, smoking, kissing, etc., are normal behaviour in western countries but in our society is termed as delinquency. Following is the list of acts which are termed as delinquent acts in our society :

(i) Acquisitive Tendency

The highest percentage of delinquent acts of children have the immediate aim of gratifying the acquisitive tendency. Stealing is the most common act which, starting from the family and if not detected at the initial stage and dealt with adequately, is generalized to other situations in neighbourhood, school, shops, etc. Stealing releases tension, particularly sexual tension and gratifies the needs of delinquents. Generally stealing is done during adolescence by groups which develop cohesion.

(ii) Forgery

Forgery is another delinquent act which is committed by adolescents. They can forge the signature of their parents on result cards and cheques to draw money from the bank.

(iii) Aggression

Aggression is found in great percentage among adolescents. It gives relief to the offender. Aggression may be direct or indirect against animate or inanimate objects of the environment. The following are the major types of aggression.

(a) Bullying and mockery

(b) Torturing of animals

(c) Damaging school or public property

(d) Committing suicide.

(iv) Sex Delinquency

Following are the major types of sex delinquency :

(a) Homosexuality

(b) Heterosexuality

(c) Prostitution

(d) Musturbation

(e) Abducting and raping

(f) Making sexual suggestion

(v) Tendency to escape

This tendency indicates the inability of the individual to face reality.

(a) Truancy from school and home

Causes of Delinquency

There are two different views as regards the causal factors of delinquency : one view is held by hereditarians who hold that delinquency is caused by inheritance; the other view is held by environmentalists who emphasize the importance of the environment in the development of antisocial behaviour. A third view lays emphasis on the interaction of the hereditary and environmental factors and holds that an individual is the by-product of the constant interaction of these two factors. It is very difficult to isolate the contribution either of heredity or environment in the development of personality. The following may be the causes of delinquency.

(a) Psychological or Hereditary factors

1. Genetic factor

Eysenck, an English psychologist, proposed a constitutional cum-learning theory of delinquency and criminal behaviour. He quotes nine separate studies which report findings on 331 monozygotic twins and 535 pairs of dizygotic times. The concordance rates of the identical twins with regard to delinquent behaviour is over four times that of non-identical times and in every investigation the concordance rate of the monozygotic pair was greater than that of the dizygotic pair. He maintains that it is difficult to account for these differences solely in environmental terms. He postulates that the personality dimensions of extraversion, neuroticism and tough-mindedness are significantly influenced by genetic factors. The delinquents score high on measures of extraversion, neuroticism and tough mindedness.

2. The XYY Factor

According to some psychologists, an extra male chromosome predisposes males with the socalled XYY condition to delinquent behaviour. There appears to be any usually high proportion of XYY men in penal institutions, mostly belonging to class IV and V, i.e., they come from lower socio-economic groups. But Radcliffe (1974) on the basis of his genetic surveys of 1000 babies has discredited this theory. It is no longer held that the XYY factor is responsible for delinquent behaviour.

3. Organic Factors

Rogers and Lilienefied (1956) suggest that there is convincing empirical evidence of correlations between complications of pregnancy and birth and behaviour disorder. Behaviour disturbances are caused by abnormalities of pregnancy and incidence of prematurity.

4. Congenital Temperamental Factors

Some psychologists take the view that delinquent behaviour is caused by temperamental factors which are the by-product of early learning and hereditary factors.

(b) Enviromental Factors

Environmentalists who emphasize the importance of learning hold that delinquent behaviour is learned like other behaviour in the environment. The environmental factors can be dealt with under four heads which are described below :

(1) Ecological Factors

Ecology means the effect of physical surroundings and climate on the growth and development of the organism. Burgess and Park applied the ecological approach to the study of human community in Chicago city. They studied the social phenomena in Chicago city and related delinquency to the growth of the city. The conclusions of their ecological studies can be summarized as follows :

(i) The highest percentage of delinquents come from densely populated areas and specially from congested wards of the city.

(ii) A high percentage of delinquents come from manufacturing commercial plants and highly industrialized parts of the city.

(iii) The nearer a given locality is to the centre of the city, the higher will be its rate of delinquency.

(iv) The slum areas of the city breed the highest percentage of delinquents.

(2) Delinquency and Home

Industrialization and mobility in the last two decades have accelerated the process of social change in India. We are proceeding from a rural economy to an urban industrial economy. There has been high increase on large scale migration from rural to urban areas. The traditional joint family is disorganizing and the process of socialization is being adversely affect.

There is a great difference in the process of socialization in rural and urban community. The family as an agent of socialization has lost its importance in cities. Parents are not able to give proper training to their sons and daughters. In big cities working parents leave their families for long hours. The women lib movement of the seventies, has adversely affected the permanence and stability of the family.

Now let us give the specific conditions within the family which may create delinquency in children.

(*i*) *Broken Homes* : All psychologists agree that the highest percentage of delinquents come from broken homes because broken homes fail to provide a conducive environment for the proper development of the child.

(*ii*) *Marital Adjustment* : If parents are not well-adjusted and quarrel, there is every possibility of children being delinquents.

(*iii*) *Employed Parents* : Homes where both the parents are in service and children are left in the care of servants may breed delinquents. Servants in big cities are responsible to a great extent in developing anti-social behaviour in children. It has been established by several studies that if the mother is employed, the child does not receive his mother's attention and the affection which he needs. Gluecks conducted research on the problems of working mothers and delinquency. Their main conclusion is that children of working mothers may become delinquents.

(*iv*) *Poverty* : Poverty is the root of all evils. Due to poverty parents fail to fulfil the legitimate needs of their children. The highest percentage of delinquents come from the low socio-economic stratum of the society. But it should be kept in mind that not all delinquents come from poor homes. As a matter of fact it depends on the moral code of the family and how far the moral values have been internalized by the child.

(*v*) *Disability of Parents* : If both parents, or one of them is physically or mentally disabled, they cannot exercise control over their children and there is every possibility of children being engaged in delinquent atcs.

(*vi*) *Defective Discipline* : Homes which do not follow any criterion of discipline, may develop anti-social behaviour in children. Parents who are sometimes too strict and sometimes too lenient may create mental tension in the minds of their children. If the parents quarrel, abuse, drink or criticise each other in the presence of their children, then there is every possibility of their children being led to delinquency.

(*vii*) *Lack of Affection* : Homes where children feel insecure and neglected may breed delinquents.

(*viii*) *Partiality* : If children are shown partiality by parents, they become delinquents.

(*ix*) *Unvocalized Tension* : Sometimes in joint families, there is unvocalized tension among the members of a family. This tension affects the children adversely.

(*x*) *Lack of Moral Code* : Homes which do not follow any moral code may develop anti-social behaviour in children because children do not have any model to imitate in their home.

(*xi*) *Lack of Recreation* : Recreation is an essential activity which releases pent-up feelings of the individual. If the pent-up feelings are not properly released they may be directed to anti-social behaviour in adolescents.

(*xii*) *Crowded Home* : Generally in big cities homes are crowded with many members accommodating in a single room. Children in such homes come to know about sex delinquency at an early age.

(*xiii*) *Company of Servants* : In big cities, and particularly, in the higher strata of society children remain in the company of servants who may induce them to a life of delinquency.

3. Delinquency and School

Next in importance to the home is the school which is responsible for training children to shoulder the responsibilities of future life. The school of today has become even more important with additional responsibilities which were formerly the exclusive province of the home. A mushroom growth of kindergarten and nursery schools has taken place in the last two decades to educate children right from the age of two in the process of socialization. The following factors in the school may lead children to delinquent behaviour.

(*i*) *Location* :

If the school is located far off from the city or in an industrial area in the vicinity of movie, halls and undesirable markets, there is every possibility that school children may be tempted to delinquent acts.

(*ii*) *Lack of Discipline* :

If the school has no discipline or it is too strict, students may revolt against authority and indulge in delinquent acts.

(*iii*) *Lack of Proper Emotional Climate* :

The emotional climate of the school exercises great influence on the behaviour of children. If the climate is conducive then there is no problem. If the relationship among students-students, students-teachers, teachers-headmaster, headmaster-students is not smooth, students may be associated in the dirty game of school politics. The incidence of delinquency increases in such schools.

(*iv*) *Partiality* :

Partiality on the part of the Headmaster or the teachers may lead to group formation among students, who may often clash on the campus and outside.

(*v*) *Lack of Facilities like Games and Library* :

Instruction in the classroom as it is practised today in our country creates monotomy and inhibits the emotional feelings of students because students do not actively participate in the teaching-learning process. The emotional stress created by teaching may be released in games and through light reading but if the students do not get an opportunity to express their pent-up feelings, they may indulge in anti-social activities. Schools which do not have these facilities may breed more delinquents than schools which have facilities for a good library, sports and games.

(*vi*) *Lack of other Extra-Curricular Activities* :

Drama, debate, excursion, clubs, scouting and educational tours and provide an opportunity to express feelings freely. students come closer to each other and the process of socialization is accelerated.

(*vii*) *Caste System* :

It is really very unfortunate that many schools in our country are still being run on a caste basis. In such institutions students of other castes are humiliated by students who form groups and often clash. Incidences of agression, rape and murder are very common.

(*viii*) *Lack of Guidance and Counselling* :

Schools which do not provide guidance and counnselling to their students produce more delinquents.

(*ix*) *Defective Curriculum and Examination System* :

A defective school curriculum which does not fulfil the needs of adolescent boys and girls contributes to a great extent to the development of anti-social behaviour. The present examination system, based on bookish knowledge, is also one of the major factors.

(x) *Lack of Moral and Sex Education* :

Our schools do not provide moral and sex education to students In the absence of these facilities many students are led to delinquent acts.

4. Delinquent and Society

Delinquency is also highly related with the social environment of the country. The following conditions may be responsible for delinquent acts in the society.

(*i*) *Class Conflicts* : Indian society is divided on the basis of religion, caste, creed and class. There have been rooted prejudices among some classes for generations. These age old conflicts still continue and consequently cause frequent riots, quarrels and clashes.

(ii) Tension in time of war, partition, floods and other natural calamities, when there is uncertainty of life, increases the rate of delinquency. International conditions also affect delinquency.

In the last two decades thousands of hippies have visited India and our adolescent boys and girls have been greatly influenced by their habits such as the use of drugs and a permissive attitude towards life.

Prevention and Treatment of Delinquency

There are two aspects of delinquency : prevention, which refers to the methods and strategies which may be used to check or to prevent delinquency in children and treatment of those who have become delinquents.

Prevention

The main objective of prevention is to develop skills, attitudes and other competencies in the individual so that anti-social behaviour may be checked in future. The task of prevention is very complex and difficult. It needs the combined efforts of home, school and society. Parents and significant others can inculcate good habits, attitudes and a sound value system, in children, because the child remains within the home in early childhood when a permanent impression can be created in his mind. It is unfortunate that in our country most parents are illiterate and themselves ignorant of the psychological principles of rearing children. The parents in most cases cannot provide proper guidance and counselling. Most children become delinquents because of the sheer ignorance of parents.

Here it is suggested that parents who are literate and familiarized with the basic principles of psychology may help their children by providing guidance and counselling in personal, educational and vocational problems. If proper guidance is provided at an opportune time, delinqency can be prevented.

The school can play an important role in preventing delinquency if the following facilities are provided :

(*i*) *Environment* :

The environment should be free of emotional tension. A conducive environment within the class and outside should be provided.

(*ii*) *Facilities* :

The School should provide facilities for games, a good library, drama, debate, excursion, tours, pinics, scouting, etc. for the maximum development of the potentialities of the students. The students should feel secure and closely affiliated with the school.

Curriculum

The curriculum should be framed in such a way that it fulfils the needs of children. The recently developed new structure of education (10+2+3) is designed to fulfil the needs of the children and the demands of society. The new educational policy (1985) which has been formulated on the initiative of our young and dynamic Prime Minister Rajiv Gandhi is expected to cater to the needs of children and demands of the society.

Provision for sex and moral education

Moral and sex education should be given to children to check their anti-social behaviour.

Emphasizing the importance of school as an agency which may help in the prevention of delinquency, Glueck suggests schools are in a position to reach children before maladjusted behaviour expresses itself overtly or becomes too deeply rooted.

Treatment of Delinquents

The treatment of delinquents are done by applying psychological techniques known as psychotherapy. The following methods can be used.

(*a*) *Re-education* :

As we know, delinquency is a learned behaviour like other behaviours. The aim of re-education is not to give the child academic information but to build his self by giving information on sex problems, family relation and morality. The re-education is to clarify the ideas of the delinquent on different problems which he faces.

(*b*) *Abreaction* :

Abreaction means providing opportunity to the delinquent to express his pent-up and suppressed feelings by means of free expression through discussion. The counsellor becomes the parent figure in whom the delinquent confides. He may use various techniques such as free association, psychodrama, play techniques, etc.

(*c*) *Persuasion* :

The therapist may persuade the delinquent not to indulge in anti-social activities in future. It is based on an appeal to the reason of the delinquent child. Persuasion should be logical so as to appeal to the delinquent. It has been reported by therapists that persuasion is not of great value because it only removes the symptoms and not the underlying causes.

(*d*) *Suggestion and Counselling* :

Children are suggestable and suggestion may produce good results provided it is given in an appropriate manner. Positive suggestions are given to delinquents to strengthen their super-ego.

(*e*) *Environmental Treatment* :

Environmental treatment is generally done by improving the home, school and social environment of the delinquent. Parents and other members of the family are advised to change their attitudes toward the child. Some psychotherapists suggest that the delinquent may be shifted to another environment for some period, preferably to a lodging or a foster home. It is hoped that by shifting the delinquent to a new environment he may give up his delinquency and start life afresh.

(*f*) *Behaviour Modification* :

Behaviour modification has been recently developed as an effective method to treat delinquents and other maladjusted persons. Behaviour modification is based on the assumption that anti-social behaviour is learned in the environment and can be modified by the principles which are applicable to learning. The following specific techniques may be applied in behaviour modification of delinquents.

(*i*) *Stimulus Change* :

It refers to the technique of removing the child from temptation. The stimulus is changed. This technique decreases the delinquent behaviour so long as it continues in operation.

(*ii*) *Overt Sensitization* :

It refers to increased emotional reactions in specified situations. The delinquent act (stealing) is paired with noxious experiences. In this technique delinquents are trained to imagine committing a delinquent act.

(*iii*) *Modelling* :

Modelling and role-playing procedures are used to teach new behaviour as alternatives to anti-social repertoire. Sarason and Ganzer (1973) developed a proforma for delinquents They used modelling experiences to counter the inadequate learning experiences that they saw as the basis for some form of delinquency.

(iv) Punishment :

Punishment is also an effective technique to cure delinquency. Burcharad (1967) used punishment to reform delinquents and he succeeded to a great extent.

Books and Snow (1972) used a procedure in which the boy received points for attendance and academic assignments. These points earned free time for the whole class. Inappropriate behaviour resulted in a response-cost-penalty. The group contingency had immediate effect on the behaviour of individuals.

Some other ways of handling delinquent behaviour are :

(*v*) Vocational skills are developed according to the aptitudes of adolescents.

(*vi*) Self Governing Behaviour.

(*vii*) Contingency Management.

B-SEXUAL DYSFUNCTION AND ABERRATIONS

Sexual dysfunctions refer to those sexual behaviours of individuals which violate the legal sexual code of the state in which they are residing. This section of the chapter deals with sexual behaviours that are indicative of maladjustment and emotional disorders, caused by a number of psychological factors.

Sexual offenses

Sexual offenses are acts that violate the norms of the particular society in which a person lives. Most societies develop norms that are supposed to govern the behaviour of people. When an individual performs a sexual act which is forbidden by the society, he is considered a sex offender.

Sexual offenses are symptoms of sexual deviation.

The so-called psychopath is a person who is not psychotic or mentally deficient yet who cannot control his sexual impulses. Karpman describes a sexual psychopath as follows :

"Any person suffering from such conditions of emotional instability or impulsiveness of behaviour or lack of customary standards of good judgement or failure to appreciate the consequences of his acts or a combination of any such conditions as to render such persons irresponsible in respect to sexual matters and thereby dangerous to himself and to other person." The sexual psychopath is a neurotic with a character disorder who lacks a conscience and has no regard for the welfare of others.

Sexual Aberrations

Sexual aberrations include all sexual acts in which gratification is obtained by practices other than the method of heterosexual intercourse. The sexual deviant achieves more sexual satisfaction from these acts than from normal sexual behaviour. Major sexual aberrations are as follows :

(1) Aberrations in choice of Sexual Partner

Homosexuality :

Homosexuality refers to the satisfaction of sexual desire by erotic interest or relations between members of the same sex. Female homosexuals are called lesbians. Sexual gratification is attained by being close to or looking at the person of the same sex. It is often attained by overt sexual act such as manual or oral manipulation of the genitals.

There are three types of homosexuals (a) active homosexual who plays the male role in the relationship whether he be male or female, (b) the passive homosexual who plays the female role in the relationship whether he be male or female and (c) the mixed type who assumes active and passive roles occasionally.

The most frequent homosexual practices include mutual

masturbation, sodomy, and interfemoral contact.

Research has been conducted to list the physical characteristics of homosexuals but so far no conclusive findings have been reported.

Causes of Homosexuality

According to some investigators homosexuality is an inborn behaviour pattern; others have assumed that homosexuality is caused by harmonal imbalance. But most researchers explain homosexuality on the basis of psychological factors: conditioning and adjustment. According to them homosexuality is the result of environmental experiences and emotional stresses.

Henry conducted a very intensive study on homosexuality. His findings are given as follows :

> "The sex variant is a person who has failed to achieve and maintain adult heterosexual model of sexual expression and who has resorted to other modes of sexual expression. The sex variant seems to be in part a by-product of civilization. In our present civilization he is an expression of his inability to meet the responsibility of establishing and maintaining a home which involves the rearing of children. The manifold demands made upon parents in recent years as a result of industrialization often discourage heterosexual adjustment and foster substitute sexual activity. The sex variant may remain at an immature level of sex adjustment because of (a) constitutional deficiencies (b) influence of family patterns of sexual adjustment (c) lack of opportunities for psychosexual development."

Kin ey and his associates also emphasize the importance of environmental factors in the development of homosexuality. According to them homosexuality is learned behaviour which depends on the mores of the culture in which the individual is raised.

The following environmental factors are important psychological forces in the development of homosexuality.

(i) Antagonism toward the parent of opposite sex.

(ii) Inharmonious marital relationship between the parents.

(iii) Treatment of the child as being of the opposite sex.

(iv) Unsatisfactory relationship with members of the opposite sex.

(v) Strong attachment to the parent of the same sex.

(vi) Faulty attitudes on the subject.

(vii) Isolation or segregation of sexes over a long period of time as in the military, boarding schools, prisons and hostels.

Pedophilia

Pedophilia refers to sexual aberration in which the adult, adolescent or person of any age satisfies sexual desire by iudulging in sexual activities with immature children. This sexual deviancy is much more common among men than women. The child is induced to manipulate the genitals of the adult or the adult fondles the genitals of the child. Sometimes the adult attempts to engage in sexual intercourse usually without success. Newspapers often report incidences of pedophilia. The pedophelic is an emotionally disturbed individual who suffers from feelings of insecurity and inadequacy. He has an intense fear of failure in maintaining a normal sexual relationship with the member of the opposite sex and avoids the complications involved in such love-making by directing his sexual desire toward immature children.

Bromberg discussing the motivation of pedophelics writes :

"Pedophelics are particularly afflicted with anxiety regarding their sexual potency...pedophelic is one whose sexual impulses are distorted by crippling anxiety. A larger number gives histories of impotence or partial impotence. It is evident that the pedophelic's inferiority feelings lead him to search for younger and less formidable love objects...The child as sexual object saves the offender's ego from blows which might prove destructive to his mental equilibrium."

According to psychoanalytic theory the desire for sexual relation with children is due to a narcissistic complex. The individual is in love with himself as a child. He treats the child in the same way as he would like to be treated.

Bestiality

Bestiality refers to the sexual aberration in which an individual satisfies his sexual desire with an animal. The most common animals used for sexual gratifications are cats, dogs, cows, sheep and goats.

Animal contact is not regarded as pathological where opportunities for normal heterosexual sex relationships are lacking.

It is said that a Zoophialic is motivated to engage in sexual relation with animals because of his strong feelings of insecurity and inadequacy. The individual is unconsciously attempting to avert a threat to his ego or sense of personal adequacy. Affection for animals as a substitute for human affection is frequently observed in modern society. His fear of being rejected or humiliated by members of the opposite sex is overcome by adopting a different sexual object of which he may be especially fond of.

Necrophilia

A necrophiliac is one who gains sexual satisfaction from the sight of or actual contact with a cadaver. These sexual deviates often gain sexual gratification by going to funerals or to the morgue whenever the occasion permits.

The causes of necrophilia are similar to those of other sexual disorders. This sexual pattern operates as an ego-defense mechanism. Strong feelings of inadequacy make it difficult for the individual to carry on sexual relation with other adults. The necrophiliac gains feelings of competency when he is having relationship with a corpse.

Fetishism

Fetishism refers to the sexual aberration in which the individual gains satisfaction from the sight of or contact with certain portions of the human body or with inanimate objects. Fetishists are usually males and the fetish is an article of female clothing such as under garments, shoes, handkerchiefs, dresses, rings, etc. The part of the body found to be the object of fetish are hair, hand, thigh, legs, and eyes, etc.

Fetishism develops as a result of the individual's faulty evaluation of himself in relation to those with whom he comes into contact.

The fetishist uses the ego-defense mechanism of substitution. He fears being rejected by members of the opposite sex and therefore guards himself against possible failure by substituting some part of the body or an article of clothing for genitila. The individual may attain sexual gratification by touching a braid of hair or gloves. The usual procedure is for the deviate to masturbate while he is looking at or touching the object.

Fetishism is adoration of something serving as a substitute for the original object. Fetishism is peculiar to man. It is an attempt to control the genital fear aroused in the child by discovery of anatomical differences between sexes.

2. Aberration in Method

Several aberrations have been reported relating to the methods of sexual gratification in book on the psychology. Some of them are given below.

Sadism

The sadist attains sexual gratification by inflicting pain upon the person with whom he engages in sexual relation. Sexual satisfaction is derived from the suffering of the sexual object. The pain may be either physical, such as whipping, biting, slapping or i'.

may be verbal in the form of sarcastic remarks, teasing, threatening or belittling. Sadism has its root in repressed hostility and childhood resentment toward a parent. The child who is harshly treated and severely punished by his father or mother reacts with hate and hostility and his feelings are repressed. But in the adult' repressed feelings are manifested in the form of hostility, attack and destruction toward a love object or parent-figure. These destructive aggressive patterns of behaviour arise from emotional insecurity caused by parental rejection.

Psychoanalytically sadism is explained in the form of fear of castration. His fear of being castrated causes the sadist to attack the supposed castrator. His torture of his sexual partner gives him feelings of power and superiority. The sadist exhibits feminine mannerism. He inflicts physical pain to compensate for his feeling of inadequate masculinity.

Masochism

The masochist is a sexual deviant who experiences sexual gratification by having suffering and pain inflicted on him or her by a sexual partner. The masochist must suffer either physical pain or mental anguish (cruel treatment, disgrace) in order to obtain sexual gratification. Masochism is opposed to sadism.

The causes of masochism are rooted in early childhood and faulty training through conditioning. The child develops feelings of guilt and shame towards normal sexual relations. The self-punishment is to reduce feelings of guilt and it also serves as a compensatory mechanism for inadequacy.

Fenichel, a psychoanalyst, explains masochism as follows :

—Certain experiences establish that sexual gratification is connected with pain.

—Masochistic activities are symbols of self-castration and are used to avoid castration.

—Playful anticipation of what is feared stares off anxiety.

—Stressing one's helplessness and littleness is an appeal to the mercy of the threatening or protecting power.

—The idea of being beaten is accepted as punishment for bad behaviour.

—By being beaten the individual is reassured that he is not being castrated.

Exhibitionism

Exhibitionism is indecent exposure of genitals to the members of the opposite sex in public places to gain sexual satisfaction.

Exhibitionism becomes pathological only when the opportunities of heterosexual relations are not available. Sometimes it has been observed that the exhibitionist gets complete sexual satisfaction by masturbating while exhibiting himself.

Karpman reports that, "the exhibitionist is quite often a young man of rather good intelligence, high culture and education, frequently from the better social strata." The causative factors in exhibitionism are the same as those in other sexual aberrations. Exhibitionism is a defense mechanism for coping with a dangerous psychological situation which is threatening to the individual's ego. Such a person suffers from inadequacy in regard to sexual activities. It is an attention-getting mechanism as well as sexual substitute pattern. By exhibiting the genital organs, the individual gains attention and feels important, Psychoanalytically, exhibitionism has been explained as fear of castration in the male. The patient feels that he can dispel fear of castration by showing his genital organs.

Voyeurism or Inspectionism

Inspectionism refers to the act of sexual gratification from looking at the genitals of the opposite sex. The deviant gets pleasure by observing the sexual act of others. Some individuals get sexual satisfaction by observing nude pictures, paintings, etc.

The dynamics of inspectionism is one of the ego-defense. It is a defense mechanism against a situation which endangers the deviant's integrity. The deviant feels frustrated and inadequate in adult heterosexual situation. According to the psychoanalytic explanation of inspectionism : "Looking is equivalent to swallowing ; thus visual observation is a means of identification with the object observed as a method of gaining control over it."

Treatment and Prevention

The sexual aberrant is an emotionally disturbed person and is in need of therapy. Punishment and segregation do not help in curing the behaviour perversion. Karpman writes : "Since his reactions are expressions of 'unconscious urges', it is no more possible to cure the sexual psycopath of his impulse by repeated punishment...Punishment is useless and irrational."

As we know, sex aberrations are most often symptoms of maladjustment. Therefore therapy must be directed to rehabilitating them in the social environment.

Guilt feeling, a sense of insecurity and inadequacy must be neutralized. Socially acceptable methods of gaining status and resolving conflicts should be introduced. The method of psychotherapy should be determined by the nature of the aberration. But it has been reported that depth interview and psychoanalysis have in majority of cases proved successful.

For an adolescent, psychotherapy entails educating him about the nature, developments and the possible effect of sexual aberration and redirecting his attitudes from fear and shame to confidence and courage adequate for making satisfactory social adjustment.

Prevention

Sexual aberrations are caused by faulty rearing of children. Therefore it is very essential that parents should be educated to charge their attitudes with regard both to general rearing and sex education. It has been mentioned above that sexual aberrations are primarily symptoms of insecurity, inadequacy and guilt. The assurance of sympathy, understanding and honest consideration of the problems of the child will help in establishing a confidential relationship between the parent and the child.

Adequate sex-education should begin at home. Parents should be able to find opportunities to give sex instruction naturally and informally. They should be well-informed about sex education.

Prescott writes on love and security ; "Given love, any human being enjoys a basic security in the world. He matters. And if he returns the love he becomes the agent of security and support toward some one else and has an important reason for courage and enduring effort..."

3. Alcoholism and Use of Drugs

A world wide phenomenon of recent years has been the tremendously increased use of all types of drugs and alochol to reduce anxiety and tension. In particular, the use of drugs by adolescents has posed serious problems in developed and developing countries. Parents, educationists and social workers are particularly worried about this as it poses serious social problems that need immediate preventive measures. The question arises : Why has the use of durgs increased so alarmingly in recent years ?

A number of surveys have been conducted in recent years to find out the causes of alcoholism and use of drugs among adolescents. The following have been listed as the important causes :

Adolescents use drugs to reduce anxiety and tension created by frustrations of the following types :

(a) Failure in examination, competition, and employment.

(b) Loss of parents and loved ones.

(c) Frustration of needs due to poverty, and barriers (social, economical and physical).

(d) Drugs are also used to act out one's repressed emotional feelings and are a manifestation of anti-social feelings against adult culture.

(e) The increasing use of drugs may be due to the availability of drugs in the market and high purchasing power of the individual.

(f) It is unfortunate that our educational system has not been able to inculcate in children some universal moral values. Due to lack of moral avlues and an ideal model for immitation adolescents are easily led to the use of drugs and alcohol.

(g) Some adolescents may start use of drugs due to the physical environment or out of curiosity in the company of their peers and gradually become addicts.

(h) Many adolescents become the victims of drugs because of :

(i) insecurity of life (war)

(ii) social conflicts, and tension.

(iii) sexual problems

(iv) constant quarrelling in the home

(v) association with gangs

Treatment and Prevention

The social evil of alcoholism and the use of drugs can be prevented and treated by improving the home, school and social environment. All the three—parents, teachers and social workers—should pool together their resources to check this menace. Psychotherapy may also prove very useful in correcting chronic cases of drug use. But there is a great need to improve the overall environment.

QUESTIONS FOR DICUSSION

1. What are the causes of delinquency ? Describe them in brief.
2. "Delinquents are born," Comment on the statement.
3. What are sexual dysfunctions ? What are their causes ?
4. Why do adolescents use drugs ?
5 What are the social causes of delinquency ?

SUGGESTED READINGS

1 Chauhan, S.S. : Psychology of Adolescence ; Allied Publishers, Delhi. 1984.

2. Crow L.D. and Crow A. : Abnoomal Psychology ; Macmillan Co. NY, 1982.

3. Mehar Joseph ; Abnormal Psychology ; NJ, 1982.

4. White, R. W. : The Abnormal Personality ; John Wiley and Sons, NY, 1981.

CHAPTER 10

Assessment of Psychological Adjustment

The success of any psychotherapeutic teatment depends to a great extent on accurate assessment of the psychological problems of the individual. There are several methods generally used to diagnose the mental disorders of the patients who are referred for treatment to psychological clinics and mental hospitals. Here it would be remember that no single method can be completely relied upon for exact assessment of mental disorders.

Therefore it is suggested that a combination of methods should be used to collect reliable information for correct diagnosis of the patient for treatment.

The main objectives of psychological assessment are : (a) to discover the sources of mental disorders ; (b) to plan the treatment of the patient to improve his efficiency, happiness and social adjustment in society ; (c) to evaluate given treatment procedures and outcomes of the treatment ; (d) to provide a basis for discussing his problems with the individual, his family or the group for further investigation.

The therapist with the help of assessment techniques should develop a comprehensive biographical-historical profile of the specific problems of the patient and his treatment.

The present chapter deals with the procedures which are normally followed in assessing the problems of maladj usted individuals.

Here it should be kept in mind that individuals differ as regards their adjustment problems in the home, at school, in society and at work. Therefore no single criterion can be prescribed to screen all maladjusted persons. The therapist will use understanding about the method to be used to diagnose the problems of a specific case. The following methods are used for screening and evaluating the nature and extent of psychological problems.

1. Observation

The simplest and the easiest methods is to observe the behaviour of the individual in different situations to diagnose his specific problems. For example, how does the individual behave with his parents and siblings ? How does he behave in school with his classmates and teachers in the class and outside it ? The behaviour may be observed several times by two or three observers to validate their observation. It will be very helpful if an observation schedule is prepared in advance to maintain uniformity in collecting information. Observation of behaviour problems may be done by parents, teachers and other adults and may be reported to the clinician.

Direct observation is essential for proper assessment but the observer's presence may affect the target behaviour. Further it is seldom possible to arrange observation with appropriate reliability checks before, during and after in all situations where the behaviour may occur. Innovative techniques of observation may be used to collect accurate information about the individuals.

2. Ratings by Significant People

Ratings by parents, teachers and peers on behaviour checklists are widely used to collect a picture of the child's behaviour. Rating of the child's behaviour should be done objectively to provide correct information on deviant behaviour. It has been demonstrated in several studies that checklist ratings discriminate significantly between clinically referred and normal children both in terms of specific items and syndrome scores,

3. Interview

An interview skilfully and extensively conducted can be a very reliable source of information about the mental abnormalities of individuals. The interview should be conducted after establishing perfect rapport with the individual so that he may disclose in confidence his past experiences without any inhibition. Observation and interview both are subjective methods and have their own limitations. Therefore some objective methods are used to diagnose the problems of mal-adjusted persons.

4. Case History Method

The case history method is generally used to find the type of mental disorder the individual suffers from. It is a very comprehensive approach and includes all possible aspects of the individual's life which influence his presonality development. Information pertaining to the past and the present is collected from every possible source: for example, from the patient's parents, relatives, teachers, school record, social worker, the employer etc., to have a comprehensive picture of the patients' problems.

5. Medical Examination

It has been observed that physical factors are sometimes directly or indirectly responsible for psychological disorders. Therefore a complete nhysical examination of the patient is essential to see if there is any physical deficiency which has caused the maladjustment. In some cases the physical examination of the patient is itself or therapeutic importance. For example, many maladjusted individuals (hypochondrics) are overanxious about their health. A physical examination helps to reduce their apprehension and anxiety. There are certain physiological methods which require technical and specialized knowledge to assess the problems. They are as follows:

(*i*) *Electroencephalography*:

It is the graphic recording of the electrical activity of the brain potential popularly called brain waves. Anomalies in brain tissues are reflected in the frequency, amplitude and pattern of electrical activity and indicate the type of mental disorders, the patient is suffering from.

(*ii*) *Encephalgraphy and Ventriculography*:

In order to detect the presence of tumours or other ventricular deformities, X-ray pictures of the ventricles are taken.

Ventriculography is a process of injecting air directly into the ventricles by trephining the skull. Myelography is a procedure when cerebrospinal fluid in the spinal arachoma space is replaced with air or oxygen to study the presence of any lesion or tumour.

6. Psychological Testing

To assess psychological adjustment, the need frequently arises for the assessment of abilities, aptitudes, scholastic achievements personality of the mentally disturbed individuals. The guidance worker or psychotherapist may use the individual test/group test to measure the individual/group of student's mental level.

The following types of tests can be used to diagnose the problems of adjustment. Here the psychotherapist should keep in mind that test developed in western countries should not be used because these tests are culturally biased and fail to provide accurate information regarding the problems of Indian clients. Therefore it is suggested that tests either developed or adapted in India should be used. The following types of tests are used in clinics and guidance bureaus to assess the adjustment problems of individuals.

Intelligence Tests:

Historicalty the development of intelligence tests can be attributed to Binet-Simon of France who in the beginning of the present century (1905) constructed a scale to identify children in the Paris schools who did not have sufficient intellectual capacity to benefit from normal schooling. The scale successfully screened such children.

The original scale was modified in 1908 and 1911 in the light of field testing. The scale was adapted in different countries according to their socio-economic conditions and cultural background. In USA ths Stanford-Binet Intelligence Scale made its appearances in 1916 and was subsequently revised in 1937, 1960 and 1973.

Dr. Bhatia adapted the test to Indian conditions and published it by the name of Bhatai's Battery.

The Wechsler Tests

Another important test which is also individually administered was published by David Wechsler in 1939. The test has three scales meant for different age-levels.

(a) The Wechsler Adult Intelligence Scale (WAIS) is designed for persons from sixteen years and above.

(b) The Wechsler Intelligence Scale for Children: (WISC). It is used for the age group 6 to 16 years.

(c) The Wechsler Pre-School Intellgence Scale. It is designed for children from 4 to 6 years of age.

The following individual tests may prove useful to measure the intelligence of Indians:

(i) Indian Adaptation of Binet-Simon Intelligence Scale

(ii) Draw-a-Man-Test

(iii) Iadian Adaptation of Wechsler's Adult Performance Scale

(iv) Pass Along Test

(v) Koh's Block Design Test

(vi) Bhatia's Battery of Performance Tests

(A) INTELLIGENCE TESTS

Group tests of Intelligence

Group tests of intelligence were for the first time developed during the first World War to screen a large number of recruits for the Armed Forces in the USA. Such tests are administered to a group of people at the same time. These tests easy to score and can give a rough idea of the intellectual development of the individuals. The following group tests may be used to measure intelligence.

(i) Group test of general mental ability. — S. Jalota

(ii) Group test of Intelligence. 10 to 16 years. — R. K. Tandon

(iii) Group test of Intelligence for College Students and Adults. — R. K. Tondon

(iv) Group Test of Intelligence — P. Mehta

Achievement Tests

It has been observed that most children who have been referred to mental health clinics have school problems. But their academic strenghts and weakness are seldom assessed precisely. Therefore it is very necessary to make assessment of academic weaknessess of children to find out the source of mental abnormality. Standardized achievement test for a specific subject or a wide-range achievement test may be used to assess the academic achievement of children.

(B) PERSONALITY TESTS

A person's abilities and skills play an important role in determining the career avenues which will lead to a better or proper personal adjustment and specific personality attributes are also important in this regard.

In planning the maximum use of capabilities, therefore, and to achieve the best possible adjustment, it is wise for individuals to spend their time in activities which are compatible with their general personality.

The other area where assessment has an important function in adjustment is, of course, the understanding of psychological problem areas, their cause and possible ways of alleviating them with the help of personality tests.

(i) Adjustment Inventories

Adjustment inventories have their origin in the First World War, when it became apparent that there were not enough psychiatrists to examine adequately all potential recruits. The ned at the time was to identify in advance persons who might suffer some kind of psychological breakdown when under the stress of battle. The first adjustment inventory was developed by R. S. Woodworth as Personal Data Sheet, a standardized psychiatric interview in printed form. Woodworth's Personal Data Sheet was very successfully used to screen adjusted and maladjusted recruits. The success of the Personal Data Sheet created great enthusiasm in psychologists for the development of adjnstment inventories. Several inventories in different dimensions of human development were made. The following inventories are generally used to assess adjustment.

— The Bell's Adjustment Inventory. The adapted form of the inventory may be used.

— The MMPI, the Minnesota Multiphasic Personality Inventory (1940) was developed to meet the practical need for rapid and standardiized psychiatric diagnosis rather than assessing overall psychological adjustment.

— Eysenck's Maudsley Personality Inventory adapted by Jalota and Kapoor.

— Personality Inventory by Y. Singh and H.M. Singh.

— Personality Adjustment Inventory by M.S.L. Saxena.

— Introversion-Extraversion Inventory by R.K. Kundu.

— Adjustment Inventory for College students by A.K.P. Sinha.

— The C.P.I. The California Psychological Inventory was specifically designed for the multidimensional description of normal personality.

— Sinha's comprehensive Anxiety Test.

— Test Anxiety Scale by U.P. Sharma.

— Behavioural Deviance Scale by N.S. Chauhan.

— Security-Insecurity Scale by H. Tewari.

— Job Satisfaction Scale.

Adjustment inventories are commonly used in routine screening procedures that attempt to identify individuals with adjustment or other problems that need professional attention. The psychological screening inventories were developed for such a purpose and are used in clinics, probation courts and other places where a brief evaluation could be helpful in the prevention of more serious problems.

(ii) Projective Techniques

The development of projective tests began in the 1930s when it was popular to regard mental problems of the mind as analogous to physical problems of the body. It was considered that the causes of mental problems lay beneath the surface of the mind in the unconscious just as the cause of most psysiological problems lay beneath the skin and thus hidden from direct observation. Projective tests are supposed to diagnose accurately the problems of the individual with the justification that they function like an X-ray of personality. Projective techniques quickly became the most popular assessment tools.

The three widely used tests of projection are briefly described hereafter.

The Rorschach Test

This test was developed by Herman Rorschach, a Swiss

psychiatrist. This is the most widely used test for projection. It is based on the assumption that the individual will project his unconscious feelings, desires and aspirations in the inkblots. The test material consists of ten symmetrical inkblots printed on cards. The respondent is shown the test cards one by one and is asked, "What you can see in them o. what do they remined you of ?" The examiner records everything the individual says does during the testing session. After the responses are received on all test cards, an enquiry or post-interview is held in which the examiner repeats the responses back and asks exactly what it was about each blot that led to each specific response.

The responses of the individual can be scored in various systems based on a number of percepts involving human or animal movement, dominance of colour versui form, reliance on the whole blot versus small details and well differentiated versus global images.

The test responses give a fairly good idea of the adjustment mental eisturbances of the individual.

Thematis Apperception Test (TAT)

Another widely used test is TAT which was developed by Henry Murray (1935). The test material consists of 30 cards depicting various situations and one blank card. In the standard presentation, the respondent is shown 20 cards chosen according to sex age and problem. The TAT is introduced as a test of imagination, and the respondent is asked to write as dramatic a story as possible on each card. The respondent is instructed that each story should include what has led up to the event depicted in the card, what is happening at the movement, what the people in the story are feeling and thinking and, finally, the outcome of the story.

After writing of the stories, an interview is conducted to determine the source of each story—whether based on personal experience, heard from friends or derived from books or movies. It is generally assumed that the resgoadeet identifies with a mjaor figure in each story so that a close examination of the stories will reveal much about the respondent and his problems and identification and aspirations. It is suggested that for Indian adolescents, an adapted form of TAT should be used.

Children Apperception Test (CAT)

In the Children Appreception Test (CAT) by Belack, the material consists of 10 picture of animals depicting psychosexual conflicts assumed to be important for children aged 3 to 10. Animals have been used in the belief that children would identify more closely with them than with the adult figures of the TAT. Children's mental abnormalities, conflicts, anxiety and emotional disturbances may be assessed with the help of CAT stories.

Children's Anxiety Scale (CAS): Several anxiety tests for children have been developed in recent years to identify children whose anxiety interferes with their school performance. The following projective tests can be used to explore the unconscious personality of the maladjusted individuals.

— TAT Indian Adaptation

— CAT Indian Adaptation

— Bender-Gestalt Test

— Rorschach Ink Blot Test

— Sentence Completion Test

— Draw-a-Man Test

— Free Association Test

***(iii)* Vocational Interest Tests**

It is well known that people differ in their suitability for different careers. Much of the difference is due to variations in skills and abilities. However, a significant part depends on personality characteristics, attitudes, aspirations, motivations and a variety of other influences. These factors, as related to vocational satisfaction are called vocational interests. Although some persons may make a decision fairly early in life as to the kind of career they would ilke to follow, many do not have the opportunity to make such a decision with any degrce of maturity. Their interests can be measured with the help of the following tests :

(*a*) *The Strong Vocational Interest Blank* (*SVIB*) :

The SVIB was developed in 1927 and has recently been updated. The test indicates the degree of similarity between a person's interest and those of successful persons in a wide variety of occupations. Test forms, scoring procedures and norms are different for men and women. Respondents are asked to indicate their likes and dislikes among a list of 400 occupations, school subjects, kinds of people, hobbies and so on regard less of whether or not they possess any special training the might be required. Longitudinal research with SVIB has indicated that vocational interests tend to remain remarkably stable from the years of career decision through middle age.

(*b*) *Kuder Preference Record* :

Kuder Preference Record was developed by G. Frederic Kuder. He developed several preference records which are widely used to assess vocational interests. The procedure is simple. The respondent is asked to indicate his likes and dislikes among a wide varieties of activities. The scoring of the test yields preference on nine different vocational interests such as outdoor, mechanical, scientific, literary and persuasive etc.

(iv) Innovative Techniques

Modern scientific inventions have revolutionized life on earth in all walks of human endeavour. For example, the concept of time and space has been reduced to the minimum. Inventions in biological and medical sciences have minimized the percentage of diseases and increased the longevity of human beings and the invention of the computer has challenged the human mind.

Computer

The most dramatic innovative technique in the field of

psychological assessment is the introduction of the computer to : (1) gather information directly from the subject ; (2) put together all information collected from different sources such as interviews, tests, rating, etc., and (3) simulate and predict the functioning of the social system.

The computer can play an important role by comparing the incoming information with data previously stored in its memory bank. The computer can perform a wide range of assessment functions. It can supply a diagnosis, evaluate the risk of certain kinds of behaviours, suggest the most appropriate form of treatment, predict the outcome and point out a summary report concerning the subject. Goldberg (1970) demonstrated the importance of the computer in individual psychological assessment. He says "a computer programmed with the assessment strategies utilized by 29 clinicians was more proficient than the individual clinicians in differentiating between neurotic and psychotic individuals on the basis of MMPI profiles."

It has been proved in almost all studies that a computer can perform better than an individual clinician in predicting the risk of suicidal behaviour. And comparing a patient's adjustment in the community prior to and after treatment show whether the outcome of the treatment was better or worse.

In addition to the use of computers, there is an effort in the direction of developing highly specialized intensive batteries of tests which may answer with a high degree of assurance specific questions relevant to the assessment of a given individual.

QUESTIONS FOR DISCUSSION

1. What are main objective of psychological assessment? Explain them?
2. What are various methods of assessing psychological adjustment ? Describe personality tests.
3. How are psychological tests useful for assessment of adjustment ?
4. What are the innovative techniques of psychological assessmet ? Describe them in brief.

SUGGESTED READINGS

1. Achenbac, J., Thomas M: Developmental Psychopathology; Wiley and Sons, NY, 1982.

2. Coleman, James C : Abnormal Psychology and Modern Life; D.B. Taraporevala Sons and Co., 1981.

3. White, Robert W: The Abnormal Personality; 5th ed. John Wiley and Sons, NY, 1981.

4. Kleinmuntz, B. Essential of Abnormal Psychology; Harper and Row, NY, 1980.

5. Freeman, S.: Theory and Practice of Psychological Testing.

SECTION B

11. Treatment ; Biological Therapies
12. Treatment : Individual Psychotherapy
13. Treatment : Group Psychotherapy
14. Indian Psychotherapy
15. Prevention of Maladjustment
16. Mental Health of the Teacher
17. Community Mental Health

CHAPTER 11

Treatment: Biological Therapies

Imagine for a moment : If there were no mental abnormalities, human life would have been full of joy and happiness. But unfortunately it is not so. Human beings are victims of a number of mental abnormalities which necessitate the development of methods of treatment that have been changed and modified in the course of increased scientific knowledge about human nature.

There are broadly two methods for treating mental disorders, namely: (a) Biological methods and (b) Psychological methods.

The present chapter deals with the biological methods which include drug therapy, electrotherapy, psychosurgery and physiotherapy etc. and the three subsequent chapters deal with psychotherapeutic practices which are usually followed in the treatment of psychogenic disorders.

1. DRUG THERAPY

There has been an extraordinary growth in the production and use of drugs in the treatment of mental disorders in the last two decades. This revolutionary change has been effected by our expanding knowlege of the importance of biochemistry in brain pathology. Drugs of different categories are primarily used as tranquilizers to relieve distrbing symptoms particularly those related to anxiety.

The therapeutic use of drugs in the treatment of mental and emotional disorders is called pharmacotherapy/drug therapy.

Types of Drugs

Three categories of drugs are generally used in drug therapy to reduce anxiety and depression in the patient : (a) major tranquilizers; (b) anti-anxiety drugs ; (c) anti-depressant drugs; and (d) antimanic compound.

(a) Major tranquilizers

The Indian system of medicines (Ayurveda) is the oldest in the world. The ancient 'Rishis' found Snakeroot (Sherpgandha) to be the most effective drug in the treatment of mental disorders. Reserpine a drug derived from rauwolfia was used in USA in early 1950 but it was found that its side effects such as low blood pressure, and nasal congestion etc. overweighed the advantages. Therefore, its use was given up.

Reserpine has been replaced by other major tranquilizing drugs such as phenothiazines which have remained the most popular drugs in modern times. Thorazine and stelazine have proved highly successful in giving relief to psychotics minifesting emotional tensions, distorted thought process and hyperactivity. Phenothiazines produce sedation and reduce chronic anxiety.

There are several other drugs that are used for mental patients such as Haldol, Taractan, Loscitance, etc.

Major tranquilizers have some side effects such as central nervous system effects, muscular rigidity, seizures, respiratory depression and autonomic nervous system disturbances as blurred vision, dry mouth, inhibition of ejaculation, allergic reaction and behaviour disturbances, etc.

(b) Antianxiety drugs

A number of minor tranquilizers have been used in recent years to reduce the anxiety states and tension of the patients. The important ones are: Miltown. Serax, Librium and Valium. These drugs are used in cases of anxiety, tension during period of severe stress as well as in the case of neurotics. These drugs have side effects like drowisness, fatigue, confusion, withdrawal symptoms, insomania, headache, and convulsion, etc.

(c) Antidepressant drugs :

In case of depression, mood elevators are used which energize the patient. The first drug for this purpose was used improvized but due to its bad side effects it was prohibited. New phenelzine (Nardil) and isocarboxazid (Marplan) are used in the treatment of depression. Other anti-depression drugs are also used such as *Tofranial* and Sinequan, Elavil and Triavil.

(d) Antimanic compounds :

Manic patients are treated with lithium, a salt which was approved in 1970 for use in experimental studies. The use of lithium on manic patients had favourable effects. Several types of drugs are used on mental patients, keeping in consideration their age, sex and the tyye of mental disorders. Drugs should be used under the guidance of some qualified doctor.

2. ELECTROTHERAPY

Electrotherapy is also used in the treatment of neurotic and psychotic disorders. There are three types of electrotherapies. A brief description is given below :

(a) Eletroconvulsion Therapy (ECT)

ECT was for the first time introduced in 1938 in Italy to produce convulsive seizures in mental patients.

This type of treatment has been found to be highly effective in the treatment of depressions and other minor mental disorders.

(b) Electrosleep

This type of treatment is used for mental patients who have sleep disturbances. It was developed in the USSR. The procedure is simple : A soft mask containing electrodes is placed over the upper part of the individual's face. A mild electric current just enough to cause a slight tingling sensation is administered. The patient does not lose consciousness and does not experience convulsions; he may or may not fall asleep during the treatment. Usually half-hour treatment is given daily for one or two weeks.

(c) Implantation of Microcircuity

One of the most important new researches in brain pathology is the electrical stimulation of the brain (ESB) that attempts to learn more about how various brain areas function. For example, ESB can produce emotional responesses from euphoria to terror. Such findings have led to research in the possibility of surgical implantation of microcircuity to control some form of maladaptive behaviour in human beings.

3. BRAIN-WAVE THERAPY

Brain-wave therapy is a recent development in the treatment of mental disorders. Brain-waves (alpha, beta, delta, theta) patterns have direct relationship with the mental conditions of the individual. Mostly people are unaware of their brain-wave patterns and unable to control them. Brain-wave therapy has been introduced in the treatment of patients suffering from blood pressure and functions of autonomic nervous system, chronic anxiety, and tension, etc.

Acupuncture is another biological therapy which has in recent years been introduced in the treatment of chronic pain. However, its usefulness in the treatment of mental disorders remains to be ascertained.

4. NARCOSIS THERAPY

Narcosis therapy refers to the process of treatment which involves prolonged sleep. By the use of drugs the patient is kept asleep for periods ranging from 15 to 20 hours a day. This method is used principally to quiet agitated and excited patients. Numerous drugs are used to produce somnolence. Sodium anatal and sodium phenobarbital are the most widely used drugs in Narcosis therapy. The therapy continues for 20 to 14 days and is gradually terminated.

5. PSYCHOSURGERY

Psychosurgery was introduced for the first time by Moniz in 1933. The treatment involves severing the fibre tracts connecting the prefrontal lobe with the thalamus. This method has been found very effective in cases of agitated depression and involutional melancholia. Psychosurgery is very difficult and needs the services of a highly skilled surgeon. Several techniques of psychosurgery have been developed since 1933 with many technical changes and improvements in brain operation.

6. PHYSIOTHERAPY

Physiotherapy refers to the treatment of psychotic disorder by the use of physical agencies. It includes the following commonly used methods :

(a) Hydrotherapy

It refers to the use of water as sedative, stimulant and tonic. Water is used in the treatment of excitement, agitation and cases of exhaustion.

(b) Electrotherapy (Heat Therapy)

It refers to the application of heat by means of electrical devices such as electric light bulb, heat bore, infra-red lamp and electric pad.

(c) Heliotherapy

Heliotherapy is treatment by light rays. Ultraviolet rays are a universally accepted and widely used form of treatment.

(d) Massage

The treatment involves rubbing, kneading or tapping the body either by hands or by some instrument. Massage can relax tense muscles and induce sleep and rest. It also offers human contact to the patient.

7. OCCUPATIONAL THERAPY

Occupational therapy is specially meant for institutionalized cases of mental disorders. Its main objective is to engage the patients in useful activities. Occupational therapy helps the patients in several ways such as engaging them in constructive activities which give them feelings of worth ; it restores confidence in them and helps in developing vocational skills for earning their livelihood independently.

The kind of occupational activity will depend on such factors as the type of patient, his age, qualification, interest, and experience, etc.

We have briefly described the biological therapies commonly used in mental hospitals and clinics, generally in combination with psychotherapy.

CONCLUSIONS ABOUT BIOLOGICAL THERAPIES

The following conclusions can be drawn about biological therapies described above. The conclusions have been drawn on the basis of studies conducted on various types of biological therapies.

—The biological therapies are effective and yield good results in the reduction of cognitive, emotional and behavioural disorders.

—They have been very successful in the most severe disorders such as psychosis.

—It has been reported by a number of studies that biological therapies have substantial risk for the patient in terms of unpleasant or even dangerous side effects.

—The biological therapies are not always effective with every person and every disorder. A substantial number of people treated this way relapsed, and in some cases, emotional disorders recurred even when treatment was continued.

QUESTIONS FOR DISCUSSION

1. What are the important medical therapies ? Describe any one of them.
2. What are the major tranquilizers commonly used in mental treatment ?
3. "Psychosurgery involves an ethical question." Comment.
4. What do you mean by Occupational Therapy ? What are its use ?

SUGGESTED READINGS

1, Bianchi, L. : Foundations of Mental Health ; Appleton, London, 1930,

2. Brown, W. : Psychology and Psychotherapy ; Arnold, London, 1934.

3. Cameron, N. : The Psychology of Abnormal Disorders ; Houghton Mifflin, Boston, 1947.

4 Groves, E,R. and Blanchard, P. : Introduction to Mental Hygiene : Howa, London, 1930,

5. Wallin, J.E.W. : Personality Maladjustments and Mental Hygiene ; McGraw Book Co., NY, 1935.

CHAPTER 12

Treatment : Individual Psychotherapy

Individual psychotherapy refers to professional efforts to correct mental disorders of the individual in order to rehabilitate him in society. The patient is helped by some professional worker to gain an understanding of his problems and to make an effort to solve them.

The earliest programmes for treating mental disorders were directed only to the most severely disturbed people and the methods of treatment were very crude.

With the development in psychological and biological healing arts, more specifically since the beginning of the present century, more systematic and scientific techniques have been evolved to treat all types of mental disorders ranging from anxiety to psychosis.

The treatment of mental disorders is primarily meant to alleviate suffering, to eliminate symptoms, to increase adjustive effectiveness and to derive maximum satisfaction from life and to develop insight in the patient. This chapter deals with the treatment of mental disorders with the help of different types of psychotherapies.

Definition of Psychotherapy

The term psychotherapy covers a wide range of treatment procedures which have been developed since the last quarter of the 19th century. During this period several techniques such as suggestion, advice, direction, hypnotism, and chemicals, etc. were used to cure mental disorders. The early 1900s witnessed a tremendous expansion of psychoanalysis and by 1940 several variations of psychoanalysis appeared on the scene. In the last four decades several methods within the ambit of psychotherapy have been developed for the treatment of mental disorders, e.g., the humanistic-existential approach, behaviour therapy, transactional analysis, etc. The common characteristic of all the methods is that they deal with psychogenic illness by psychological methods. They aim at modifying the patient's personality and changing his social and material environments for proper adjustment in society so that the individual can develop his potentialities maximally and utilize them for his own benefit as well as for that of society. In a basic sense psychotherapy is a process of emotional re-education of the patient.

According to Lazarus, Psychotherapy "is basically a face-to-face situation in which one person agrees to provide assistance to a patient or group of patients who have sougnt help with their problems of living." Psychotherapy can also be defined as guidance provided by a professionally trained person to a mentally disturbed person or group of persons.

Objectives of Psychotherapy

According to Thorpe and associates, the objectives of psychotherapy can be classified into two categories : immediate and ultimate.

A. Immediate Objectives

These objectives are generally meant to provide immediate relief from the mental disorders and the ultimate objectives are aimed at uprooting their causal factors and to develop insight in the patient to enable him to rehabilitate himself in his environment. Following are the important immediate objectives :

1. Elimination of symptoms

The elimination of symptoms of maladjustment does not mean that the basic cause of maladjustment has been cured but there certain situations where immediate elimination of the symptoms is needed by the patient. For example, a stenographer who develops a contracture of the left hand, needs immediate removal of the symptoms and an insomanic needs immediate relief from his disease.

2. Release of repression

The second important immediate objective of psychotherapy is to release the repressed emotional feelings of children, adolescents and adults by using vicarious aggressive actions such as use of play materials for children and use of football, bowling, debates, etc. for adolescents and adults.

3. Promotion of efficiency

Maladjusted individuals are not as a rule as efficient in either their social or occupational activities as an evaluation of their potentialities would lead one to expect. It is one of the immediate objectives of psychotherapy to aid them in the release of inhibitions which prevent the use of such capacities

4. Adaptation to environment

Man has survived because of his unique capacity to modify the environment to suit has needs and also the capacity to adapt himself to the requirements of his environment. Maladjusted people become rigid and prejudiced to make such adaptation but the objective of the psychotherapy is to develop flexibility in the patients so that they may make adjustment to both the material and social demands of the environment. The therapist must develop insight into the patient regarding the nature of social relationship and also intelligent discrimination in dealing with interpersonal problems.

5. Satisfactory physiological functioning

Another important immediate objective of psychotherapy is the attainment of proper physiological functioning by the patient. Many patients suffer from physical dysfunctions such as lack of appetite, insomania, hypertension, headache, ulcer, chronic fatigue, etc. which need the immediate attention of the psychotherapist.

B. Ultimate Objectives

1. Removal of causes

The ultimate objective of psychotherapy is to remove the root causes of the mental disorders. The therapist helps the patients by developing feelings of security, personal adequacy and of acceptability in the eyes of the individuals who are important in the eyes of the patient.

2. Development of insight

Development of insight into his problems helps the patient to understand the true nature of his defense mechanisms and makes it possible for him to secure his needed status through more desirable channels.

3. Continuous personal adjustment

Psychotherapy is not meant for the purpose of assisting a patient in solving a particular behaviour problem. It is a life-long process. The objective is to bring about changes in the personality of the individual conducive to the continuous solution of recurring problems of a psychological nature. It does not seek only immediaie relief from mental disorder but aims at paving the way for a programme of adaptation to the requirements of both personal needs and the social structure involved which will be as permanent as possible. It is the objective of psychotherapy to relieve the patient permanently of insecurity and inadequacy in favour of desirable activities.

4. Growth in social adjustment

The long term objective of psychotherapy is also to help the individual to adapt to group life by developing in him self-confidence and willingness to work consistently for self-improvement. The patient after cure of mental disorders should improve interpersonal relationships for his social growth by participating in social activities, games, plays, etc. It is the therapist's aim to enable the patient to make mutually satisfying adjustment to his home, friends and his community.

5. Attainment of personal goals

Psychotherapy promotes the fullest development of the potentialities of the patient. It helps the patient to formulate positive personal goals in accordance with his capabilities in order to help him to adjust adequately in his social environment.

A. The following Psychotherapeutic Methods will be described.

I. Psychodynamic Therapies

II. Behaviour Therapy

III. Humanistic-Existential Psychotherapies

(a) Client-centred therapy

(b) Existential therapy

(c) Gestalt therapy

(d) Transactional analysis

(e) Rational-emotive therapy

(f) Reality therapy.

(I) PSYCHODYNAMIC THERAPIES

Psychodynamic therapies cover a wide range of approaches which emphasize the discovery of various causal factors that impair the proper functioning of the individual to work effectively in his environment. They refer to the forces or influences that account for one's actions and reactions. All psychodynamic therapies share the following major and common unifying and interrelated features :

(a) All employ talking as the primary instrument of treatment. It is the patient who determines what he wants to talk about.

(b) The professional attitude of the psychotherapist rather than his personal attitude is important in the treatment of mental disorders.

(c) Insight is the basic principle of all Freudian therapies. The therapy assumes that the patient has not been able to follow Socrate's injunction "Know Thyself". Aspects of the patient's unconscious childhood life give important clues for treatment.

(d) Symptoms are secondary surfacc manifestations of some basic underlying neurotic process. To treat the patient it is important that he must discover the nature of his misconceptions about himself and of the faulty beliefs which guide his life course inappropriately.

(e) As a patient starts to explore his problems, an outpouring negative pent-up feelings occurs. Freud called this process of outpouring as "Gatharsis" which helps in cleaning the inner-self of the patient.

Freudian Psychoanalysis

Sigmund Freud was the first psychoanalyst to develop a method of therapy for the treatment of mental disorders. The basic concepts of Freudian therapy are catharsis, resistance, transference, and re-education which will be briefly described in the subsequent pages.

Psychoanalysis has made several important contributions to the exploration of the personality of an individual. Important among these are : an individual's mental life can be understood and this understanding can be applied to cure human sufferings. Human behaviour is governed by unconscious motivation. Early childhood experiences have a profound effect on later development stages. This theory has provided a meaningful framework for understanding the ways in which an individual attempts to cope with anxiety by postulating defense mechanisms. It offers ways of tapping the unconscious through the analysis of dreams, free association resistance and transferance.

Resistance

The first essential step in psychoanalytic therapy is that the patient talks about his problems. The patient will usually begin with a story that he is prepared to tell, one that is coloured by his self deceptions. It often consists of descriptive intellectual statements. It involves a flood of emotions that are forms of resistance.

Resistance is considered to be an inevitable process in psychoanalysis by which patients protect themselves from painful discoveries about the real nature of their problems. The patient is reluctant and seems to resist such help by refusing to expose impulses, attitudes and experiences which are responsible for his problems.

The process of resistance manifests itself in many ways. For example, the patient may protest at a therapist's interpretation to avoid talking about certain matters, leave treatment, or show inability to associate freely. The process of resistance is unconscious. If the resistance is stronger, the wish to remain in treatment decreases and the patient may leave. One of the major tasks of Freudian therapy is to overcome the patient's resistance but this cannot be done by direct attack. The psychoanalyst must be careful in dealing with the patient. He should not press the patient too hard to break his resistance.

Transference

It has been observed that as the therapy proceeds, the patient develops certain emotional attitudes towards the therapist. He or she may show evidence of an emotional attachment or perhaps of hostility toward the psychoanalyst. Patients sometimes express resentment about the time the therapist spends with other patients, solicit affection and approval from the therapist, seek more attention, criticize the therapist for indifference or give other evidence of a childish emotional reaction.

Generally Freudians take the view that the patient transfers to the therapist childhood emotions that he has experienced toward his parents.

According to Freud the seeds of neurosis are planted in the very earliest years of childhood. He considered it essential that the pathological emotional relationship of childhood be reenacted via transference in order to be understood and corrected in therapy. It has been established by the treatment of mental disorders that psychoanalysis is suitable only for those neurotic disturbances where the transference neurosis is possible.

The transference relationship may work in both directions. The analyst may develop a counter-transference reaction with the patient. The analyst transfers his emotions to the patient. Counter-transference may interfere with the process of objective analysis of the problems of the patient.

Re-education

Re-education is one further step in which patients are helped to learn new and more adequate ways of dealing with the neurotic conflicts before they can function successfully. They must apply the insight they have gained in a wide variety of situations The patient learn new ways of behaving. The basic purpose of Freudian Psychoanalysis is to aid the patient in developing general resources with which to solve any emotion-producing problem. The patient's general capacity to make satisfactory adjustment to new as well as to old interpersonal problems must be enhanced.

Techniques of Psychoanalysis

Generally psychoanalysis employs the techniques to explore the unconscious structure of the personality of the patient ; Free Association and Dream Analysis.

Free Association

The principal procedure in psychoanalysis is free association. This method is used to explore the content of the unconscious as well as for encouraging resistance and promoting transference. The free association method is employed by having the patient lie on a couch where he cannot see the analyst, relax and tell everything that comes to his mind, no matter how embarrassing or foolish it may be. The relaxation and reeling position tend to minimize the influence of repression and to induce attitudes of submission and dependence. The patient must also be seen frequently if the necessary data for interpretation by the analyst are to be available. The responses of the preceding day should be fresh in the patient's mind as he endeavours to talk freely.

Maslow and Mittelmann commenting on the method say: "The analytic procedure has unique features which are offered in no other situation. The patient learns to behave, speak and think in a way which is possible at no other time—he is encouraged to describe to the analyst, another human being, all his attitudes towards him; he is encouraged to reveal feelings which under ordinary circumstances are conventionally completely hidden ; finally, in talking, he has to discard shame, embarrassment and his desire to maintain a good impression. It is due to the uniqueness of procedure which incidentally, the patient learns gradually, that remarkable data are revealed and that the treatment can be so successful."

Psychoanalysts are insistent that in free association everything must be told because one association leads to another and father into the unconscious. These associations are, of course, only disguised expressions of the repressed urges of early childhood.

The analyst must use his imagination in interpreting the associations of the patient. He must penetrate and recognize the repressed complexes that are unintelligible to the patient.

Dream Analysis

The second important technique is dream analysis. According to Freud, dreams manifest our repressed needs and desires. Dreams and their analysis may serve as an important source of valuable information regarding the unconsciousness. The dream content in some instances contains a universal symbol readily recognizable by the analyst. The dream is not, of course, interpreted literally for its associations. The latent content which can be penetrated only by an expert analyst, contains the real meanings needed for the solution of the patient's difficulties.

The analyts's interpretation of the dream thus plays an important part in the free association process and may be considered as part of the therapy. Dream analysis is designed to break down resistance by pointing out to the patient its association with infantile complexes.

The individual is said to be well in the way to adjustment when he understands the infantile nature of the causes of his symptoms.

The theory of dream analysis is based on the assumption that once the libido has been freed, the ego will be sufficiently strong to enable the patient to dispense with his symptoms and to solve his problems.

Steps in Psychoanalysis

Generally, the following steps are followed in psychoanalytic therapy.

(1) Establishing report : The psychoanalyst establishes perfect rapport with the patient.

(2) Structuring the situation : After establishing rapport, the psychoanalyst prepares the room, furniture, curtains, etc. where the sessions are to be held.

(3) Explanation of procedure : The psychoanalyst explains clearly what is to be done by the patient. Free association and dream analysis are explained.

(4) Resistance : When the first resistance appears, the analyst helps the patient to overcome it. The patient begins to talk about his problems, a process and called catharsis.

(5) Transference : When the patient brings back his repressed childhood emotions that were directed toward his parents and transfers these to the analyst, transfer occurs.

(6) Insight : Gradually, the patient removes the group of emotions and gets insight into his problems.

Neo-Freudian Concepts

Neo-Freudian views have influenced the psychodynamic therapy theory and practice. They have greatly emphasized the importance of social forces that shape the person. Adler who was once an associate of Freud broke with him in 1911. He was critical of Freud's emphasis on sexual drives as the mainspring of neurosis and his emphasis on the discharge and blockage of instinctual drives in the formation of personality.

Adler emphasized the inevitable helplessness of the child and the feelings of inferiority that were fostered by this helplessness. The neurotic solution was to compensate for the inferiority feelings by striving for power. According to Adler, in order to be healthy, the person has to develop the inherent humanneed to involve oneself unselfishly with others, to indentify with the group, and to express a healthy social interest. He believed that a person has the urge to grow and to strive for perfection through social identification. In Adler's psychotherapy more attention is given to the 'persons' conscious intentions and sense of the future than to the past and to unconscious forces. Individuals are encouraged to give up their neurotic style of life.

Carl Jung agreed with Freud that human beings' animal instincts had to be discharged or gratified for psychological health but like Adler he emphasized much more than Freud the struggle of the individual to develop in a positive direction to become self-actualized by which he meant achieving harmonious integration of all the conflicting and diverse aspects of the personality.

Otto Rank, another Neo-Freudian, emphasized the constructive striving of the person to grow, to break with the past in order to live independently in the present. According to Rank, human life is a struggle between two basic tendencies, on the one hand to be in safe union with the protective mother and on the other hand to become a separate and distinct individual. Gratification of one of these tends to thwart the other. This struggle between two opposing tendencies in the cause of maladjustment, and the objective of psychotherapy is to resolve this struggle. He set a time limit to force the patient to face the inevitable separation.

Erich Fromm can also be regarded as a Neo-Freudian. He showed role of the society in facilitating or undermining healthy personality development. He gave more importance to the social character which is the product of the culture in which one lives. According to him, there is struggle to grow and to synthesize the need to feel secure as part of the sociai environment with the need to be independent of that environment. As children develop, they become free to express their individuality which is a strong inherent need but in the process they feel isolated and helpless, a situation that he saw as distinctively human. One inadequate solution to this conflict is to try to escape from the frightening condition of freedom and to submit to social authority. Fromm see failure of adjustment as largely a result of the failure of society in meeting basic human needs.

According to Karen Hroney, basic anxiety is the cause of mental disorders which is the child's feeling of being isolated and helpless in a world that is potentially hostile. Anything that disturbs the child's basic security in relation to the intimate family relation produces anxiety.

Stack Sullivan emphasizes the role of personal relations and the study of humans in relationship with significant others. The self-system of an individual develops as a reaction against the anxiety produced by interpersonal helplessness.

Erik Erikson conceives ego identity as a polarity of what "one feels one is and what others take one to be." One who achieves ego-identity feels a sense of belongingness. There are 8 stages of human development which are related ot each other.

Critique

No doubt psychoanalytic therapy is the oldest method of treating mental disorders and has been widely used all over the world but critics have made the following attacks against psychoanalysis as a method of treatment.

— The concepts of psyhoanalysis are mushy—Freud, Jung and other psychologists used large global concepts such as the Id, the ego, the superego, shadow, self, collective unconscious and so forth. These concepts are not well-defined in antecedent and consequent events. It is difficult to point a finger at exactly what events in a person's life history these large global agents create. It is also difficult to specify what behaviours are being caused by the inner agents. Critics of psychoanalysis, argue that the inner agents represent nothing more than a new demonology.

— The conclusions of psychoanalysis are based on clinical data, not on the basis of experimental method, which is an essential condition for scientific study. For example, many psychologists, particularly Rogerians, question the wisdom of dream interpretation given by an analyst on the grounds that it is difficult if not impossible to differentiate between the patient's true problems and those given to and accepted by him through directive interpretation.

— Psychoanalysis tends to perpetuate dualistic thinking, regarding mind and body as separate realities. Freud divides the personality into two realms—conscious and unconscious and treats them as distinct entities.

• •

— Psychoanalysis is not humanism. It is modelled too much after the natural sciences in that it places too much stress on cause and effect. Freud was a strict determinist. Nothing happens in the mind that is not caused.

— Psychoanalysis places too much stress on man's animal nature. Freud's Id and Jung's shadow are all representations of biological drives. Psychoanalysis makes the inborn biological drives, the foundation of human personalty.

— Freud over emphasized the importance of sex and aggression in the development of neurotic reactions. Critics point out that they are not the only themes in human existence. There are other great drives in life which are more important than sex.

— The process of psychoanalytic therapy is slow and very expensive. It is very difficult for an average income group person to take psychoanalytic therapy for treatment of mental disorders.

Implications for Adjustment

Now the important question is : how can psychoanalytic therapy be helpful to individuals for making adequate adjustment in society ? The following are some of the ways psychoanalysis can contribute to the adjustment and growth of the individuals.

— Extensive reading of psychoanalysis is a mind-expanding activity. It gives a broader prospective on life and a different perception of the human conditions which contribute towards more effective living.

— The subject of motivation is of great importance in psychoanalysis. It makes the individual feel that he is not a mystery to himself. The doctrine of unconscious motivation explains the sources of his actions.

— A knowledge of psychoanalysis makes an individual more tolerant of the behaviour of others.

(II) BEHAVIOUR THERAPY

Behauiour Therapy is a term used to describe a number of new psychotherapeutic methods which have been developed in recent years of a common theoretical basis.

Behaviour therapy derives its impetus from experimental psychology and is essentially an attempt to apply the findings and methods on this discipline to disorders in human behaviour. The area of experimenlal psychology which has the most immediate and obvious value for psychotherapy is the study of learning processes. The early experience of behaviour therapy seems to vindicate these attempts and one can draw further encouragement from the very extensive information about the learning process which has yet to be typed by therapists. The rationale of behaviour therapy is that neurotic behaviour is acquired like other behaviour patterns. If neurotic behaviour is acquired, then it must follow that such behaviour will be subject to the established laws of learning. Current knowledge about the learning process concerns the acquisition of habits and how habits are eliminated. The elimination of learned responses occurs either by a process of extinction or by inhibition.

Wolpe has defined neurotic behaviour as, "any persistent habit of unadaptive behaviour acquired by learning in physiologically normal organism. Anxiety is usually the control constituent of this behaviour, being invariably present in the causal situation." Similarly, Eysneck postulates that, "neurotic symptoms are learned patterns of behaviour which, for some reason or another, are unadaptive." It should be noted, however, that neurotic symptoms may under certain circumstances result, "not only from the learning of an unadaptive response, but from the failure to learn an adaptive response."

The re-learning and unlearning techniques which have been used include :

1. Desensitization based on relaxation
2. Operant conditioning

3. Aversion conditioning
4. Training in assertive behaviour
5. Use of feeding response
6. Avoidance learning
7. Anxiety relief
8. Use of sexual responses
9. Extinction

Behaviour therapy has been successfully used in the treatment of a wide range of neurotic behaviours including phobias, hysteria, enuresis, sexual disorders, tic, and tension states, etc.

Origin

Modern psychology is dominated by what are known as theories of learning. The two theories of learning which are of direct relevance are those of Hull (Reinforcement theory) and B.F. Skinner (Operant conditioning). These theories are in a sense the modern version of Behaviourism. Some of the most significant improvements are the insistance on quantitative studies, increasingly flexible methods and theorizing and in the case of Hull, the use of hypothetico-deductive method. In the past thirty years psychologists have acquired a considerable amount of qualitative information concerning various human processes, particularly in the field of learning. The word learning, it should be noted, is used in any extremely broad manner and includes any aspect of behaviour which is acquired by experience. This includes changes in behaviour which result from maturation or by direct intervention in the functioning of the nervous system.

Behaviour therapy has developed partly as a consequence of these advances in psychology and partly as a reaction to psychoanalysis and its derivatives. The need for a new approach to psychotherapy is emphasized by the disappointing results obtained with prevailing techniques. Since 1948, systematic attempts have been made to apply the facts, theories and methods of learning to the practice of psychotherapy. Wolpe developed several therapeutic techniques on the basis of the learning theory and the most prominent of these is systematic desensitizati on.

Systematic Desensitization

An inquiry is first conducted in order to ascertain which stimulus situations provoke fear or anxiety in the patient. The patient is told that he can add to or modify this list at any time. The stimuli are then categorized by the therapist and the patient is asked to rank the stimuli in order, from the most to the least disturbihg. The ranked list of noxious stimulus conditions are referred to as the hierarchy, ambulance hierarchy and the hospital hierarchy. Hierarchy may contain from 5 to 25 items.

When the hierarchies have been worked out, the subject is told which stimuli are to be presented in each session and is advised to signal with his hand if a stimulus presentation disturbs him unduly. This is an important instruction and should cn no account be omitted, for the arousing of anxiety during the session can be damaging. In the experience of several psychotherapists it has been found that with most patients it is possible by observing his facial expression, bodily tension, respiration and so forth, to perceive such disturbances before the patient actually sigbals when such disturbances occur. The therapist immediately withdraws the stimulus and calms the patient. No session should be concluded when a disturbance occurs but before rousing the patient, the therapist should continue and present a further easy stimulus which has already been successfully overcome. The reason for this is to be found in the commonly observed fact that the last item of any learning series is well retained. Anxiety which occurs at the end of the session is likely to require a longer period before dissipating. When the preliminary instructions have been given, the patient is relaxed and then told to visualize the various stimuli. Each stimulus is visualized for 5 to 10 seconds and 2-4 different items are presented each session. Each item is generally presented twice. When the requisite number of stimuli have been presented the patient is slowly roused and then asked for a report on his reactions. If the items were visualized vividly and without undue disturbance, the therapist then proceeds to the next items in the following session. The item lowest in the hierarchy (the least disturbing) are introduced first and the therapist proceeds slowly up the list depending on the progress achieved and the patient's reactions In this way it is possible for the patient to eventually picture formerly noxious stimuli without any anxiety whatever. This ability to imagine the noxious stimulus with tranquility then transfers to the real life situations.

Operant Conditioning

The work of B.F. Skinner on operant conditioning has recently been applied to problems of psychotherapy. Although Skinner's theoretical views differ from those of Hull, the practical application of his work to psychotherapy involves a similar rationale. Behaviour disturbances are regarded as problems in the acquisition and retention of complex responses. Consequently these disturbances are open to manipulation and modification by the recognized process of learning. Skinner argues that the use of appropriate learning technique should enable the therapist to shape human behaviour in the desired direction of improved mental health. Operant conditioning has been the subject of intensive research and the information which has been collected can be fruitfully applied to the training and re-training of maladjusted behaviour.

From the therapeutic point of view the four most significant concepts are reinforcement, intermittent reinforcement, selective reinforcement and successive approximation. In operant conditioning the strengthening of the response is dependent on the response itself. Reinforcement cannot follow unless the response appears. It is the response which causes the reward to arrive and this reinforces the responses. This process is, of course different from that described by Pavolv. It will be noticed that the subjected in an Operant Conditioning situation plays an active role in the learning process whereas the subject's part in classical conditioning is a relatively passive one. Considerable research has been devoted to the analysis of rewards (reinforces) in the operant-conditioning situation. A highly significant finding is that if reinforcers are presented irregularly (in time or sequence) they are more effective. This intermittent reinforcement produces stronger responses than can be obtained by rewards presented on a regular basis Apart from its value for the therapists, this observation is useful in the analysis of many aspects of human behaviour. For example, it helps to account for the often surprising effects of inconsistent parental care on the behaviour of children.

Experimental work has led to the development of the technique known as selective reinforcement. The use of this method enables one to simultaneously strengthen a desirable. response and extingiush an undesirable one. Briefly this method involves rewarding the appearance of selected response and with holding rewards when the undesired response appears. In this way the person's behaviour can be shaped in the desired direction. The skilful use of this method coupled with successive approximation brings a wide variety of human behaviour into the range of therapeutic manipulation. Successive approximation refers to the gradual and graduated building-up of a new response on the basis of the person's existing repertoire of responses. By careful planning it is possible to build up the person's simple responses into a complex pattern of socially cooperative behaviour.

Evaluative Comments

Historically, behaviour therapy was developed when psychoanalysis was passing the peak of its popularity. Psychoanalysis was considered to be an obstacle to further progress. Therefore, learning theorists on the basis of their experimental studies developed behaviour therapy which has become very popular in recent years.

An objection which is frequently presented by critics against behaviour therapy is the concept of basic causes. They argue that this therapy deals only with symptoms and leaves the basic cause untouched; that this superficial approach to the treatment of neurotic behaviour is destined to bring about only temporary alleviation of symptoms and may well aggravate the patient's conditions.

They claim that it is only when inner forces of the psyche have been restored to harmony by free association, transference and interpretation that the person is normal again. The major objections against Behaviour Therapy may be summarized as follows ; it (a) is superficial (b) is symptom-oriented (c) ignores the deep inner causes of neuroses; (d) can effect only temporary improvement; and (e) smothers certain symptoms only to provoke new ones.

McGaugh considered the learning principles invoked too simple and asked that a larger place be made for the more complex characteristics of human experience as contrasted with animals.

In spite of the above criticism, behaviour therapy is being increasingly practised to cure mental disorders. Behaviour therapy is likely to prove of particular value in the treatment of deficit behaviour disorders such as aphemia, alexia, anorexia and so forth. It may be used in developing psychological functions which are only partially or improperly operative. It is hoped that behaviour therapy may prove valuable in the treatment of children's disorders.

There is no doubt that behaviour therapy has now developed to the point where large-scale field trials with adequate control can be carried out.

In conclusion, it may be said that behaviour therapy offers substantial advantages as a method of treating mental disorders. It has developed out of established psychological theories and has a large body of experimental evidence on which to proceed. The therapeutic process and its outcome are both open to quantification. It permits precision and a systematic planning of the treatment required.

(III) HUMANISTIC-EXISTENTIAL THERAPIES

The humanistic-existential therapies have recently emerged as a third force in psychology. They have developed in reaction to psychoanalytic and behaviouristic view-points which many feel do not take into account either the existential problems or the full potentialities of contemporary men and women. According to humanistic-existential psychotherapists, most problems stem from alienation, loneliness, depersonalization and the lack of a meaningful and fulfilling existence which are not met either by psychoanalysis or behaviourism. The humanistic-existential therapies are based on the assumption that human beings have the freedom to control their behaviour—that they can reflect upon, make choices and take positive action and feel that the client take most of the responsibility for the success of therapy. Major humanistic-existential therapies will be described in the following pages.

(a) Client-Centred Therapy

Carl Rogers introduced a method of psychotherapy which is popularly known as client-centred or non-directive method of treating mental disorders. This method widely differs from the psychoanalytic method and behaviour therapy in its approach to the treatment of mental disorders. Rogers developed a theory of personality based on his observation in psychotherapy. He argued that in order to understand a person, a scientist must try to explore his subjective world, the world as he experiences it.

The basic assumption of this theory is that human beings are capable of understanding their problems and removing them. Therefore in his therapy it is the client (Patient) who takes the lead in the therapeutic process. The counsellor does not intervene by asking questions or by giving information and advice of any type or even by directing the course of conversation. His main objective is to help the client grow in his own direction and his role is confined to encouraging and ratifying this growth. To achieve this goal he employs tools of the acceptance, recognition and clarification of feelings. He simply restates what the client has just said but he restates the feeling side of it rather than the content.

Rogers later on amended his account in order to avoid the elussiveness of the word 'feeling'. The counsellor must learn to perceive things as the client perceives them, to enter as fully as possible into the client's internal frame of reference and to indicate to the client the extent to which he securing through the client's eye.

Client-centred therapy has been widely adopted by non-medical counsellors. The method is simple, clean and consistent in its approach. It does not do any harm to the client.

Harper (1959) commenting on the usefulness of clientcentred therapy has pointed out: "This method of therapy is popular because nothing fits our democratic outlook better than the assumption that even the mental patient can become a new self-made man." Critics of this method point out that regardless of the wide individual differences among the clients the rigid use of a single therapeutic process is made. Perry and Estes pointed out that counselling ceases to be client-centred the moment the counsellor does any thing except recognize feelings.

Throne considered client-centred therapy an incomplete answer to all therapeutic problems, even in mild personality disorders. He laments the failure to obtain any kind of history, pointing out that the counsellor cannot be sure he has really uncovered the major problems if he does not ask questions about the patient's past life. Furthermore what facts the patient elects to reveal are not checked by corroborative evidence from other sources. As a result, it is open to question that a "comprehensive evaluation of the dynamic mechanism operant in the total personality has been made." Not enough is done to prevent the treatment from concentrating on one small and secondary portion of the patient's difficulties. Client-centred therapy is not a panacea for all types of mental problems. It is just an approach to resolve the problems of a client, to rehabilitate him in his environment.

(b) Existential Therapy

Existential therapy is based on the existential model of human beings. Let us first acquaint the readers with the basic concepts of the model.

1. This therapy lays emphasis on the importance of the human situation as experienced by the individual.

2. The second basic concept which bothers existentialists is the break down of traditional faith, the alienation and depersonalization of the individual in the society. There is a lack of meaning in the lives of many people.

3. The existential therapist sees the individual as having a high degree of freedom and thus as capable of doing something about his predicament. Human beings are superior to animals and have the ability to be aware of, reflect on and question their existence.

4. The individual's freedom confronts him with the responsibility for being; for deciding what kind of person to become, for establishing his own values as a human being.

The existential therapist does not follow any rigidly prescribed procedure in the treatment of mentally disturbed people. His main emphasis is on the uniqueness of the individual and his way of being in the world. He stresses the importance of confrontation, challenging the individual directly with questions concerning the meaning and purpose of his existence and the encounter, the complex relationship that is established between two interacting human beings.

In contrast to behaviour therapy, existential therapy calls for the therapist to share himself, his feelings, his values and his existence and not letting the client respond to him as anything other than he really is.

The focus in therapy, is on the here and now—on what the individual is choosing to do and therefore be—at the moment. This sense of immediacy, of the urgency of experience, is the touchstone of existential therapy and sets the stage for clarifying and choosing alternative ways of being.

(c) Gestalt Therapy

Gestalt Therapy is a new approach to understanding mental disorders and resolving them. It was developed by Fredrick Pearls The main assumption underlying it is that individuals must find their own ways in life and accept personal responsibility in order to achieve maturity in life. It emphasizes the importance of the *what* and *how* of behaviour and experiences in the here-and-now by integration the fragmented and unknown parts of personality. The basic assumption of Gestalt therapy is that individuals are capable of dealing with their life problems. The task of the therapist is to assist clients towards fully experiencing their being in the here-and-now by helping them become aware of how they prevent themselves from feeling and experiencing in the present.

The Gestalt view of human nature is rooted in existential philosophy and phenomenology. It lays emphasis on the concepts of awareness, accepting personal responsibility, the unity of mind and body and experiencing the ways in which awareness is blocked. It further holds that every individual has the capacity to assume personal responsibility and live fully as an integrated person.

The Now:

In Gestalt therapy it is the "Now" which is important in understanding the problems of an individual. The main emphasis in therapy is on the here-and-now and on learning to appreciate and experience fully the present moment.

According to Polster and Polster (1973) "Power is in the present". There view is that, "a most difficult truth to teach is that only the present exists now and that to stray from it distracts from the living quality of reality". It is observed that mostly people engage in endless resolutions and plans for the future.

They direct their energy toward what was or what might have been and thus their capacity to capitalize on the power of the present diminishes.

According to Pearls, anxiety is "the gap between the now and the later." People create anxiety by living in the now an attempt to fill the gap between the now and the later with resolutions, plans and visions. The Gestalt therapist does not bother about the past and the future but rather concentrates on the present. He asks the client "what", and "how", questions but rarely asks "why"?

Role of the Therapist

The main role of the therapist is to assist the client, to make him aware of the here-and-now experiences. He provides the climate where the client taps his own developmental process and becomes more clearly focused on his changing awareness from moment to moment. He tries to remove the blocks which prevent a person from standing on his own feet. Polster and Polster (1973) discussing the role of the therapist observed that like artists who need to be in touch with what they are painting the therapist is an artistic participant in the creation of new life. The therapist in order to function effectively must be in tune with the person before him. He must also be in tune with himself.

The therapy is a two-way engagement on a genuine—I-and-Thou basis.

Therapeutic Techniques:

Several techniques are used in Gestalt therapy to help the client gain fuller awareness, experience internal conflicts, resolve inconsistencies and work through impasse that prevents completion of unfinished business.

(*i*) *The Game of dialogue*:

The Gestalt therapist pays close attention to splits is personality function. A main division is between "top dog" and "under dog". The top dog is righteous, authoritarian, bossy and manipulative. This is the critical parent.

The underdog plays the role of victim, by beings defensive, apologetic, helpless and weak. The top dog and undergo are engaged in a constant struggle for control. It is said that:

> "The conflict between the two opposing poles in the personality is rooted in the mechanism of introjection which involves incorporating aspects of another, usually parents, into one's ego-system."

To externalize the introject. The empty-chair technique is used. In this technique two empty chairs are placed in the centre of a room. The therapist asks the client to sit in one chair and be fully the 'top dog' and then to shift to the other chair and become the 'underdog'. The client plays the roles of top dog and unper dog and thus the client can experience the conflicts more fully. The conflicts can be resolved by the client's acceptance and integration of both sides.

Pearls in his apprach to Gestalt therapy has a good deal of emphasis placed on dreams, "...all the different parts of dreams are fragments of our personalities since our aim is to make every one of us a wholesome person which means a unified person without conflicts. What we have to do is put the different fragments of the dream together. We have to reown these projected, fragmented parts of our personality and reown the hidden potential that appears in the dream."

(d) Transactional Analysis (TA)

Transactional Analysis (TA) was developed by Eric Berne, (1910-1970). He was dissatisfied with the traditional methods of psychoanalysis to cure mental disturbances and was constantly in search of any method that would be more effective than the traditional methods of psychotherapy and counselling for the treatment and prevention of mental disorders,

He started his work in the Army Medical Corps as a psychiatrist in 1941. He practised group psychotherapy in the army and suceeded to a great extent in curing mental disturbances in army men.

His first book 'Transactional Analysis as Psychotherapy' was published in 1961. He wrote several books which deal in detail with the coneepts to Transactional Analysis. He rose to international prominence with the publication of his book "Games People Play" in the year 1964.

Encouraged by his innovative techniqne of interpersonal therapy, he started the Transactional Analysis Journal in the year 1962 to popularize his new method of psychotherapy. The journal was well-received by the members of the profession and the general public. The International Transactional Analysis Association (ITAA) was formed in 1964. It publishes a Quarterly journal presenting theory, methods and researches being conducted on TA in differnt parts of the world. Though Berne died in 1970, the interest and the enthusiasm created by TA continues even after his death.

Theory of Transactional Analysis:

The Theory of Transactional Analysis (TA) is very comprehensive. It is not possible to describe it in detail. Therefore a berief summary of the basic concepts is presented here to acquaint the reader with the innovative technique of interpersonal therapy for treating mental disturbances. The following are the basic operations which are followed in TA psychotherapy.

Structural Analysis:

Structural Analysis is the segregation of three ego states, namely Child, Adult and Parent, which, according to Berne, comprise the individual personality. William Wordsworth once commented, "The Child is the father of the man." It means that a child contributes to the adult as he is to-day and the child is retained in our personality throughout life. Three ego states are shown in the following diagram.

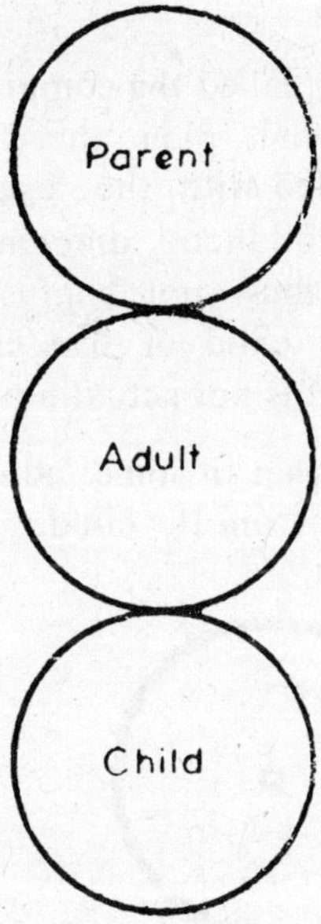

Fig. : 3 Basic structure of Personality

The Child ego state

The child ego state may be equated with the Id of Freud. This ego state contains all the natural feelings, needs, impulses and potentialities of an infant. According to Berne, the child may be divided into there levels (a) the adapted child (b) the rebellious child and (c) the natural child.

The Parent ego state:

The parent ego-state has certain similarities to the child ego state. Like the child, the parent also consists of a set of recordings carried forward from childhood. The parent recordings often have to do with 'oughts' and 'shoulds'. Parents in early childhood interaction inculcate moral values and good habits in their children. The part of the parent that moralizes and issues advice is called the controlling parent. The parent has another aspect which is ealled the nurturing parent.

The Adult ego state:

The adult ego state is called the computer of the personality. Its function is to be rational, plan ahead and take reality into account. It may be equated with the 'ego' of Freud. the adult beings to form in early childhood, differentiating itself from the child and parent. You must not confuse the term Adult with an actual adult. Thus a child of five can be said to have an adult, although this child is not actual adult.

It has been observed that in some adults, the Adult is not sufficiently discriminated from the child. The following figure shows the contamination.

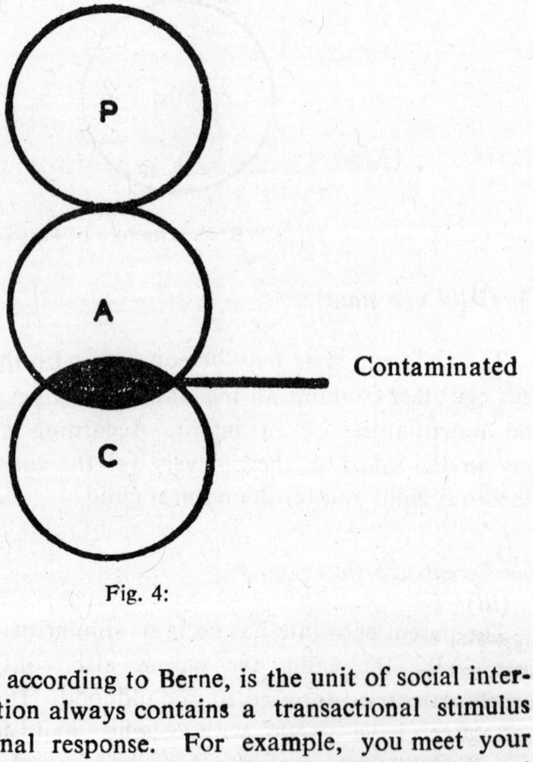

Fig. 4:

Transactions:

A transaction, according to Berne, is the unit of social intercourse. A transaction always contains a transactional stimulus and a transactional response. For example, you meet your friend on the road and greet him by saying, "Namaskar" and in response he also says, "Namaskar". Your namaskar is stimulus and his namaskar is response and both form a unit of simple transaction. Now the question that may be asked here is: why do people engage in transactions ? According to Berne, transactions provide use with strokes which may be either positive or negative. Strokes satisfy the basic human needs of affection and love. Transactions may be of the following types :

(*i*) *Complementary transactions* : It is defined as a "no conflict" transaction. Had all transactions between human beings been complementary, there would have been no conflicts and hostility among the members of a society.

(*ii*) *Crossed transactioni* : They refer to the condition when there is conflict between two or more members.

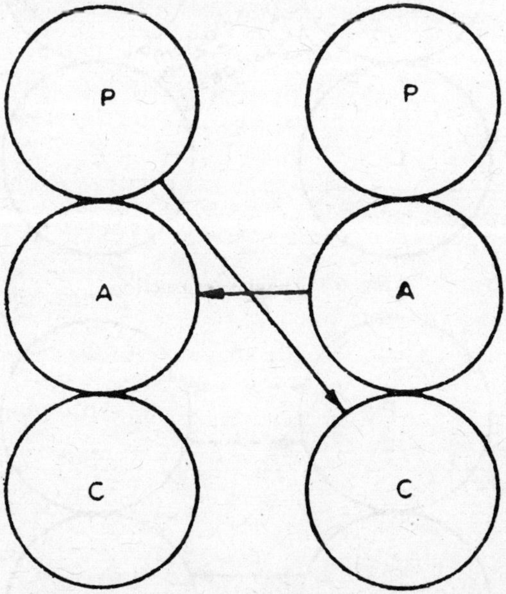

Fig. 5 : Crossed transactions adult and parent-child,

(*iii*) *Ulterior transactions* : These transactions, as the name suggests, are hidden. They have a hidden aim and are the real trouble makers in hdman communication. They have two levels namely : the social level which contains the manifest message, a message that is being communicated in an obvioos sense and the psychological level which contains the latent message, a message which hides behind the surface message. The latent message is the real message. There are two types of Ulterior transactions : angular and duplex. The following diagrams show both types of transactions.

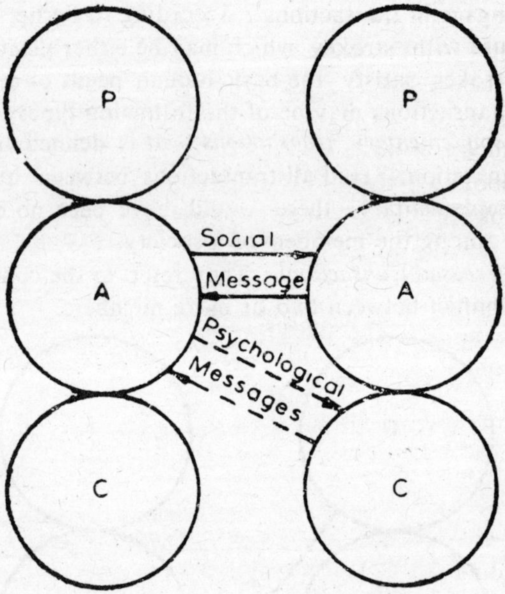

Fig. 6 : Angular transaction.

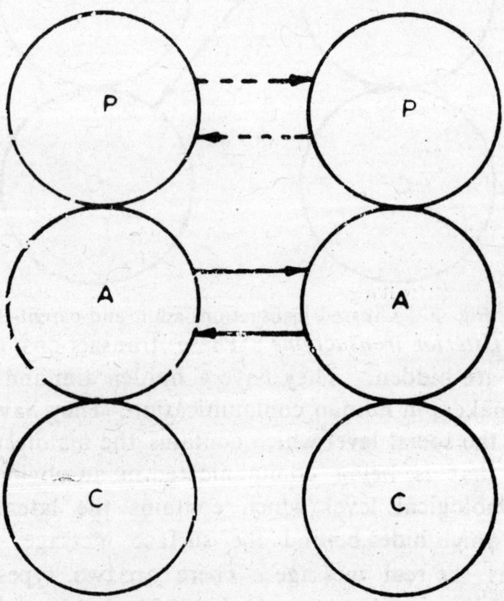

Fig. 7 : Duplex transaction

The Four Existential Positions :

According to Berne, we are all born princes and princesses but early childhood experiences with parents and authority figures turn us into frogs. We develop basic outlook to life in early childhood interactions with parents and significant others. These outlooks are called existential positions. The following four outlooks are given below :

(*i*) *I am not NK—You are OK* : It refers to the outlook of some people who suffer from low-self-esteem and inferiority complexes and consider other people more intelligent, superior and handsome.

(*ii*) *I am OK—You are not OK* : The person having this outlook considers himself superior to others and that consequently he has a right to use others for his own ends.

(*iii*) *I am not OK—You are not OK* : This outlook refers to the conditions when people feel that they are inferior in some way.

(*iv*) *I am OK—You are OK* : A person in this position is in the healthiest life position. He feels that he is reasonably competent and that life is worth living. He trusts himself others.

Games Analysis :

Games analysis is the series of social transactions that are accompanied by covert ulterior transactions which lead to a well-defined pay off.

According to Berne, a game is an ongoing series of complementary ulterior transactions progressing to a well-defined, predictable outcome. Descriptively it is a recurring set of transactions, often repetitious, superficially plausible with a concealed motivation or more colloquially a series of moves with a snore or gimmick. A game is called a game because it is played according to a set of rules by two or more people. Why do people play games ? The answer to this question was given by Berne. As people are alive they must spend their time on Errth in some way. The need to structure time arises due to the following reasons.

(*i*) *Stimulus hunger* : It refers to the human craving for some kind of sensory output.

(*ii*) *Structure hunger* : It refers to the craving for something to do or to go somewhere.

(*iii*) *Recognition hunger* : Every one in the world wants to be recognized by others, People structure their time for the short run in the following ways.

(*a*) *Withdrawal* : The first choice open to us is whether we should play or not to play ; we can engage in social interaction or we can refuse to interact with others.

(*b*) *Rituals* : It consists of a series of predictable complementary transactions. A ritual may be formal or informal.

(*c*) *An activity* : It is a form of social interaction in which the transactions are programmed by the nature of the material with which people are working.

(*d*) *Pastimes* : Pastimes are a step on the way to games. Tney are a series of transactions on a particular subject.

Trading Stamps and Rackets :

The main characteristic of a game is that atleast two people manipulate each other for personal and ulterior ends. Before describing the different types of games, let us introduce two important concepts. Psychological trading : stamps and rackets.

The notion of psychological trading stamps in TA is similar to actual trading stamps given by merchants. Psychological trading stamps can be cashed for various kinds of feelings. There are two colours of psychological trading stamps ; brown and gold. Brown clour stamps are associated with bad feelings whereas gold colour stamps are associated with good feelings.

A racket, then is a feeling out of all possible feelings that is habitually turned on by a given person as his pay off in the games he plays.

Kinds of Games :

TA has identified many kinds of games. The major games are marital games, party games, sexual games, underworld games, consulting room games and good games. In addition, there are several types of games as :

Mine is better than yours : This is a basic game. The reason is that it best represents the raw power struggle between two or more persons. The aim of the game is to be one up, to place the other person in the one down position.

Life-Seripts

TA asserts that we not only tend to live by games but also by scripts. A script is defined as an unconscious life span. TA, however, does not see one's life script in terms of interpersonal fate determined by planetary bodies. On the other hand, the life script is the person's own choice. It represents a decision made in early childhood out of the child ego-state. It is difficult to change.

Kinds of script

As remarked above games are one of the ways people, structure time for the short run. Scripts represent a way that people struccture time for the long-run. Scripts represent an unconscious life plan adopted by the child ego state. There are three types of scripts :winning, non-winning and losing.

Autonomy and Intimacy

The principal goals of TA are autonomy and intimacy for the individual. Autonomy may be defined as a game force and script-free living. The autonomous person tends to be non-manipulative in his personal relations. It does not mean that a person without a script has no plans or goals. On the contrary he has flexible plans and realistic goals made out of his thinking adult not his irrational child.

The other main objective of TA is intimacy which may be defined as game of free exchange of emotional expression without exploitation. The concept of intimacy is particularly impor. tant when it is applied to the way we relate to significant others, When there is intimacy in a relationship, there is mutual respect for each individual's status as a real person.

Process of Transactional Analysis

The success and effectiveness of TA largely depends on the setting and the environment of the room where the session of TA is held. The furniture, colour of curtains and the wall and the dress of the therapist all constitute the setting.

In the initial interview, the therapist very carefully tries to assess the ego-states the client seems to be in. The therapist makes an analysis of the initial transactions and draws certain consclusions. TA can be used in individual therapy but much of its power comes from its use in group transactions analysis. Interview records are kept for future reference.

Mechanisms of TA Therapy

The first stage of TA relationship is that of meeting a confused client with benevolent parents. The therapist seeks the necessary information from the client in order to establish a contractual relationship. The main objeetive of the first stage is to create a safe environment in which the client may begin to reown his adult.

The TA is usually carried out in groups. The initial stage also serves to develop the group into a community of meaningful others. Improved communication among participants is hoped for.

In the second stage, the therapist explains the client's behaviour to him using the information obtained in the first stage. The therapist's tools are structural analysis, transactional analysis, script analysis and games analysis. The principal and specific objective of this stage is to familiarize the client with the vocabulary and principles of TA. The therapist can use various techniques to make the client aware of his areas of conflicts.

The third stage is marked by confrontation. The therapist keeps the client in the present time frame while eliciting a commitment to some action : It is during this stage that clients begin to appreciate their own value in the therapeutic process. The clients come to accept their own adult as the true base of support for them in life activity.

Advantages of TA

—The greatest advantage of Transaction Analysis is that it focuses on the communication process. It suggests ways of improving the quality of messages exchanged by human beings.

—Transactional Analysis is self-help psychology. The literature is simple and understandabld even by a layman. People can help themselves by reading the basic concepts of TA.

—TA helps to see the destructive and self-destructive traps of larger patterns identified as games and scrips.

—The insight offered by TA suggests practical ways of coping with destructive and manipulative people. TA gives us strategies to defend ourselves. TA as a matter of fact is psychology of change. It is aimed at changing what people want to change in their behaviour.

—The TA goals of autonomy and intimacy create powerful images of what thc good life can be.

—Transactional analysis gives us many ideas for becoming more effective parents.

(e) Rational—Emotive Therapy

Rational-emotive therapy was developed by Albert Ellis, an American psychologist, to prevent the mental disorders produced by unnecessary reactions of anger, guilt, anxiety, etc. According to Ellis, the main objective of rational-emotive therapy is to educate the emotions of the individual so that he can adjust adequately society.

According to Ellis, "Rational-emotive therapy is like the science of psychology. It teaches the client how to discriminate more clearly between sense and non-sense, fiction and reality, superstition and science."

Rational-emotive therapy places great emphasis on cognitive change designed to help the client to deal effectively with his emotional 'shoulds' and 'musts' to grow as a creative person. It is based on the premise that an appraisal of threat is the critical link in the stress-threat-anxiety chain.

Irrational Ideas

According to Ells, excessive guilt, anger and anxiety are the result of various irrational beliefs. These irrational beliefs are consciously held by the person and he makes himself sick by repeating the idea over and over again to himself. Thus one factor emotional illness is the pattern of self-indoctrination with false notions.

Human beings suffer largely because they confuse desires with needs. They make their wishes into demands and they feel miserable if they cannot make their wishes come true. It is an irrational idea to think that wishes must come true or life will not be worth living.

The Ellis theory of human suffering revolves around man's cognitive capacities. People think that they have conscious ideas and it is these conscious ideas which lead to emotional reactions.

An anxiety-prone person suffers from chronic negative emotional states and does a lot of catastrophic thinking. For example, he rails in the examination and thinks, "I will never pass." He over-generalizes his experiences from one situation to other situations.

Another emphasis of rational-motive therapy is on long-range hedonism. Ellis has no argument with a basically hedonic attitude toward life : the view that pleasure is good and that it is an important end in itself. He contends, however, that much suffering is the result of short range hedonism—living only for immediate gratification. The rational-emotive philosophy teaches that one should attempt to maximize one's total happiness, not just the pleasure of the moment.

List of major irrational ideas

- The idea to be loved or approved by virtually every significant other.
- One should be thoroughly competent, adequate and achieving in everything.
- Certain people are bad, and wicked. They should be punished.
- It is awful when things are not the way one would like them to be.
- Human unhappiness is caused and people have no control over their errors.
- It is easier to avoid than to face life's difficulties.
- Past history is an all important determiner of one's present behaviour.

ABC of Emotional Self-Control

Ellis believes that training and self-control of emotinns is possible. He developed the rational-emotive therapy to help people find freedom from the constraints of excessive and unnecessary emotions. He proposed a systematic approach called the ABCs of rational-emotive theray which is given below :

Point A

According to Ellis at point 'A' there is some even that starts an emotion-producing change. This event actualiy takes place in the real world. This event can be called activity or action or agent. For example, a person has a quarrel with wife, fails in an examination, loses a job, is disappointed by his son's choice of a career. Many of these events can be the real world agent that evokes an emotional response.

Point B

At point 'B', the person has a belief about the activity, action or agent. If the person has a rational belief than there is no problem but on the other hand if the person is irrational and is rigid in his belief, then there is problem. Irrational beliefs cannot be sustained by the facts of life.

Point C

Point 'C' represents the consequence of a belief. If the belief is rational, the consequence will be an emotion that is appropriate to the situation. If the belief is irrational, the consequence will be some thing unusual an emotional outburst, excessive guilt, anxiety, depression or anger, etc.

Point D

This is a point which is not added by typical person. Most of us accept our emotional states uncritically. The feeling at point 'C' is one that we deem to be legitimate simply because it is ours.

Point 'D' stands for dispute. Ellis contends that the key to emotional education resides in the capacity to challenge the irrational belief of point B.

The dispute of irrational beliefs at point D is not designed to replace negative emotional states with bliss. The goal is more limited: the idea is to bring the emotions into balance, to make them oppropriate tó one's life eircumstances.

Ellis and Harper summarized the ABC of rational-emotive therapy in the following words :

"Combat the idea that it is terrible horrible and catastrophic when things are not going the way you would like them to go. When conditions are not the way, you would prefer them to be, calmly and determinedly try to change them for the better; and when for the moment, they cannot be changed, the only sane thing to do is quietly to accept them: The greater your loss or frustration is, the more philosophic you must be in regard to it; the more you must accept the fact that it is bad and undesirable but not catastrophic or unbearable."

Self-esteem and Perfectionism

One of the important themes in the RET approach is the teaching that many people suffer needlessly because they expect too much from themselves. You will recall that one of the cardinal irrational ideas residing behind irrational reactions is this one: the idea that one should be thoroughly competent, adequate and achieving in all possible respects to consider onself worthwhile. Ellis contends that a person who holds this idea is bound to experience low self-esteem, no matter what his objective accomplishment in life is. From his point of view, he has not lived up to his possibilities. His internal standards are too high, so high that they are unrealistic; and when he fails to reach his own high standard, he develops low self-esteem, living one's life by a doctrine of perfectionism is just irrational and does not fit with reality.

Summarizing the theory of RET we may conclude that there is rational thinking and there is irrational feeling. Thinking and feeling are closely connected. Irrational thinking leads to such unwarranted emotional states as excessive anger, depression and anxiety. According to Ellis, the source of personal distress is not unconscious repressed ideas.

A number of personal problems are manufactured out of consciously held irrational views or beliefs.

He encourages people to fight irrational conscious beliefs with conscious rational beliefs.

It is asserted that rational thinking frees one from the bonds of negative emotions and helps one become more self-accepting.

(f) Reality Therapy

Reality therapy was propounded by Glasser. It assumes that in early life the individual develops a basic sense of right or wrong that provides the basis for later values. Difficulties arise when the individual's actual behaviour is in conflict with the basic sense of right or wrong.

Reality Therapy focuses on helping the client clarify his basic values and evaluate his current behaviour and future plans in relation to these basic values.

The therapist works as a moral agent and helps the client to differentiate a clear set of values. Sometimes difficulties arise in helping the client to live responsibly in accordance with his values. The client is helped to perceive the aversive consequences of living irresponsibly and the sense of personal fulfilment that results from clarifying and living in accordance with one's basic values.

Glasser found favourable results with reality therapy in dealing with delinquents and wives of military personnel.

Basic assumptions

One can have a rewarding life only by living a responsible life. The essence of responsibility and of facing reality, is finding effective ways to meet two psychological needs : (a) the need to love and to be loved; and (b) the need to feel that we are worth-while to ourselves and others.

Reality therapy rejects the value of traditional categorization of mental disorders. According to Glasser, conventional clinical pigeonholes are only descriptions of various forms of irresponsibility.

— The present and future are more important than the past.

— There is greater stress in reality therapy on conscious problems than on unconscious conflicts.

— Values and moral principles are important in daily living. Reality therapy holds that it is appropriate to think in terms of right or wrong. When people cannot fulfil their needs, their behaviour is wrong. Glasser observes, "we believe that almost all behaviour which leads to fulfilling our needs within the bounds of reality is right or good or moral behaviour, according to the following definition; 'when a man acts in such a way that he gives and receives love and feels worthwhile to himself and others, his behaviour is right or moral."

— We grow as persons by setting up definite plans and followng through with the plans. Peopleneed goals. People without igoals drift.

Facing Reality

It is very essential for all of us to face reality. It is the only way to meet our basic psychological needs for love and sense of worth.

Identity

Glasser stresses the importance of the concept of identity. According to Glasser and Zunin, identity is defined as a need. They say it is, "the need to feel that we are somehow separate and distinct from every other living being on the face of the earth, that no matter where we go we will not find another person."

They further note that people seek to have meaning associated with their identity. In other words they try to take their rightful place in society. They seek a relationship with other people.

A person struggles for an identity within the society and he forms a polarized concept of self : either a success identity or a failure identity.

Individuals are responsible for themselves. They can choose their identity.

Implications of Humanistic-existential Psychotherapies

No doubt the humanistic-existential psychotherapy has certain inconsistencies and inherent difficulties but still it can help a lot in the process of adjustment, prevention and eradication of mental disorders. Following are the major implications.

— One of the principal values of the humanistic-existential psychotherapy is the reminds us our humanity.

— It teaches us to respect our own experiences. Our anxiety, anger or joy is not explained by psychological jargon. Feelings are taken to be real and there is an insistence on their validity. We are advised to respect our own feelings and the feelings of others.

— The humanistic-existential psychotherapy places importance on the individual and his unlimited capacity to shape his destiny. Human beings are not seen as passive victims of fate but as authors of their own future.

— It gives us a set of positive images about the way life can be. It speaks of the self-actualizing person who is leading a meaningful life. These images set a standard suggesting that authentic living is important.

— It sounds on optimistic note about the possibilities of human existence. It points upward to a life beyond the gray zone of mundane existence.

— It asserts that it is our responsibility to make the most of our possibilities. It challenges us to become the best and brightest that we may become.

Critique

— The psychoanalytic school of psychotherapy criticizs the

humanistic-existential psychotherapy on the count that it attempts to completely discredit the significance of unconscious motives. It makes the conscious mind king of one's fate. But through observation of every day life activities we cannot ignore the importance of unconscious motives.

— The behaviourists oppose the humanistic-existential psychology on the basis of its unscientific methodology. It says little about the learning process, the most important process underlying human behaviour. Humanistic-existential psychotherapists seldom talk of conditioned responses and habits as important variables in determining behaviour.

— Humanistic-existential psychologists talk about the absolute freedom of will. Even if the freedom of will is granted, serious thinkers would be unwilling to say that there are not many constraints on its action.

— Humanistic-existentialists hold contradictory views regarding human development. For example, Sartre says that we create our personalities, that an individual does not have an inborn essence. On the other hand Maslow suggests that each person has an inborn set of talents and potentialities which can be looked on as 'seed.'

— Humanistic-existential psychology stresses the importance of the subjective point of view. We live our lives from the within and this internal frame of reference is considered to be more valid than the external one. But other schools of psychology, particularly behaviourists, hold that human behaviour can be as objectively studied as the motions of the planets.

— The humanistic-existential approach is replete with such mystery ideas as being, the will, the creative self, consciousness and self-actualization which are not really amenable to scientific validation.

— Humanistic-existential psychologists are of the opinion that in modern society minds are being destroyed haphazardly, that every one is self-alienated. These contentions seem doubtful to more cautious thinkers.

Comparison of Pscyhotherapies

No. Therapy 1	Key Figure 2	Basic Philosophy 3	Goad of therapy 4	Techniques of therapy 5
1. Psychoanalytic	Freud	Eariy experiences and unconscious motives are important. Sexual and aggressive impulses	To make the unconscious conscious	Dream analysis and free association
2. Existential Humanistic	May, Maslow Frankl	Self awarenss, responsibil,ty, freedom and self actualization	Providing conditions for self awareness & growth	No definite technique
3. Client-	Carl Rogers	Inner-directedness, trust in self and spontaneity	Providing for self exploration N and greater trust in self	Active listening, reflection of feeling.
4. Gestalt	Fritz Pearls	Integration of thinking, feeling and behaving is emphasized	Providing awareness moment to moment expericncing	Confrontiation, Dialogue, role playing, Gestalt dream work

1	2	3	4	5
5. TA	Eric Berne	Human beings can change self defeating tendencies by awareness	To help client to become script free, game free	Script analysis contracts and questioning
6. Behaviour	Wolfe, Eysenck Lazarus, Salter	Behaviour is the product of learning and conditioning	Removal of mal-adaptive behaviour pattern	Desensitization implusive threapy operant conditioning
7. R.E. Theory	Albert Ellis	Human beings have potential for rational thinking	To remove clients self-defeating outlook	Teaching, reading Home assignment
8. Reality	William Glasser	Human beings need identity.	Guidance for developing success identity	Contract and active, directive

QUESTIONS FOR DISCUSSION

1. Define psychotherapy and describe its objectives.
2. What are the major operations of psychodynamic therapy ?
3. What do you mean by Behaviour Therapy ? What are its advantages and limitations ?
4. What are the basic principles of client-centred therapy ?
5. What are the advantages and limitations of transaction analysis?
6. Write detailed notes on
   (a) Reality therapy
   (b) Rational-Emotive therapy
7. Compare transaction analysis and psychoanalysis as techniques of psychotherapy.

SUGGESTED READINGS

1. Adler, A. : The Practice and Theory of Individual Psychology; Harcourt, New York, 1927.
2. Blum, G. : Psychoanalytic Theories of Personality; McGraw Hill NY, 1953.
3. Cameron, N. : Personality Development and psychopathology. Houghton Mifflin, Boston, 1964.
4. Corey Gerald : Theory and Practiec of Counselling and Psychotherapy, Books/Cole Publishing Co., California, 1977.

CHAPTER 13

Treatment: Group Psychotherapy

Man is a social animal. He is born in a group. He spends much of his life in different groups. He is educated in groups. He earns his livelihood in a group. In brief it can be said that the harmonious development of an individual without social interaction in a group is beyond imagination. We can say that an individual from birth to death lives in a group and dies in a group and many of his problems stem from group interaction. Some psychologists, in the beginning of the present century, realized that the best place to seek a 'cure' for the problems of individual was in the very environment in which the problem was experienced i.e., the group.

The history of group psychotherapy can be traced to the year 1905 when J. Pratt initiated the use of didactic discussion and inspirational meetings to bring about desirable behavioural changes in physically illpatients. Being successful in his attempt to bring favourable changes in his patients, he applied his technique to mentally disturbed children, adolescents and adults. But the actual widespread use of group psychotherapy was made during the first World War as a time saving device, when thousands of soldiers suffered from war hysteria and other mental disturbances which necessitated the use of some effective and time-saving device for their treatment. Group psychotherapy methods of treating mental disorders are congruent with important recent trends in the understanding of the dynamics of human behaviour approach, away from an individualistic toward a social or interactive conception. The patient is an individual. He is also a member of a family and other social groups which influence his personality development. His complaints are often rooted in his defective interaction with these other people and their behaviour may have a good deal to do with what is wrong. Therefore, treating people in groups is in a sense more realistic than the one-to-one interaction. According to Slavason, certain patients manifest aversion to the individual therapy because of fear, distrust of antagonism towards all parental figures. Such patients find in the group the acceptance and the support necessary for the examination of their problems.

Patients of low intelligence may also benefit more from group therapy in peer groups than from individual therapy. It has also been observed that children with certain adjustment problems are successfully cured by group therapy. As a matter of fact all individual psychotherapies described in chapter 12 can also be practised in groups. But here we have selected some widely used group psychotherapies such as family therapy, marital counselling psychodrama and play therapy with children. A brief description of these therapies is given below to acquaint the reader with the basic mechanism underlying them.

Family Therapy

Psychologists and sociologists have in the last two decades conducted a number of studies to investigate the mechanisms of family dynamics and its role in the personality development of its members. On the basis of the findings of various studies, it has now been recognised that interaction among family members plays a crucial role in shaping and maintaining the mental health of the individual members.

Family therapy emerged in the process of psychoanalysis which therapy traditionally based on a one-to-one relationship. When psychoanalysis was applied in the treatment of small children it was felt that without the active cooperation of parents no change could be effected in the behaviour of children. Therefore, psychologists developed family therapy in which all members of family cooperate actively in the treatment of a sick member. The primary aim of family therapy is the mobilization of a rational and effective communication system among the family members in order to bring to awareness the hidden and distorted expressions of emotions which pervade the disturbed family and adversely affect the sick family member.

The first essential step in family therapy was the practice of drawing the mother into a simultaneous therapeutic relation. This soon became the standard practice in child guidance clinics. The mother who is most upset by the mental disorder of the child usually brings the child to the office. Before the advent of family psychotherapy the treatment of child and mother was generally done on a two-to-two basis.

The bold step of trying to influence the whole family is certainly in accord with the present theories about the nature of the social system. In practice it is no small feat to secure the cooperation of all the members of a family. All members of the family are interviewed to collect useful information about the sick member and the inner relations among the members. Much can be deduced from the member enter the room of the therapist, offer greetings and distribute themselves among the available chairs. Conflicts, confision, the dominance hierarchy and preferred modes of acting as a family may reveal themselves sharply in the problem of seating. Significant family alignments, alliance and scapegoating may come to light early in the proceedings. The therapist tries to create an atmosphere of rapport that will help reduction of concealment and defenses. He must permit himself to be drawn into the centre of the family disturbances but he must also preserve objectivity and freedom so that he can serve as an umpire and even as controlling authority if things threaten to go out of hand. Family psychotherapy is obviously no job for a novice. To improvise appropriate action in what can easily become a whirlpool of passions; to grasp the meaning of behaviour of the family members requires the rare gift of alertness and seasoned skill. Haley brings out the difficulties of family therapy. He says that trouble begins with the world 'patient'. When the family is brought for treatment, one member is considered the patient by the other members of the family. As Haley puts it "the experienced family therapist...struggles to find out a better term than patient for the family member chosen to be it. The trouble is not inside one person; it lies in the entire family system, in the whole set of relations prevailing among all the members and it will not be resolved without bringing changes in the entire family system."

Ackerman describes the method of family therapy as, "therapeutic intervention in the emotional processes of the natural living unit, the family entity, viewed as an integrated behaviour system." The interview unit consists ideally of the whole family, although at certain points some members may be excused in order to concentrate on a particular pair, possibly the husband and wife, or a child and a parent. The goal can be described as producing a more healthful, satisfying family life. This implies easing the anxieties, competition and resentment that spoil the positive aspects of interaction. The therapists' task is to provide a timely challenge to the rationalization and defensive disguises whereby the members conceal from themselves the destructive aspects of their relationships. This is mainly accomplished by a device which Ackerman calls, "tickling the defenses."

This is essentially a technique of confrontation which points, especially, to contradictions between conscious attitudes and patterns of action, to discrepancies between verbal utterances and non-verbal communication as reflected in facial expression, movement, mood, posture and gesture. Especially important here is the exposure of unreal and impossible demands, the challenge of fruitless blaming and vindictive encroachment on their family members and the undermining and challenging of hypocritical self-justifications. Family therapy can be of great value in relieving the suffering of the person designated as patient and of improving the general conditions of the family life. But it should be kept in mind that it is not a panacea and cannot be expected to work in all circumstances. Ackerman points out that, "for some families, realistically speaking, it may be too late to reverse the forces fragmentation. There must be hope and desire for an improved life together. Success is sometimes blocked when the family contains in one member, a concentrated focus of malignant destructive motivation."

The therapist should keep certain important points in mind before he attempts family therapy. He must be well-aware of the forces of relation already existing in the family and patterns of communication between the members. He must clarify the communication between family members because confusion in communication creates misunderstanding in the family. Direct and explicit communications are very helpful in making the family members feel part of the process. The therapist may also make the family rules explicit so that every one knows what they are and why they exist.

The therapist can also model how to make decisions collectively so that members of the family feel they have power and importance.

Marital Counselling

Marital counselling is becoming increasingly important in modern times because cases of divorce and bride burning are being reported in the national newspapers in large number in metropolitan cities. Marital counselling is best performed by bringing the married couple in the presence of a counsellor who can point out the failures of communications at the time they occur.

Discrepancies of expectations with regard to dominance, submission and initiative can also create frustration and resentment between husband and wife.

More factors other than failure of communication are involved in marital discord. The counsellor must try to reach the root cause of the discord.

Psychodrama

Psychodrama as a method of group psychotherapy was originated by J.L. Moreno in 1921. It is an important form of psychotherapy in which people in groups participate to stimulate the expression of feelings through unrehearsed and spontaneous acting on the stage. Some patients take part in the action and some act as audience along with the observer who is generally a trained psychotherapist. The central principle underlying the psychodrama is that drama stands mid-way between fantasy and reality. It is real because there is an audience, a stage and a drama that is played. It is unreal in the sense that the whole thing is only a play. Unrehearsed drama has a certain similary to free association. Free association is real in the sense that a therapist is listening and that relief from neurosis is being sought. It is unreal in the sense that what one says is illogical and fantastic, quite unsuitable for communication in every day life.

Proponents of psychodrama maintain that it is better than free association as a means of securing expression of pent-up emotional feelings. Psychodrama is best suited to patients with a certain degree of generalized inhibition and difficulty in expressing themselves. It helps in overcoming inhibitions that are not too deeprooted.

Psychodrama was successfully used by Moreno to resolve marital discord between a couple. As a matter of fact psychodrama was developed under strange circumstances. Moreno founded a theatre and engaged Barbara, a young, beautiful lady as a stage actress. After some time she married Mr. George, a young man who was a first row spectator of Barbara's acting on the stage. After some time the relationship between Barbara and George became strained. Moreno advised and instructed them to act out their conflicts and tensions on the stage. The technique was successful in curing their strained relationship and both of them led a happy married life. Thus psychodrama as a technique for treating emotionally disturbed persons was developed. According to Moreno, "it is a reliable psychodramatic experience that once the subjects are working on the therapeutic stage they are carried by the momentum of psychodramatic dynamics from the surface to the deeper level of their relationship." In spite of the fact that psychodrama is an effective method to resolve mental disorders, it has made less rapid progress than family psychotherapy. Psychodrama as a technique makes use of the following participants : (a) Protagonist : the patient ; (b) Director Chief therapist ; (c) the auxiliary egos and the group ; other participants or other patients who make up the audience.

Group Psychotherapy

Family therapy and psychodrama certainly qualify as group psychotherapy but in practice this more general term has come to imply groups of a particular kind. Typical of group psychotherapy is a meeting of a therapist and eight ault or adolescent patients who at the outset are unacquainted with each other. In the course of a series of sessions the members of the group become well-acquainted and sometimes lasting friendships may be formed. Group psychotherapy involves work with a group of strangers and the members are bound by no formalities after the work is completed. In this respect, is differs from family therapy. Before, psychotherapists made no difference in the method of individual and group therapy. But now different approaches are being used in group therapy. For example some workers advocate a strictly group-centred procedure that copies the permissiveness and non-directiveness of Roger's client-centred psychotherapy. Some adhere to Freudian Psychoanalysis and concentrate on interpreting the transference reactions that occur during the meetings. Others favour a principle of flexibility using different degrees and kinds of activity according to the nature and circumstances of the group. Still others, chiefly those working with more seriously disturbed patients, find it advisable to use tactics of a more directive character. Similarly, there is a range of opinion about the length of time required to secure good results. 20 to 40 weekly sessions representation of an average duration is suggested.

The Course of Group Therapy

Though it is difficult to give a standard account of the course of group therapy, certain common steps are followed which are given below :

—The group consists of about five to eight neurotic patients or other individuals having some problems.

—Meetings are held once a week with the leader or group members sitting informally around a table,

—Initially members direct all their remarks toward the leader and expect answer and advice from him.

—The leader simply says, "Let me hear what you think about this question."

—Patients begin to talk among themselves.

—Now the leader works as interpreter.

—He raises questions.

—Discovery of mental tension is made spontaneously or with the help of group members.

—Patients discuss symptoms and other things troubling them.

—Feelings and past experiences are freely narrated.

—Human relations are developed.

Group Psychotherapy which was once considered superficial and ineffective is now accepted as a method having properties of its own that makes it for many purposes superior to individual therapy. Some of the advantages are :

—Quick decrease in the sense of isolation of members.

—The therapist controls the social behaviour of the patients.

—He offers more a realistic identification figure. He is seen in action with the social group.

—The patients from the start share the therapist with other group members.

—It is effective for delinquents, character disorders and problems of passive dependence on others.

Psychotherapy with Children

The psychological treatment of maladjusted children is not basically different from the treatment of adults. Though the same basic principles operate, their emphasis and application have to be adjusted to the needs of children who are completely dependent on their parents and are immature in their behaviour.

The following significant differences have been reported by psychotherapists in the treatment of children.

—The language of the child is not so advanced as to enable him to explain his problems to the therapist. He cannot communicate effectively with the therapist on his problems,

—The personality of the child is less structured and formed. The child shows rapid fluctuations in his behaviour. He is not able to differentiate between facts and fantasy.

—As already remarked the child is emotionally dependent upon his parents. Therefore, the psychotherapist has also to deal with parents because the problems of the child are inextricably involved with that of the parents who bring the child to the psychotherapist for treatment.

—Another important difference which requires an understanding of the child's behaviour involves the transference situation. Since a child is still living with his parents, he has not repressed his feelings for them but is rather in the midst of a struggle to express them. Instead of showing the adult type of transference, the child relates emotionally to the therapist as a third parent.

—The therapist has to create a situation in which the child can express his pent-up emotional feelings without inhibition.

Play Therapy

Play therapy is a most effective method for the treatment of emotionally disturbed children. It is based on the assumption that play provides a very satisfactory catharsis in case of children. Play therapy mostly involves the use of toys as a means of giving overt expression to the repressed needs and emotions of the child. The child in play therapy is permitted to give vent to his aggressive and hostile feelings through the medium of play material and other materials in child guidance clinics.

Play therapy may be used as a diagnostic instrument to get an understanding of the conflicts, anxieties and other problems of children. Play therapy provides opportunity to the child to act out his repressed feelings through play material. It enable the child to gain insight in to the meaning of his behaviour. It also provides parents with an understanding of the causes of the child's undesirable behaviour.

Child-Centred Therapy

Axline and associates have recently developed child-centred therapy on the model of the Rogerian client-centred therapy. They allow the child to play and to be as permissive as possible. But they prevent the child from harming himself or the therapist seriously. The child may be allowed to throw water and sand and may disturb and destroy toys but it does not mean that he may be permitted to throw sand in the eyes of the therapist.

The therapist tries to let the child know that his rights and freedom will be respected. If the child does not want to play, he may sit and do anything else he likes.

The therapist strives to be warm and affectionate, accepting and understanding. He will reflect and clarify what the child expresses. He attempts to create an atmosphere conducive to the relaxation of defences. Gradually, it is assumed that the child will work through his inner conflicts, expressing in his play, the hostility and other negative feelings that in time give way to positive emotions and insight.

Child Guidance Clinic

The child guidance movement is attributed to Healy who founded the Chicago Juvenile Psychopathic Clinic in 1909 where problem children were referred and treated for mental abnormalities. Another clinic was started by the Judge Barker Foundation in Boston in 1915.

The child guidance movement got a spurt during World War II due to specific reasons : The ravages of war brought in its train separation from and loss of parents, disruption of normal academic life and other privations. The second development in the same period came from the growth of clinical psychology. A large number of psychological tests were evolved and standardized to assess ths various aspects of mental functions. In India, child guidance clinics started in the fifties. There are very few child guidance clinics which work independently ; most of them are housed in big hospitals. There is a great need to establish independent ful-fledged child guidance clinics for the treatment of children.

Requirements for Clinics

A. Staff

The staff of a child guidance clinic may differ from city to city regending on the work-load but generally the following technical staff is recommended for an average city.

1. *Paediatrician* : He is responsible for the physical check up of the patients.

2. *Social Workers* : He is responsible for bringing data from the children's home, the school or the social agencies.

3. *Clinical Psychologists* : He undertakes specific mental assessment to arrive at a proper diagnosis of the problems of the children. The speech therapist and the school counsellor may also be associated with the treatment of the problem children.

4. *Nurse*

5. *Non-Technical Staff* : Clerk, peon, sweeper, gardener, etc. according to the requirements of the child guidance clinic.

B. Materials

1. Toys of different colours and sizes according to the age and sex of children.

2. Dolls representing father, mother and siblings, animals, house building blocks.

3. Toys of transportation.

4. Running water, clay, plaster of paris sand.
5. Drawing and painting material.
6. A small garden having pets, cats, deers, rabbits and small dogs.

C. Building

The child guidance clinic should be housed in a building of 5 to 6 rooms. The rooms should be well-furnished and decorated with appropriate material. The building should be constructed keeping in consideration the requirement of the community.

QUESTIONS FOR DISCUSSION

1. What is group therapy ? What are its advantages and limitations ?
2. What are the basic principles of family therapy ?
3. "Play therapy is a diagnostic method of diagnosing children's problem" Comment.
4. What is child-centred therapy ? Describe in detail.
5. What are the requirements of a Child Guidance clinic ?

SUGGESTED READINGS

1. Axline, V.M. : Play Therapy ; Houghton, Miffiin, Boston, 1947.
2. Balint, M. : Psychotherapeutic Techniques in Medicine ; Tavistock Publication, London, 1961.
3. Ginott, H.G. Group Psychotherapy with Children : McGraw Hill, NY 1956.
4. Winnicott, D.W. and Howel set al, : Child Therapy in "Modern Perspective in Child Psychitary" (Ed) ; Edinburg, 1965.

CHAPTER 14

Indian Psychotherapy

In the preceding chapters we have described the major psychotherapeutic practices developed mostly in the present century. The present chapter will deal exclueively with Indian psychotherapeutic practices which were developed thousands of years ago in the *Atharva-vedic* period. Documentary sources as well as survey reports right from the Vedas to the present day affirm the system of Indian psychotherapy.

The *Atharva-veda* is possibly the most ancient document of Indian psychotherapeutic science. It is a basic book which deals comprehensively with psychogenic problems of human beings. It deals not only with cures of all types of ailments but also attempts to solve all problems of humanity and prescribes methods to control events in the physical world with psychological practices. Here we will confine ourselves to the study of the psychotherapeutic practices of the *Atharva-veda* the *Charak samihita*, the *Susruta samihita* and Yoga—the Indian science of psychic sublimation and achievement.

(1) THE ATHARVA—VEDIC PSYCHOTHERAPY

The Atharva-veda is according to some western scholars like Winternitz, older than the *Rig-veda* and is specifically related to *Atma* and *Mana*. It shows ways and means to do everything from removal of illness to victory in war through energy of *Mana* (Psyche). It is said that the Atharva-veda is the basic book of Indian psychology. The psychology of Atharva-veda is both theoretical and practical. On the practical side its approach is psychogenic and shows the psyche to be all energetic in solving all problems and achieving all ends in life. The Atharva-veda is psychogenic in nature and its importance is in the practical application of psychic energy over matter.

Concept of normality and abnormality

According to the Atharva-veda, human personality on the physical side has three components or *gunas* like *vata*, *pitta* and *kaph*. These three *gunas* varying in degrees are in every human body since birth. They maintain a certain equilibrium in the body. So far as this equilibrium is present, it indicates physical normalcy and no diseases arise. But whenever the equilibrium of these three components (*Gunas*) is disturbed due to increase or decrease in any of these three *gunas*, it gives rise to different diseases.

The mental personality also consists of three *gunas* or characteristics such as, *Sattav*, *Rajas* and *Tamas*. These three *gunas* are in the *Manas* (mind) since birth and a certain equilibrium is maintained among them indicating mental normality. *Sattav* is pure and true and never gets corrupt. *Rajas* means the expansive impulse tending to errors, pleasure and enjoyment while *Tamas* means the impulse tending to *thanatos* an evil and downward trend. *Rajas* and *Tamas* get corrupted. When they increase or decrease in degree, it leads to abnormality.

Human personality, according to the Atharva-veda, at any stage, on both physical and mental planes, is a matter of the degree *Vata*, *Pitta*, *Kaph* and *Sattav*, and *Rajas* and *Tamas*. A personality is not the sum total of all these gunas but a combination and an organization that gives the individual his individuality.

Behaviour disorders

The Atharva-veda has described mental behaviour in detail, listing a number of mental abnormalities. Since the present chapter is meant to acquaint the readers with the psychotherapeutic practices of ancient India it is not possible to give a detailed account of all the mental abnormalities listed in the Atharva-veda. The following, according to it, are the major mental disorders :

1. *Unmad* (Insanity)
2. Mania
3. Apasmar (Seizure-hysteria)
4. Grahi (Epilepsy)
5. Bhaya (Phobia)
6. *Manaspap* (Schizophrenia)
7. *Krodh* (Anger)
8. *Irsha* (Jealousy)
9. *Pap* (guilt feeling)
10. *Moh* (Eroticism)
11. *Duswapna* (evil dreams)
12. *Shrap* (compulsive evil suggestion)
13. *Medha-vardhan* (memory and learning improvement)
14. *Atma-bal* (energizing ego)
15. *Samanasayani* (Integration and social harmony).

Atharva-vedic psychotherapeutic practices

Karambelkar has divided Atharva-vedic therapies into two broad categories : 1 psychological and 2. physical. Here we will describe only the psychological methods of treatment of mental function disorders.

The main objective of Atharva-vedic psychotherapy is to help humanity to live a happy life for more than 100 years and beyond it to get cosmic integration. It applies psychological methods to avert mental disorders, danger and calamities and to gain health, security, social integration and happiness in life. The important Atharva-vedic psychotherapeutic practices are briefly described as follows :

1. Mantra Vidya

Mentra ts related to *Manas* (psyche) whsle *Tantra* is related on the one hand to *Manas* (psyche) and on the other hand to physics. *Mantra* is secret talk. According to Niruk, *Mantra* is silent talk.

Kapali Shastri gives his views regarding *Mantra* as : "It is not a mere meaning, letter or a collection of letters with some meaning, It ts the sound body of a power charged, with intense vibrations of the spiritual personality of the creator or the Seer of the *Mantra*. The *Mantra* is an everliving embodiment of the truth and power which have found expression in it through the medium of the *Rishi* or *yogis* who has given it that body. The *Mantra* may be in the form of coherent words or single letters arranged in a certain order."

Hans Jacobs writes about *Mantra*, "Mantra or sound pregnant with meaning plays a central role in the religious practics of the Hindus. Now a *Mantra* is a combination of letters, sometimes it is monosyllabic. In which case it belongs to no particular language, sometimes it consists of one or several words, in which case the language used is always Sanskrit. A *Mantra* if it really lives is always a powerful instrument.''

Sir Yogendra says. *Mantra*, therefore is not enly a co-joined word but a particular sound body of consciousenss." Summarizing we can say that a *Mantra* is a silent or loud pronunciation of words in poetry, prose or a syllable with definite meaning and energy in itself.

Kinds of Mantra

There are two types of *Mantra* : (1) Vedic *Mantra* and (2) Tantric *Mantra*. The Vedic *Mantras* are older than *Tantric Mantras* and are recited weile Tantric *Mantras* are for *Japa* (repetition) and for keeping with oneself in the form of Yantra. The Vedic *Mantras* are longer and meaning is most important in them whereas the Tantric *Mantras* are very short, may be monosyllabic or in figures and graphs called *yantra* . Language and meaning have no importance in Tantric *Mantras.* They are mechanical and related to the psychophysical process of the individual and the universe in contrast to Vedic *Mantras* that are based on Brahma i.e., psychic and sound phenomenon of the individual and the universe.

Basis of Vedic Mantra

The Vedic Mantra has two bases : psyche and sound. It believes that every individual is a constituent of some energy which is essential for his survival and well-being. Psyche and sound are the two sources of his energy which can be increased or decreased in certain ways. The *Upanishands* being directly based on the Atharva-veda, their philosophy of *Brahma* and *Atma* is the philosophy of the Atharva-veda. Its theory believes that the individual *Atma* (psyche) is a part of the supreme energy called *Brahma*, from which it has temporarily been separated due to illusion but as a matter of fact it is always connected with *Brahma*. What is required is to shake off this illusion (*Maya*) and feel oneness with *Brahma.* When this oneness with *Brahma* is realized, one derives enormous energy from him through one's own individual psyche. So to derive energy and to use it depends on the psyche. But yow is *Mantra* related to psyche ? The *Mantra* is related to the psyche in that it is used by the psyche only after attaining oneness with *Brahma* and deriving energy from him. The *Mantra* is ineffective if used by and individual without realizing oneness with *Brahma* in the true sense.

The next source of energy is sound. It works in two ways : gaining energy in oneself by way of *Japa* (repetition) and enforcing energy on others to produce an effect on them. Out of the five motororgans, the month is one. Sound which is produced by the throat goes upto the other individual through vibrations and affects the inner part of his ears. Sound is the direct source of contact with the psyche of other.

Hans Jacobs, writing on the subject, says : "Sound is the subtle word stuff out of which the phenomenal world emanated, wherein it lives and to which all objects of thought are reduced on the destruction of their particular names and forms. *Shabda* (sound) thus conceived therefore, represents that and embracing creative power of *Brahma.* Finally sound-vibrations and though-vibrations melt into one. "Science has discovred ultrasonic sound therapy to cure septic focuses, etc. According to the theory abvanced, every object is the sound of a particular concentration. When reaching a special density and vibration it creates light ; and another level, electricity or mangnetism. Sound vibrates in the sap which rises in a tree. At another plane, it becomes though. It is (*Mantra*) is repeated (*japa*) either loudly or at more advations are practice silently, certain vibrations produced within the organism which depend in kind and in degree on the particular letters used and on their connection. It has been established that some sort of ultrasonic waves are produced in the organism by the *japa* of *Mantra.* Modern science has discovered that sound has therapeutic value.

Karambelkar says. "The curative effect of charms is through their sound vibration which are recognized to be effective by modern science also." So we can assert with some confidence that the charms were not simply witchcraft and deception but has a scientific basis. It is concluded that the Atharva-vedic 'mantras' are based on a psychic aspect. They were replaced by the psychophysical aspect in the Tantric *Mantars* in which oneness with *Brahma* is not essential.

It is now clear that some sort of energy is produced in a *mantra*, Dr. B L. Atreya says that in the letters of a *Mantra* teere is effective energy like medicine but the effect of the *mantra* is due to psychic feelings. Dr. Karambelkar says : "The charm was, best of all hunderees and thousands of medical herbs."

A. Samkalp (Self-determination, Auto-suggestion and self-Hypnosis).

Smakalp is a process of psychotherapy in which the therapist and the patient is the same person. It is self-direct autotherapy. It can be both individual and group therapy. In the former, the individual gives suggestion to his own psyche; it is group therapy when many persons do so together with their own psyches at one place. *Samkalp* is *Atmabal* (will-power). In psychological language, it is energetic ego. *Samkalp* is a method to make the therapy ego energetic and adjusted in behaviour.

Procedure

In *samkalp*, the psyche heals its own self. So it is necessary for it in the initial stage to be devided into two—to act as therapist and as patient. One part acting as therapist takes the help of several devices such as free association, analysis, suggestion and hyphotism and the other part follows its direction and suggestions. In the beginning it is the 'I' and 'You' process. But when proper analysis has been reached, this role is over only the ego dominates and suggestions work hypnotically.

According to the Atharva-veda, *Manas* and *Vani*, i.e, consciousness and suggestion generate *samkalp*. There are two essential conditions to give suggestions to himself.

Stages of Samkalp :

There are four stages which are followed in *samkalp* :

(a) Conversation between the ego and different functions of the mind such as *Budhi*, learning, memory, dream and sex etc.

(b) Harmony among different functions is established and the ego dominates. Suggestions are repeated several times to produce a hypnotic effect.

(c) An unconscious faith is created that, "I am without aliments, energetic and healthy".

(d) The fourth and the last stage is achieved when determination and will for future course of behaviour are decided and adopted.

Samkalp as a technique of therapy has been applied for a

variety of diseases both physical and mental. Mental abnormalities such as auditory, hallucinatory, *Pap bhavana*, phobia, evil dreams, *Medha vardhan*, *paustikarni*, etc. have been successfully treated by *samkalp*.

In *samkalp*, *vani* (language) is asked to create *samkalp* in the mind. Auto-suggestion is considered the best of all. It creates sweetness in the language, *Mans* (pspche) and behaviour. For example, a phobia is dealt with by giving auto-suggestion to *Manta* (psyche) not to have fear as many are fearless.

In there auto-suggestions, the law of similarity is widely used. While giving suggestions associations are made with energetic things of the universe. For example, with the lion, the elephant a warrior, the sun, the fire, the gods, the bull, etc. Auto-suggestion may also be used for self-defence and a long life. In modern psychotherapy, the equivalent of *samkalp* is auto-suggestion which has been successfully applied to cure mental abnormalities. Coue has recently popularized the use of auto-suggestion through his book. "Conscious Auto-suggestion". He developed the formula to strengthen the will power of the individual to overcome diseases. The formula runs, "Day by Day, in every way. I am getting better." He believed that the patient could give continued encouragement io himself even in the absence of the therapist. In conclusion, it can be said that *samkalp* is a mixture of three modern techniques of therapy : auto-analysis, auto-suggestion and auto-hypnosis.

Commenting on the western psychotherapeutic methods, Swami Akhilananda says : "The various methods prescribed by the western schools of thought lack considerably in the technique of developing donamic functioning of the will, inspite of their ameliorating effect. Psychoanalysis, self-analysis of various types, autognosis and insight, no doubt help in the understanding of the causes of mental problems and may often help in removing a certain amount of tension. Yet they do not seem to seem to unify the will". Thus we may conclude the Atharvavedic method of *Samkalp* is not only scientific and in line with modern methods but far better because it includes will training which modern psychopathology lacks.

B. Sadesh (Adesh or Suggestion)

Sadesh is a directive therapy in which the therapist gives suggestions to the patient. The therapist plays an active and directive role while the patient plays a passive role. P. Arsh says : "*Sadesh* is energetic and successful assurances or effective suggestions which are used to cure difierent personality defects, specially mental disorders." *Sadesh* is theoretically based on two things : (a) the language (sound-ideas) produced by the therapist ; (b) the will and inner will-wishing psychic energy of the therapist. According to P. Arsh some sort of energy emanates from the therapist and it affects the patient. Its practitioner is a *Brahmagyani* : one who has realized unity with *Bramha*. So he works through the energy of *Brahma*. It the thergpist is serious, truth speaking, self-controlled and of a helping nature, he will be mare effective. Saffer and Lazarus describing the importance of suggestion say. "The therapist because of his prestige and authority as well as helpfulness and prospectiveness is in a position to exert unusual influence on the attitudes of the patient."

Procedure :

Sadesh involves the therapist and the patient. The therapist ; plays the role of guide, teacher, therapist, authoritative priest, etc. He must be will-versed in the theoretical and practical knowledge of the Atharva-vedic practices. If he has no practical knowledge of acquiring energy from *Brahma* and using it on patients, he cannot produce therapeutic effects on the patient. It has three stages :

(1) The therapist gains the confidence of the patient (Rapport) ;

(2) He applies energy on the ailment and at the same time analyses and synthesizes the patient's thought process ; and

(3) He assures that the ailment is thrown out.

Applicant :

Sadesh is used to a certain degree in almost all physical and mental diseases in which the patient is able to understand the ideas. It is generally used for *Grah*, phobia. epilepsy, *krodh*, *irsha*, *shrap*, anger, etc. There is great similarity between the *sadesh* therapy and the suggestion therapy of the west. *Sadesh* is scientific and based upon the language and psychic energy of the therapist. It is not bare suggestion but better than that because it involves analysis and synthesis.

Samvashikaram (Hypnosis)

Western psychotherapists opine that Indian resourcefulness succeeded in discovering early autohypnosis and hetero-hyphosis. According to P. Arsh, when suggestion is very effective it becomes *Samvashikaran* (Hypnosis) and is very useful in curing mental disorders.

Drake says : "Hypnosis is a condition of heightened suggestibility and use of verbal suggestion is the technique to induce it." The suggestions given are, "Relax, let yourself go ; listen only to may voice, relax to sleep ; your eyes are closing, you are fast asleep ; etc." The Atharva-vedin believed in the process of hypnosis as a from of intense effective suggestion and used it for several purposes. It is the advanced effective stage of suggestibility in which the therapists' personality and psychic energy are the dominating forces.

Samvashikaran (hypnosis) is induced by the therapist whose mind becomes the charioteer of the hypnotee's mind who follows him and surrenders his ego to the will of the hypnotizer.

Samvashikaran was used to cure minor mental diseases. It had been used in Vedic period to acquire bravery, release from passive hysteria, and consumption, etc.

It had also been used for defeating the enemy and promoting integration, harmony, love, and long life, etc.

Ritualistic Therapy (Drama and Demonstration) :

In order to gain the confidence of illiterate patients and children, the *Atharva-veda* adopted several minor processes and aids. Rituals serve definite purposes. When performed with mantras, they become more effective. In ritualistic therapy, somatic phenomenon is added to psychic phenomenon. This approach becomes psycho-somatic. Ritualistic therapy make use of some material things which have scientific value and produce physical effects on the body of the patient.

The ritualistic therapy is psycho-somatic. It uses material things along with demonstration of certain ideas. Usually the following person participate : (i) The therapist (ii) patient (ii) relations of the patient.

The Atharva-vedic therapist plays different roles. Max-Muller says about the practitioner "*Brahman* is as it were the stage manager in the sacradotal drama. The physician of the sacrifice when it is attacked by the disease of faulty execution, he is the mind of the sacrifice."

Karambelkar says about the practitioner : "He is a physician, magician, priest, adviser, protector, phliosopher and friend all in one ; without him nothing can be done. He is equally helpfull to man, woman, young and ald, in private and public life. Thus the whole field of Atharvan practices in the stage for the activities of the Atharvan priest". Ritualistic therapy is based on so and psychological principles of symbolism. The actors and articles symbolize certain personalities, concepts and events. It uses the mechanisms of personification, identification, projection and transference and the laws of similarity and contrast of the association of ideas. Symbolism is the soul of Atharvan practices. They symbolic nature of drama and demonstration creates psychological effects of cure in the patient.

The Atharva-vedic practitioners use ritualistic therapy

(drama and demonstartion) for a wide range of mental abnormalities. To acquaint the readers with its application to mental abnormalities. two examples are given, Max Muller explains the process "Pulverised fragrant substances mixed with the Ghee are sacrificed and the patient is anointed with what remains. The patient is next placed upon a crossed road, a wicker work of Darbha grass containing a coal pan upon his head and upon the coal the previously mentioned fragrant substances are again offered. The patient going into a river against the current throws the same substance into an unburned vessel moistening the substance (ghee). Placing the vessel into a three footed wicker basket made of Munje, he ties it to tree in which there are birds nests."

The complicated ceremony is largely symbloic ; it aims at purifying and indicates the passing out of unhealthy conditions, for integration and establishing harmony in a group. The second example as explained by Max Muller runs as : "A jar full of water anointed with the dregs of ghee is carried about the throng quarrelling and poured out in their midst. The same proceedings are taken with a jar full of brandy (sura). They who desire peace are given to eat the pickled flash of a cow three years old. Food, brandy and water from the public drinking place are anointed with the dregs of ghee and consumed". The whole symbolic process is practised along with *Mantras* nnd *Havana*,

(3) **Brahma Kavach** (Psychological Defensive Beliefs)

Brahma Kavach is a psychological defence from external danger. There are two kinds of *Kavach* (a) *Bhantic* (physical, which is a garment-type like common battle armour and (b) *Brahma Kavach*, (Psychological) defence which on the subjective side is belief and self-confidence and on the environmental side an invisible force emanated from the psyche of the individual for defence from destructive forces. It is a psychological defensive atmosphere created around the personality of the individual. The theoretical bases of *Baahma Kavach* are both subjective and environmental. Any one who needs defence loses self-confidence and fears of the environment. This subjective feeling is recovered by creating self-confidence and belief of perfect defence in oneself. Thus his reactions to the external environmental become normal and energetic.

Brahma Kavach is a deeice to defend and improve the behaviour of the individual and is successfully applied where there is a fear or danger from the environment. *Brahma Kavach* is a unique technique of personality improvement used in the Atharva-veda. It has not equivalent in modern psychotherapy.

(2) Utarna (Transference)

Utarna (transference) is a process of transferring or sending symptoms of physical and psychic ailments to other objects or persons. There are two kinds of utarna (transference) : (a) Transferring the physical symptoms of a disease to plants and animals and (b) Transferring the psychological symptoms to all living beings—man, animal and plant.

According to Atharva-veda, the therapist can command and transfer psychio symptoms to other persons and objects by his own psychic energy and suggestion. The approach is psychosomatic. The utarna is supportive therapy used with other therapies such as suggestion, drama, demonstration, medicine, etc. Its process is very simple. First objects and persons similar in nature to the symptoms of the patient are brought near physically or mentally through association and then under ritcalistic performance, suggestion is given for transfer of symptoms to a person or object. The technique of transference, as a supplementary tool has been prescribed for a variety of diseases such as evil dreams, *Grahi pap*, love and other mental abnormalities.

The transference practice of Atharva-veda is totally different from transference of the modern psychoanalysis.

(3) Ashvasan and Upchar Chikitsa (Persuasion and Desensitization)

Ashvasan and *upchar* are preliminary techniques to win the confidence of the patient and create hope and satisfaction in him *Upachar* is used to control the environment and to redirect and to reeducate the behaviour of the patient. Thus the will and ego of the patient are strengthened. He feels enlightened, satisfied and cured.

Ashvasan and *upchar* are directive therapies in which the therapist plays a domination role. Therapist by his words and activities creates hope, confidence and satisfaction in his, patient and moderates his behaviours. There are certain *mantras* in the Atharva-veda which are used for creating *Ashvasan.*

Ashvasan and *upchar* therapy can be used in almost all diseases to educate the will of the patient and make his ego energetic to face the ailment with confidence. The Atharva-vedic therapy of *Ashvasan* and *upchar* hes similarity with modern therapeutic practices of persuasion, desensitization and reeducation.

4. **Daiviya and Havan Chikitsa** ((Spiritual Healing)

The trend of making offerings and praying to different gods and goddesses in order to achieve something or to cure diseases which started from the Rig-veda has been maintained by the Atharva-veda. Satavalkar has explained the Atharva-vedic *Havan chikitsa* as : "In such practices, the therapist who is usually the religious-priest acts as *Brahma*, the chief managing priest in the sacerdotal ceremony of curing mental abnormalities. The prayers are sometimes made by the therapist on behalf of the patient and sometimes the patient is also made to offer prayers. The religious therapy though mostly accompanied by *Havan*, is sometimes without it.

Havan therapy is the originality of the Athara-veda which claimed that not only known but also unknown diseases and even consumption can be cured by Havan. There is no set process for conducting the therapy. Sometimes it is conducted with *Havan.* Sometimes with rituals, some times with offerings. The deities who serve different purposes are innumerable. The therapist acts as their agent, making liaison between the deity and the patient. Material things are offered to the deity and his powers and deeds are defined in connection with the present ailment.

The Atharva-veda has used this practice on functional abnormalities of behaviours such as phobia, inferiority, guilt, erotic anomalies, evil dreams ; for long life and for compulsions etc.

(5) Prayaschittani

It is a unique psychogenic approach of the Atharva-veda which comprises several techniques, *Prayaschittani* bymns make up one of the major practices of the Atharva-veda. There are more than fifty that broadly deal with errors in sacrifice, expiration of *pap bhavna*, evil omens, shrap, unlucky star, delinquency, schizophrenia and prosperity. The word *prayaschitta* has been differently explained. According to Radha Kant Dev Behadure: "Whatever sublimates or catherizes *pap* is *prayabhitta*" and doing *tapa* after voluntary decision is *prayaschitta* according to V.P. Apte.

There are three aspects of *prayaschitta* (1). Is *tapa*—self-mortification or penance ; (2) It is done aftey a voluntary decision and (3). Its purpose is to purify the ego and get rid of *pap bhavna*.

Theoretically the Prayaschitta is based on the dynamics of the psychic personality which consists of the three gunas (characteristics) of *Sattav*. *Rajas* ad *Tamas* that always try to increase their strength and dominate *purush* (the ego) to get it to work according to them. There is often disequilibrium in their strength. Ignoring *sattva guna*, *purush* works to much under *Tamas*. After the energy of the *Tamas* has been discharged, the *sattav guna* again takes hold of purush. It penalizes itself for following *Tamas* too much. This penalization is *prayashittani* and brings equilibrium again.

The ego analyses all the factors and grievances of the supper-ego settles affairs. Then ego willingly undergoes self-imposed penalty which broadly takes three forms :

(1) *Suekarokti* (Confession)

(2) *Tapa* (Penance)

(3) *Tyag* (Sacrifice)

In cases where the ego is too weak to take a decision, its role is played by an outside person, the therapist, Guru or other prestigious person who prescribes the mode of *prayaschittani* after a deep understanding of the inner personality of the patient.

In the *Atharva-veda*, many methods have been prescribed for *prayaschitta* which can be grouped under three categories namely : confession, penance and sacrifice. Confession is a method of disclosing immoral, shameful deeds done by onself either to the person who has been harmed or to some deity if the action done against religion or to family members if the action done is against them or to a public gathering if the action done is against society. While disclosing the wrong promise is made for future abstinence from such acts and request is made for excuse.

Penance is to psychosomatic approach to behaviour abnormalities. The ego makes an agreement with the super-ego and voluntarily decides the penalty. This penalty may be both psychic and physical. When this penalty is in the from of control of drives, motives, errors, and emotions, it is psychic *tapa*. But when the penalty is in the from of physical pain-bearing and penance it is called somatic *tapa*.

Tapa has been described as an energy-producing device and is used successfully for the removal of ailments and abnormalities and for the gain of health and wealth.

Tyag (Sacrifice) is economic. If the ego voluntarily penalizes itself to pay some economic holdings either in cash or kind then it is *tyag*, It is made to deities, sadhus, brahmins, the poor, social organizations, religious, and temples in the from of cash and cattle, a house and grain, etc. *Prayaschittani* ts used in many diseases such as expiation of mental delinquency, evil eye effect, unlucky star and evil dreams, etc.

2. CHARAK SAMIHITA

Charak was a greal Indian physician of ancient times who was a master of Ayurveda (the science of life). The *Charak samihita* is in the from of question answer. It is a very comprehensive book which gives detailed discussions of all sorts of diseases. Here we shall describe only the therapeutic practices of the *Charak samihita.* According to him the main causes of bodily disease are mental.

Psychic Disorders

Bhut Vidya: The material on *Bhut vidya* is scattered in the literature on Ayurveda. Charak is primarily concerned with a somatogenic approach so he has not deat with *Bhut vidya* which is primarily a psychogenic approach originating in the Atharva-veda.

Concept of Normality

Personality, according to Charak, works as a whole but for therapeutic purposes it is divided into *soma* (body) and psyche (*mind*).

The disease may start either from the body or the mind but in the long run the other part also gets affected and diseased. The mental personality is composed of three *Gunas* (characteristics).

Sattav, *Rajas* and *Tamas*. These *gunas* keep a certain equilibrium among themselves in a normal personality. But when the equilibrium is lost and becomes inharmonious in degree it is abnormality. According to *charak*, a personality is the sum total of hereditary, family climatic, seasonal, periodic and idosyncratic tendencies with make for individual variations. Due to their different degrees of interactions in different persons there arise differences in personality make-up. He has classified personality into three types on the basis of dominance of three *gunas* (characteristics).

Personality Types

Sattavic	*R. jesic*	*Tamasic*
Brahma	*Asura*	*Pashav*
Rishi	*Rakshas*	
India	*Pisach*	*Matsya*
Yama	*Sarpa*	*Vanaspatya*
Varun	*Prera*	—
Kuber	Shakun	—
Gandharva	—	—

In the *Bharak Samihita* no new psychotherapeutic practices were developed but the practices of the Atharva-veda were followed. Therefore, there is no need to repeat the Atharva-vedic psychotherapies.

(3) SUSRUT SAMIHITA

The *Susrut Samihita* is famous as a treatise on surgery. It is an old scientific documentation of India medicine—Ayurveda. Susrut has also described the mantal diseases of children and adults and has dealt in detail with psychotherapy to cure these diseases. *Mantras* are given with methods of use for the cure of psychic diseases.

Susrut has given a long list of psychic diseases such as *grah* diseases (neuroses) *Apasmar* (epilepsy) *unmad* (psychosis) *Bhayonmad* (Phobia) *Murchha*) Psychosomatic diseases, alcoholism, etc.).

Psychotherapeutic Practices

According to Susrut, psychotherapy is the therapy of mental disorders through psychogenic methods. He divided therapies into broad categories : psychogenic and somatogenic. Here we shall briefly mention the psychogenic therapies as practised by Susrut.

The major psychotherapies are as follows :

(a) *Mantravidya* : Suggestion, auspicious reading and repetition

(b) Religious practices : Worship, prayer

(c) Re-education and desensitization

(e) Recreation

(e) Environmental change

(f) *Bali*, *Dan* and *Tap*.

(1) *Mantra Vidya* : In *mantra vidya*, definite groups of words are made *siddhas* and then used for therapy. The following types of *mantra vidya* are practised.

(a) *Sabda* (suggestion) : Mental diseases are cured by suggestion mantra, analysing, and talking, etc.

(*b*) *Auspicious reading* : *Shanti-path* is the reading of *mantras* or passages from different religious books in which soothing. quietning and consoling words are mostly recited.

(*c*) *Sh nti Karma* : Susrut has spoken very highly of *Shanti Karma*. It is the most effective psychotherapeutic practice for mental diseases. Along with *mantra*, some ritualistic ceremony is also performed in *shanti-karma*. It is a mixture of *shanti-path* and dramatization: She use of cooling things like *Khus*, bath and *sharbat* etc. and performing other ritualistic ceremonies which create calm and soothing effects are its specialities. Prayer may also be included.

(*d*) *Japa* : A few mantras or syllables are repeated innumerable times and by so doing, a psychic effect is created in the personality of the repeater.

(*e*) *Religious practices* : *Puja*, prayer, offering and *havan* have a soothing effects on the mental patients.

(*f*) *Upadesh and santvana* (*Reeducation and desensitization*) : Re-education means imparting good teachings or suggestions to the patient. *Santvana* means consoling and desensitizating the anxiety and sorrow-stricken patient.

(*g*) *Recreation* : Susrut has prescribed recreation for all types of mental patients. It is a new approached which is not found in the Atharva-veda and the Charak Samihita. In order to divert the attention of an anxiety stricken patient, different types of recreational activities are organized for him so that he may involve himself and the conditioning is broken.

(*h*) *Gaman* (Environmental change) : Susrut recommends environmental change for mental patients in order to decondition anxiety-producing stimuli.

(*i*) *Prayaschitta* : *Prayaschitta* (*Bali*, *Dan* and Penance) has been prescribed by the Atharva-veda and the *Charak Samihita* as a very effective method of curing all types of mental disorders.

(4) The Ashtang Sangrah

The *Ashtangh Sangrah* is a collection of eight branches of Ayurveda. It was written by Vagbhatt, a Buddhist, in 5th A.D. The *Ashtangh Sangrah* is a collection of all important learning from Atharva, a *Charak Samihita*, the *Susrut Samihita* and all other writers. Vagbhatt, being a Buddhist, added Aprajita Vidya and *Tantric mantras* for therapeutic use. Samadhi was also added by Vagbhatt as a technique to purify mind and body to attain peace and comic integration. He explains the therapies in detail.

Psychic Disorders

A. Bhutvidya and the concept of normality

Vagbhatt has described *Bhut vidya* as the science of psychic diseases and related it to *grah* diseases. He called the psychogenic diseases of children, as "*Grahas*" and that of adults, as "*Bhut Grahas*".

According to Vagbhatt, *Bhut Grhas* are eighteen in number. The concept of normality and abnormality is the same as given in the *Charak* and Susrut *Samihitas*.

Psychotherapeutic Practices

Vagbhatt has classified all therapies into two broad eategories: Psychogenic and somatogenic. Here was are concerned with psychogenic therapies. A brief description of important psychotherapies is given below :

1. Mantra Vidya :

(*a*) *Tantric Mantra* : Vagbhatt has used *mantra* therapies for all types of psychic disorders. He added *tantra vidya.* He did not believe in *Brahma* like the Atharva-vedic therapist, but he was a psycho-physicist and believed in deriving energy from physical and cosmic elements and from the goods.

(*b*) *Japa* : He prescribes *japa* for *Grah* diseases and epilepsy of the psychogenic type.

(*d*) *Ritualistic Bath* : Vagbhatt has given a full chapter to ritualistic bath and has prescribed it for *Grah* diseases of children. The ritualistic bath is technical and dramatic and accompanies *Mantravidya.*

2. Religious Practices :

Only two religious practices related to offerings and *havan* are given.

Desensitization :

Faith and insight. These techniques of psychotherapy have been prescribed for the treatment of anxiety end psychic shocks due to loss of loved objects and *Grah* diseases.

4. Recreation :

It has been prescribed as a subsidiary therapy used after epilepsy and coma fits.

5. Virodhi Bhuvana (opposite passion)

It has been prescribed for hyper function of different passions.

6. *Gaman* :

Environmental change has been prescribed for neurosis and anti-social behaviours in the order to decondition anxiety states of the patients.

7. *Samadhi* : (Concentration and Meditation).

8. *Paryaschitta* : (Confession)

This has been already been described under Atharva-vedic therapies.

4. YOGA THERAPY

The science of yoga, as Indian mythology goes, was originated and practised by Siva who revealed it to various yogis later on. But the ancient literature tells that the original philosophy known as the *Sankhya Barshonam* from which some of the fundamental principles of yoga were supposed to be borrowed, dates from the time of Kapila. However, from the time it was first revealed, about three thousand years ago; it was successfully interpreted and preached in India. Patanjali, the father of the yoga philosophy, merely put it into words. But the real philosophy remained to be learned by practice.

The philosophy of the *Sankhyas* can be regarded as the origin of the system of yoga. It can also be assumed that both Patanjali and Kapila may have been students of one common school of philosophy and might in time have developed their own branches of yoga. Even before Kapila and Patanjali, we find the germs of the system in the Jain and Buddhist yoga and later in the earler *Upnishads*.

In the begining, yoga was more of a practice that a theory. But practice was always kept secret by the teachers who never went out of their own circle. Yoga in ancient times was spiritual, but as time passed the intelligent students wanted to investigate it further and apply their spiritual experiences to the more subtle and the grosser plane of life. This process changed the philosophy into a proper science of mind and body. Yoga developed itself in course of time into philosophy, religion and science. Havell speaks of yoga as both science and philosophy remarking that "whereas the western mystic seems to have allow himself to be carried away more or less unconsciously by an imbalanced and uncontrolled emotionalism, the practice of yoga in India, recognized as a branch of physical which is a science, the knowledge of suksma or mental is philosophy, religion aad metaphysics". The word yoga in original sophy, religion and metaphysics". The word yoga in original Sanskrit means, "Ekagrata" or oneness. It is derived from the Sanskrit root "Yoga" to join or to unite and literally it means union. We have the word Yoga in English which means the same thing

Patanjali, the first commentator on the yoga philosophy writes that, "yoga is the scientific process of restraining the mind stuff from taking various modifications". It is a philosophy which first establishes, through pure common sense and logic, the necessity of such restraint of the various mental modifications as a means to the attainment of Absolute Freedom. So the system that teaches us to restrain all activities of the mind and the senses so as to make them, one is yoga.

The word yoga underwent many changes as regard its meanings and interpretations.

According to Yogavasisth, "yoga is thus controlling of out going energy, and directing it to Him." Here the question is of energy and its control. Hence it is mors physical than spiritual.

In one place the Bhagavad Gita speaks in the same strain. Thus it says. That in which the mind finds rest, quieted by the practices of yoga, that in which he seeing the self by the self in the self is satisfied : that in which he findeth the supreme delight beyond the senses wherein established the moveth not from Reality, which having obtained, he thinketh there is no greater gain beyond, it that should be known by the name of yoga and wherein being settled he can move even by the greatest sorrow".

It may be said that whatever act of body mind or will that tends towards the controlling of other senses excepting the one that as intended for the purpose of concentration, is nothing but an unconscious move towards the attainment of yoga. Adi Sankaracharya defined yoga as : "To bring the external and internal senses into centre is the yogi's aim".

Thus the practice which teaches us to control the external and internal senses in known as the yoga-practice. Yogic exercises if continuously practised train the body and mind for spiritual perfection.

Types of Yoga

There are several sub-branches of yoga whose ultimate aim is attainment of self-realization. Here we will mention only four important branches.

1. Jnana Yoga

It refers to the science of acquiring proper knowledge about the ultimate reality. It includes all types of knowledge pertaining to nature, society and the self essential for warding off sorrow and maintaining a healthy and happy life in society.

2. Hatha Yoga

It is primarily concerned with making bodily postures and practising various *kriyas* (exercises) with air. It is comprised of Asanas, Pranayamas, Bandhas and Mudras. Though it is basically a science of physical excellence, its practice generates mental health as well,

3. Karma Yoga

This is a science of action. It teaches how to avoid undesirable elements in the various actions of an individual and how to act so that a satisfactory result is obtained.

4. Raja Yoga

It is a science of mental excellence. Its three basic steps are (1) concentration, (2) meditation and (3) contemplation. The system of Raja yoga shows how to practise these three steps and explains what can be achieved and accomplished by their power and practice.

Advantages of Yoga Therapy

— Yoga helps us to keep our body fit.

— Yoga promotes inner health and harmony. It also enables one to have complete control over the mind and mental activity.

— Conscious control and toning up of the autonomic nervous system can be attained. This is not possible through other system of physical culture.

— The limbs of the body become symmetrical and body figure improves.

— A high degree of physical endurance and resistance to diseases develops by regular yogic exercises.

— Yoga teaches the art of relaxation. Muscular and nervous tension is removed. Both body and mind work in harmony.

— Yoga practices bring about better training in serenity and increased will power.

— Continued yoga practice enables one to get better control over emotions and the mind gradually gets freed from the way of the senses.

— It increases the power of concentration and helps to control the wandering and wavering mind. Resistance to mental diseases increases by regular yogic exercise.

Yoga is a sacred science of India, a practical method of spiritual emancipation practised from time immemorial. Now-a-days its usefulness in attaining quietitude, bodily and mental health is being increasingly recognized alike in the east and the west. The earth with its over-population, mechanization, urbannization and scientific inventions has lost all peace and human being have strayed from nature. Humanity as a whole is suffering from innumerable ailments of the body as well as of the psyche. This feverish life has proved to be futile and meaningles and hence people of all countries long for a means to ensure happiness.

Practical Ideas to reduce tension

Man is filled with tension and insecurity. This is because he has not paid attention to the teachings of Buddha, Christ, Lord Krishna and other spiritual leaders. In other words so long as we think, as we have for centuries, that the way to peace, happiness and freedom is through aggression so long will man not know peace of mind. Negative feelings and attitudes, selfishness, hatred, greed, prejudice, worldliness creat tension within the individual and on a universal scale.

Here are a few practical ideas on how to avoid tension that can benefit all of us.

— *Keep the mind calm through meditation* : All our physical responses originate in the mind; so to overcome tension, we must first bring the mind under control. When we learn to calm the mind, we can calm the body.

— *Think one thought at a time* : When too many thoughts crowd in on us, pressure begins to build up inside. Cultivate the habit of thinking calmly one thought at a time,

— *Do not interrupt others while they are talking* : We have a tendency to interrupt others when we feel under pressure. Learn to let others finish what they have to say before you respond, The individual who talks too much is insecure. He feels that he must constantly explain his ideas and actions to others. Learn to be a listener.

— Read books that require deep concentration. Do not read trash.

— *Learn to eat slowly* : Learn to eat more slowly and in silence.

— *Exercise regularly* : Try to cultivate the habit of physical exercises daily either in the morning or evening.

— *Relax* : Do not get bogged down in little things.

— Set aside time for seclusion, when you can be alone with God and have time to think.

Features of Indian Psychotherapy

Indián psychotherapy is unique in its approach to mental disorders. It was originated thousands of years ago by the *Rishis* of ancient India. Some of its salient features arc as follows :

1. Existence of psychotherapeutic practice—past and present

Documentary sources affirm the existence of therapeutic practice in the past. The Atharva-veda is the oldest possible document on Indian therapy. It is a very comprehensive treatise which deals not only with cures of all types of ailments but also solves all p oblems of humanity and even describes how to control the events of the physical world by psychological practices. There are 5 major and 11 minor practices of psychotherapy.

2. Existence of psychotherayy both in theory and practice

The Indian psychotherapeutic practices are based on sound theoretical foundations as well as being a practical approach to mental disorders.

3. Wide range

Indian psychotherapeutic practices have a wide range—from abnormality through normality to suppernormality. It is an inter-individual and cosmic psychosynthesis.

4. Individual and group

Old documents affirm that both types of psychotherapies : individual as well as group were practised in ancient India.

5 Psychogenic approach

The approach of Indian psychotherapeutics is psychogenic in nature, The challenge of the Atharva-veda is to control the physical world through the psyche. Charak and Susrut also followed the Atharva-vedic practices. Yoga is a simple, ideal psychogenic approach to mental disorders.

6. Directive, semi-directive and non-directive

All Indian therapies can be classified under three heads namely : directive therapy in which the therapist is active while the patient is passive; non-directive therapy in which the patient is active and semi-directive in which the therapist and the patient play somewhat equal roles. Therapies are conducted by a single therapist or by a battery of therapists. No doubt most of the Indian therapies are conducted by a single therapist. But there are certain therapies in which a battery of therapists works simultaneously on the patient. It is a multiple therapy. In the battery of therapists every member of the group does a particular job in which he is specialized. The noteworthy battery-of-therapists conducted therapies are *Gayan Nrtya* and *sir*, *Hilana* therapy of *sayana*, and the famous group therapy of Balaji where two to four therapists perform specialized duties.

7. Unipractice and multipractice therapies

In Indian psychotherapy, sometimes only one therapeautic element or practice and at other times several practices are applied at the same time and to the same case. In chronic cases they usually multipractice therapy. It is very clearly seen in *sayanas*, therapy of music, dance and convulsive shocks. Indian psychotherapy is a technical and skilled job.

8. Symptomatic and Dynamic therapies

There are two kinds of cures : symptomatic and dynamic. Some of the Indian therapies cure the symptoms of the diseases only. They do not go deep into the dynamism of the psychic personality and their main aim is the removal of outer symptoms. But some of the others attempt at the personality make-up and their aim is a dynamic cure.

9. Economical

Indian psychotherapy is economical in respect of money and time to a great extent in comparison to western psycho. therapy. Most of the traditional psychotherapists do not charge any fee from the patients.

10. Original approach

Indian psychotherapy is an original and independent approach to mental disorders out of 36 Indian practices only 15 practices have any equivalents in the west.

QUESTIONS

1. What are the salient features of Indian Psychotherapeutic practices?
2. What are major psychotherapeutic practices as given in the Atharva-veda?
3. What is the basis of *Mantra Vidya*?
4. What is yoga? What are its advantages?

SUGGESTED READINGS

1. Karambelkar V.W. : The Atharva-Veda and th. Ayurveda; Usha Karambelkar, Nagpur, 161.
2. Max Muller Sacred Books of the E st-Hymns of Atharva-veda; Motilal Banarsidas, Delhi, 1964.
3. Shastri, R.G. : Vedon Me Ayurveda.
4. Singh H.G. : Psychotherapy in India; National Psychological Corporation, Agra, 1977.

CHAPTER 15

Prevention of Maladjustment

In the preceding chapters we have described the major Western and Indian psychotherapeutic practices generally followed in the treatment of maladjusted persons. This chapter deals with programmes and methods which can prove useful in preventing maladjustment and in preserving and promoting the mental health of those who are sound.

That "Prevention is better than cure" is proverbial wisdom. The huge task of prevention of mental disorders is primarily concerned with two things. The ffrst is locating and eradicating the causes of maladjustment. The second task is aimed at preserving and enhancing the mental health of those who are already mentally healthy.

There are three types of preventives measures which may be taken. A brief description of them is given below:

A. PRIMARY PREVENTIVE MEASURES

Primary preventive measures include all programmes for fostering healthy growth and development or individuals and inculcation of effective coping behaviours on biological and socio-cultural levels. A brief description of each of them is given below:

1 Biological Measures

Biological measures refer to all methods and techniques which directly or indirectly emphasize the importance of sound physical health for better mental health. Some of the important measures are:

Improving Physical Health

Sound physical health is very essential to prevent the occurrence of mental abnormalities. But the basic puestion is how to improve the physical health of the present and future generations in such a big country as India where the population has touched 68 millions (census 1980); where we are adding an Australia to our population and where more than half of the population is living under the poverty line. However, efforts are being made to control the menace of a rapidly growing population and to raise the general standard of living of the people. The following specific measures are being taken to improve the standard of physical health of the population.

(*a*) *Family planning*:

The Government of India has launched a massive programme of family welfare and planning for educating population on the advantages of a small family. Medical facilities are being provided for prenatal and postnatal care of children. Incentives are given to motivate the public to undergo operation after two children in order to check the growth of population. It goes without saying that the smaller the number of children, the better their care.

(*b*) *Adult education programme* :

In 1980 a comprehensive scheme of adult education was started for the 15 years to 35 years age group with the purpose of educating the people to understand their general problems. Educated adults need to understand the importance of the small family norm, nutritive food, etc.

(*c*) *20-point programme* :

The programme has been started with the main purpose of eradicating the poverty of the weaker sections of the society and raising their general standard of living.

(*d*) *Genetic counselling* :

A breakthrough in genetic research has made it possible to

detect genetic defects potential parents to assess their risk to having defective children.

(*e*) *Parents' education* :

Parents are being educated in child rearing methods to minimize the physical as well as mental diseases of their would be children.

(*f*) *Mid-day meal* :

A programme of mid-day meals has been launched in primary schools of the children of weaker sections of society to make up the deficiency to nutritive food in them.

2. Psychosocial Measures

Normality has been defined as optional development and functioning of the individual that implies opportunities for learning and needed competencies to lead a normal life. If one fails to learn skills required for effective problem-solving, for handling emotions constructively and for establishing satisfactory inter-personal relationships, he faces serious problems in the process of adjustment.

The following psychosocial measures may be taken to avoid mental health problems.

(*a*) *Proper training for child birth* :

Parents, particularly the mother should be given proper training as regards the care and precautions to be taken during child birth.

(*b*) *Emotional training* :

Emotions play a crucial role in the development of the human personality. It has been observed that children who are deprived of proper emotional development develop feelings of insecurity and inadequacy that may cause maladjustment.

(*c*) *Preparation for developmental tasks* :

Havighurst developed a comprehensive list of developmental tasks appropriate for a particular age. Children should be given proper training to acquire skills and competencies to perform developmental tasks for their age-group. If this is done well in time, children will feel confident when the actual tasks is performed. Though in India, research has not yet been conducted on developmental tasks for Indian children, for the present we can adapt with certain modifications, the tasks developed by Havighurst.

(*d*) *Proper training for interpersonal relationship* :

Man is a social animal. His development depends on proper interaction in society. By interpersonal interaction, children develop social competency and social skills which are essential to lead a happy social life and moral education should form an integral part of the school curriculum right from the primary classes to prevent delinquency and sex aberrations.

3. Social-Cultural Measures

Recent researches in the field of sociology and anthropology have thrown light on the role of pathological social conditions in producing maladaptive behaviour. Therefore, more attention is being focused on broad socio-cultural measures that will foster the healthy development and effective functioning of members of society.

The following socio-cultural measures may be helpful to check maladjustment.

(*a*) *Public education* :

The general public should be educated through TV and Ratio programmes to maintain communal harmony, feelings of brotherhood among the members of different communities.

(*b*) *Economic planning* :

Economic Planning should be done in such a way that

benefits should be equally distributed among the different sectors of society. The weaker sections should be helped financially by the government to improve their socio-economic status.

(c) *Health care for all citizens* :

Physical health care centres should be opened to cater to the needs of all citizens of the country.

B. SECONDARY PREVENTIVE MEASURES

Secondary preventive measures should be taken at an early stage within the family for checking maladaptive behaviour. Secondary prevention is primarily concerned with the incidence and scope of maladaptive behaviour in a specific population; with early detection of such behaviour; with the variety and availability of mental health facilities, and with crisis intervention.

Research studies have revealed that most contagious physical diseases can be brought under control once their distribution and modes of communication are discovered via empidemiological studies. Studies have revealed that high school drop outs, recently divorced or widowed people, physically handicapped and elderly persons living alone are high risk groups for various mental disorders.

C. TERTIARY PREVENTION

It has been observed that despite secondary preventive measures, some persons to require hospitalization for emotional and other mental disorders. Tertiary prevention involves prompt and intensive in-patient treatment for such disorders. Its main aim is to prevent the disorder from becoming chronic and to enable the individual to return home as soon as possible. Now we will describe in detail the role of the family and school in promoting mental health of children.

MENTAL HYGIENE AND FAMILY

Mental hygiene is, as already defined, the science which aims at achieving mental health for the maximum development of people's potentialities in order to enable them to adjust adequately in society. The family, as the first institution of social interaction, plays an important role in the process of maintaining and promoting the mental health of individuals. This part of the chapter deals with conditions within the family which are conducive for maintaining the mental health of its members.

Everybody agrees that societies in the course of their development evolve certain values, norms, traditions, customs, etc. which are transmitted to the future generations through the process of socialization. The process of socializ tion being from the moment of the birth of the child, and continues thoughout his life span. During this period, different persons, groups and institutions have their influence on the developing individual, modifying his ideals and beliefs and changing his behaviour. Some social institutions and systems such as religion, school and political systems were developed, specifically, to perpetuate and maintain cultural knowledge and stands. Other groups such as the community, peers and the family serve the same functions although their roles may not be formally prescribed. It is obvious that some groups involve relationships that are more intimate and salient in shaping the individuals' moral values, attitudes and behaviour than are others. Cooley named these groups as peimary and described them in detail. Explaining the primary group he says, "By primary group I mean those characterized by intimate face to face association and cooperation. They are primary in several senses, but chiefly in that they are fundamental in forming the social nature and ideals of the individual...Primary groups are primary in the sense that they give the individual his earliest and completest experience of social unity and also in the sense that they do not change in the same degree as more elaborate relations but from a comparatively permanent source out of which the later are even springing".

The family in terms of the above description by Cooley is a primary group which provides freedom to exchange intimate knowledge within the groups, depth of emotional involvement and acceptance among the family members and spontaneity of interpersonal behaviour. It is the unique and enduring quality of the affective relationship and mutual concern in the family that distinguishes it from other groups. The reader should keep in mind that the it is not intimacy and face-to-face quality of relations in the family group that is important but that these contacts of the child occur early and serve as the foundation for values and attitudes that will shape later his social relations.

The family, undoubtedly, is the most influential primary group in the socialization of the child shaping the personality of the child in the early, formative years.

Characteristic Structure of the Faimly

— *Earliest and most enduring*: The family is the earliest social group existing since human life on earth. Its characteristics :

— Structured social institution

— Differentiation of roles and division of labour

— Spontaneous and role-prescribed

— Face-to-face interaction

— Strong emotional bonds among the members

— Power relation unequal

Socialization is a continuous process through which new members are taught the moral values and norms of social behaviour evolved in the course of development. Now we will analyse of socialization.

The process of socialization starts from the birth of the child and involves a complex interactional process between the in need of the child and the relationship he develops with socializing agents and the techniques and manners in which these agents either attempt to or inadvertently influence his behaviour. For example, the infant has biological needs for whose satisfaction he requires the mother's care. During early childhood, the mother's ability to meet the various needs of the child plays a crucial role in shaping the personality of the child. How the mother attempts to control the child's behavi ur and his reactions to different stimuli is also important. It is a very complex web.

The process of socialization involves the transmission of social values, skills and roles and is effected through the following interactional techniques.

Direct Tuition, Reinforcement and Punishment

Much of the systematic moulding of social behaviour is done by parents and significant others though direct tuition : that is, the child or adolescent is given verbal instructions or directions and is praised or reprimanded in response to his/her performance. The more precisely and consistently the rules are stated the easier it for the child to learn what is expected in the situation. Such verbal instructions of parents or significant others help to clarify to 'dos' or 'don'ts' of a situation for the child. Once the child attains some degree of verbal comprehension, it is more efficient to instruct the child as to desirable behaviour, than to wait for it to occur spontaneously. However, it is impossible to anticipate all the actions of a child. Behaviour must be encouraged or discouraged in a child by rewards or punishments after it has occurred. This process differs from direct tuition in that the response is emitted by the child, whereas in direct tuition it is elicited by another person through language.

Invariably all studies conducted in the field of child development and behaviour modification emphasize the use of reward rather than punishment in the socialization of the child because the side effects of punishment are distressing, anxiety-provoking and injurious to the mental health of the child.

Experts advocate rewarding positive behaviour and ignoring rather than punishing negative behaviours at home. But it is not always practical as in some cases behaviours of children are so intolerable and damaging to the child that parents want to eliminate them as rapidly as possible and resont to punishment. There is sufficient evidence that mind punishment in the from of verbal rebukes, especially if used in combination with rewards for desirable behaviour is an extremely effective means of socializing the child. This is especially true if the punishment is administered immediately after the undesirable act, accompanied by an explanation for the punishment and suggestions for alternative actions.

Both reward and punishment should followed immediately upon the performance of the act by the child, since delay diminishes their effectiveness. It is very unfortunate that, in real life situations, the misbehaviours of children are often not discovered until some time after they are committed.

Finally the relationship between the child and the person punishment or rewarding is an important determinant of how effective the adult will be in modifying the child's behaviour. It has been established by researches that even punishment is more effective controlling technique when it is exercised by a nurturant rather than a hostile parent or teacher.

Observational learning

Children learn many attitudes and actions by imitating the behaviour of models to whom they are exposed. These models may be parents, teachers. friends. siblings, or characters seen on TV, screen or in a book. Different psychologists have explained the selection of models, in accordance with the age, sex and intelligence of the child.

Fear of Punishment

This refers to the process of identification with the aggressor A threatening model is selected because of an individual's fear of injury from the model secondary reinforcement.

— Fear of loss of love

— Status envy

— Social dominance

— Similary

Family

The family is social system with a formal structure and inter-dependent system of functioning among its members. The family structure may be of two types : nuclear family with two parents and their children or an extended family (joint family) with grand parents and other relatives living together.

When a child is born he becomes a member of an already established primary group with its own rules, roles and relationships.

Mentally Hygienic Conditions

As has already been mentioned, early childhood interaction within the family lay the foundation for the personality patterns the individual will develop in later years. Psychanalytically; the foundation of the personality is laid down by the age of five years and in later years they are merely strengthened. Here we will describe some of the conditions within the family which may help in preventing maladjustment among family members and preserve their mental health for better adjustment.

Environment of the family

The environment of the family plays a very crucial role in shaping the behaviour of its members. The environment should be free from all types of anxiety and unvocalized tensions among the members.

2. Fulfilment of needs

The needs of children and adolescents who are entirely dependent on parents should be fulfilled in order to avoid any feeling of frustration or tenison in them.

Certain studies have been conducted on infants to show

that meeting satisfactorily the physiological and psychological needs of children is very essential for the harmonious development of their personality.

4. Feeling of security

Early interaction with the parents and significant others must emphasize the development of feeling of security and adequacy in children.

5. Parental relationship

The attitudes which parents hold toward each other definitely affects the attitudes and behaviour of children. A number of studies have been conducted on parental relationships which have invariably proved that the majority of the problem children and adolescents come from (a) broken homes (b) homes wtih marital friction or those with a step mother, or step father. If the parents maintain cordial relationship with affection, mutual respect for eace other and cooperation in the solution of problems, the create desirable atmosphere for the development of feelings of security and self-esteem in their children.

5. Parental rejection

Rejection means over behaviour toward an individual leading him to believe that he is neither loved nor valued by his parents. Such behaviour on the part of parents threatens a child's security and creates in him a feeling of uncertainty and helpless. The rejection may be through the following types of parental behaviour :

(a) Emphasis on the child's physical and mental shortcomings

(b) Negative attitudes (scorn, humiliation, threats, and ridicule)

(c) Severe punishment

(d) Desertion or eviction

(e) Unfavourable comparison

(f) Deliberate statement to the child that he is unwanted.

Parental rejection in early childhood is very harmful for the mental health of children which may be manifested in attention getting, delinquency and temper tantrums, etc.

6. Dominant parental behaviour

Dominant parental behaviour is another source of maladjustment in children. Dominant parental behaviour is based on the traditional philosophy of severe and determined regulation of the proper development of children. The rigid imposition of a diciplinary code creates resentment in children and may lay foundations for later rebellion.

7. Submissive parents

Submissive parents are those who for one reason or another fail to establish legitimate authority over the child and always agree to his demands and requests. The causes of submissive parental brhaviour may be several, such as illness of the child, an only child born atter a long period of marriage.

It has been observed that submissive parental behaviour develops in children undesirable traits such as conceit, disobedience and disrespect for authority. Such children fail to adjust in society and constantly experience emotional tension and feelings of insecurity.

8. Do not overprotect the child

Overprotection of the child by parents or significant others is also harmful for his/her harmonious development because an overprotected child does not get the opportunity to make decisions, assume responsibilities or to face and solve his own problems.

Such children develop a constant threat to their personal worth. They face frustration, feeling of failure and may consequently withdraw from social situations.

9. Parental mishandling of the child

There are certain other unfovourable parent-child relationships which may also prove harmful to the adequate adjustment of the child in society. They are :

(*i*) *Projection of parental ambitions* : Parents who could not accomplish their ambitions try to acheive them through their children. Such parents project their educational, vocational and professional ambitions without any regard to the suitability and interests of their children

Children who attmpt to live upto their parents' expections are constantly in a state of emotional tension. Such children develop feelings of insecurity and threats to their self-esteem.

(*ii*) *Preference for child of given sex* : Parents who express a strong preference for a child of one sex obviously make the child of the other sex feel unwanted. It is very unfortunate in India that we culturally prefer a male child to a female child. This bias creates anxiety in the mind of the female chtld.

10. Development of independence and adequacy

Parents and significant others should try right from early childhood to develop the feeling of independence and adequacy in children so that they may face problems in neighbourhood, school and society without being emotionally disturbed.

11. Inculcate sound moral values

All agree that in the last three decades the traditional moral values have degenerated to the lowest level in our society causing great harm to the mental health of the individual. Therefore, there is a great need to develop or to revive old moral values which develop self-confidence and self-esteem in individuals.

We have suggested certain measures which if followed by parents and significant others in their interaction with the child would help them is bringing about desirable changes in the behaviour of children. There are no two opinions that the home lays the foundation of the child's future personality. Therefore, it is the home where we should provide a conducive environment for the proper development of children.

MENTAL HYGIENE AND SCHOOL

If we trace the history of the development of the school as an institution, we find that in the nomadic stage of civilization, there was no formal schooling. The needs of the individual were limited and knowledge of skills necessary for livelihood was acquired in the process of apprenticeship working with parents. But gradually as civilization progressed to the next stage of permanent settlement, needs multiplied and new professions emerged Parents were not capable of training their wards in the new skills that were essentially required for adjustment in society. Therefore, a separpte institution—the school, was established where the accumulated experiences of the race and new skills were transmitted through a planned curriculum. Thus we can say that the school is an institution established by society where the knowledge, skills and attitudes needed in adult life are learned by young ones to equip them with the essential competencies for coping with the problems of life.

We have discussed above the role of the family as primary group of socialization and conducive conditions within the family that help in the development of the harmonions personality of children.

This part of the chapter deals with the school and its role in the process of adequate adjustment. We will deal with the contribution of school under the following headings:

A. Physical setting

Recent research in the field of environmental psychology has thrown light on the impact of the physical aspects of an environment on the behaviour which takes place within it. The school in no exception. The physical environment of the school affects the students and the teachers. Physical characteristics such as location, size, design, furniture and light arrangments affect both teachers and students.

It has been suggested that the school should be located outside the city, a way from the hustle and bustle of the city life because students are under constant strain and stress in schools that are situated in the centres of big cities.

Barker and Gump have studied high schools ranging in size from 35 to 2287 students. Their findings showed that while larger schools hove more diversified extracurricular opportunities available to student, they often did not take advantage of them. The small school setting produced more, pressure on students to participate in such activities. Indeed the small school had more involvement of students in order to maintain the existence of the various programmes they had. The result is that students in small schools participate more in extra curricular activities and thus a greater "we" feeling is apparent. Another important factor is the size of the class. This directly affects the amount of pupli participation during discussion; smaller classes not only have more discussion but also draw participation from a larger proportion of class membrrs. The seating arrangement in the class also has it effect on student's participation in the teaching-learning process.

B. Classroom climate

Lewin, Lippit and White conducted a study on classroom climate in relation to the teacher's behaviour. The teachers/leaders were instructed to be either democratic, authoritarian or laissezfaire in their orientation. The task was to prepare masks by groups of 5 ten year-old. The tree types of leadership produced striking differences in the behaviour of children. The authoritarian leader produced rither aggression a apathy in children. The laissez faire leader induced hostlility, lack of output and disorganization. The groups under a democratic leader were the most cohesive and least hostile. The authoritarian leader produced the highest rate of output on the assigned task but only when he was present. As soon as he left, work ceased and the output was reduced. Thc democratic leader's presence or absence, however, did not affect productivity.

The teacher plays an important role in creating a conducive atmosphere in the class. Classroom climate largely depend on the consistency in the teacher's behaviour.

Consistencies which are particularly noticeable occur in interaction with the class as a whole. However, each child in the class reacts in his own way to the teacher's group-directed behaviour and the tone or climate it creates. The impact on each child is unique because each child brings a singular pattern of needs and characteristics to the class room setting.

C. Variations in teacher's behaviour

Some of the variations in teacher behaviour reflect an important acknowledgement on the part of the teacher that children are individuals and that each one can respond best to a different treatment. Differential treatement of children by teachers may be based on his beliefs associated with the apprearance, race, caste, sex and socio economic status of students.

Generally in society people like an attractive child and the teacher is no exception. But does not prevasive preference for an attractive child lead to differences in expectations about good and bad behaviour ?

A study conducted by Dion (1972) suggests that physical attractiveness does make a difference. Though discrimination based on a child's attractiveness is unfortunate, it is there.

D. The effects of race and caste of the child

India has always been a multi-racial society. There are hundreds of castes and creeds.

However, there is discrimination on the basis of the race and caste of children.

In a school run by Hindus, teachers are mostly from the same community. Teachers in school discriminate between Hindu Muslim and Christian students.

Caste also plays an important role in deciding the behaviour of the teacher. Upper caste teachers discriminate between upper caste and scheduled caste students. It is really very unfortunate that even ofter 40 years of independence caste feelings continue in our society irrespective of the fact that our constitution does not allow discrimination on the basis of religion, sex, caste and creed.

E. Effects of socio-economic status on teacher behaviour

The majority of the teachers come from middle class families. Culturally disadvantaged and scheduled caste students who do not share the teacher's values on matters such as neatness, punctuality and seriousness of learning are therefore more likely to come into conflict with him. More generally, it seems safe to say that the middle class child experiences a continuity between his home and school environment while the lower class child feels inadequate and insecure and out of place in school.

These feelings of inadequacy and iesecurity in children of lower class/castes create a number of adjustment problems in them. Whether teachers are baised toward children of lower castes in the prejudicial sense or whether their behaviour and attitudes represent a realistic apprai sal, the result seems damaging and injurious to the mental health of children.

The sex of the child also affects the teacher's behaviour. Schools, especially, nursery and kindergarten ones are 'feminine' places: the general environment in these seems more suited to girls than boys.

Girls in these schools receive better treatment at the hands of their teachers who are in 98% cases ladies.

Fagot and Patterson conducted a study and observed that teachers reinforce behaviours associated with the female sex role (such as quiet play) more frequently than male sex role behaviours. Such behaviour produces more rewards for females but also leads to conflict for male children whose peers and families are likely to encourage them to engage in more made appropriate behaviour.

It has been observed that one of the major problems for the male child in the early school years is the lack of a suitable male model in the classroom.

F. Contribution of teaching learning to mental health

"Nothing succeeds like success" goes the proverb. It means that success in any walk of life brings confidence and enhances the self-esteem of the individual. It also develops emotional stability. The school is the place where damage done to a child in his home or neighbourhood may be partially repaired by satisfactory school experiences.

Learning experiences acquired in school develop self-esteem, self-respect and feelings of adequacy in students enabling them to master their environment. Successful learning perform the same function for mental health that proteins do for physical health. Learning can help you, "belong". A childwhose knowledge or silks are markedly below those of other children soon has problems in group relationship. On the other hand a child has learned things his group admires, is more firmly established in his social life.

In school a child not only learns how to learn but may find security in knowing. Therefore in modern society when changes are occurring speedily, the child has to keep pace in learning with other children. This will give him a feeling of belongingness and encourage him to face new situations boldly.

Learning builds confidence

Experimental studies on the importance of success in children show that successful children set higher and more realistic goals for themselves because of the feeling of confidence created by success. Successful learning also helps children to deal with certain inner tensions confidently.

Teaching is domonstration of affection :

Over and over again we hear that people are helped by the feeling that they are loved and wanted. This feeling is very important for children. The teacher can help in developing this feeling by friendly assistance in learning activities. He can give Warmth and affection which are essentially needed.

Learning difficulties :

Researches on classroom teaching-learning process have reported a number of difficulties that may damage a child's self-esteem and cause emotional disturbances which lead ultimately to mental disorders. Net let us specifically list problems that cause difficulties.

The first problem is instructional methods. In our classroom teaching traditional methods are being used wihch have become obsolete in the light of the findings in the field of educational psychology. Children in such classes find it much harder to learn and express their dissatisfaction.

Maturation and learning ability

Maturation and learning are closely related. For learning a certain level of maturation is essentially needed. For example learning to write and to read needs formation of concept and maturation to a certain level of the nerves and muscles. It is very unfortunate that learning of reading is introduced at a very early stage when children are not able to respond properly.

Small children should be sent to reading readingness where they should acquire concepts necessary for tackling the reading material with success. Early mishandling of children is very harmful for their future success because it develops in them confusion frustration and self-distruct. Other difficulties include no provision for individual differences among children. Chidren at the high and low extremes of scholastic attainment are the worst sufferers. These children may develop behaviour problems in course of time. Children with physical handicaps do not receive proper individual guidance. The existing curricula for different classes contain a great deal of subject-matter which has no functional utility for children. Poor classroom organisation and discipline are other factors which create learning difficulties for children.

Consequences of poor learning :

Poor learning situations are reflected in restlessness, disorder and fighting among children. It creates frustration and tension. It leads to lethargy and failure.

Emotional disturbances and and learning :

Not doubt learning difficulties are created by factors like poor methods of teaching, inept teachers and bad curriculum but there are certain difficulties in learning which are due to the child.

Specific emotional blocks :

Sometimes a single subject or even a small event in the class creates emotional tensions and learning is blocked. What specific factors will cause emotional blockage in learning cannot be predicted.

General block—the emotional tensions may be related not to a specific subject but to the school as a whole.

Examination panic :

Examinations have acquired an important place in our education system. Some students fare very poorly because of the effect of "examination panic".

General anxiety :

The upbringing of many children has been so full of scoldings and ridicule that they are terrified making mistakes. Such children suffer from floating anxiety.

Sibling rivalries :

The effects of rivalries between children from the same home may disrupt school work. For example, a child whose older brothers or sister had a highly praised school record develops a distaste for studies. Parents sometimes compare the schoalstic achievement of their children which creates anxiety.

Relationship to teacher :

Emotional forces centering around teachers may also block learning. A teacher who does not provide any guidance to his students may create emotional blockage for learning.

Frustrations due to physical conditions. When children want to learn and physical conditions interfere, the result is frustration. Badly crowded classrooms, a poor library and bad sitting and lighting arrangements may cause constant worry.

Poor timings of learning activities :

Poor timing of learning may also cause conflicts in the minds of children. Therefore, it is suggested that learning activities in school should be during morning hours.

Curriculum :

Mental health is very closely related with the curriculum which is taught to the students. Is is very unifortunate that even after 40 years of independence we have not been able to plan our curriculum in accordance with the various needs of children. The fulfilment of the legitimate needs of the children is very essential for maintaining their mental health. Needs have been classified differently but all needs can be grouped under three broad categories, namely :

(*a*) *Physical and physiological* needs include water, oxygen, food, sex, etc. Without these the individual cannot survive.

(*b*) *Psychological needs* are those needs which become essential in association with basic needs. These needs include safety needs, belongingness, love, prestige, esteem needs and self-actualization. It will not be out of context to describe in detail the emotional needs of children which are essential for maintaining their mental health.

(*c*) *Emotional needs*: Emotions play in important role in the development and maintenance of mental healths. Let us describe some emotional needs which if not adequately fulfiled may cause emotional disturbances. The following are the basic emotional needs:

(*i*) *Sense of security*: For emotional stability and mental health, an individual must have a reasonable sense of security. Anxiety, worry, fears and tension adversely affect the physical as well as mental health of individuals. A number of research studies confirm that persons who are anxious and insecure cannot think and reason well to solve any problem.

(*ii*) *The need to be loved*: The need to love and to be loved is basic and universal. Therefore it is very essential for parents and significant others to inculcate and develop love in their children so that later they might not face any problem.

(*iii*) *The need for independence*: The psychological structure of human beings is such that they are happiest when they have independence. Independence of the individual implies respect and due consideration for other. The most effective kind of independence is that which support the emotional needs of the individual without taking from others their instinctive right to be independent. Independence should not be granted indiscriminately. It should be associated with a sense of responsibility. Ind pendece should be gradually given right from childhood to adolescence. Every parent should have a dsliberate programme to yield independence to his/her children. In the long run it pays dividends of happiness for all members of the family.

(*iv*) *The need to be successful*: To be emotionally stable and mentally healthy all people need to feel that they have acccomplished something worthwhile. Parents should inculcate in their children right attitudes towards life and the smaller successes of daily life should be recognized and cumulated deliberately as a contribution to the meeting of their emotional needs.

(*v*) *The need for recognition*: Recognition by others give us pleasure and a feeling of importance. It is an indication of regard, respect and friendship that enhance our self-eatcem. Recognition may take, many forms. For example, recognition of an adolescent by associating him in taking a decision in the family; by a friend, braising one's achievement; granting certificate of merit or rewarding in any other way are acts of recognition.

(*vi*) *The needs for self-respect*: A mature person, aware of his responsibilities, should not see himself as an utterly insignificant part of the family and community. The ego is a powerful force in emotional life and must be sustained at a normal level. Self- respect rests mainly upon an independent spirit, a sense of having accomplished something worthwhile and recognition by others of the useful things you have done in life. Self-respect is recognized by others even though they do not know what that self-respect is grounded upon. To live will with one's self is to assure an orderly progress through life.

(*vii*) *The need to be taken as we are*: The personality of an individual cannot be changed overnight, but it can be gradually changed in course of time with certain limitations. It adjustment.to others is always one way, then this giving in and modifying of our own way of living and thinking must eventually lead to a disturbing surrender of independence and self-direction. There is a fundamental emotional need for acceptance as we are. Each of us has a basic personality structure beneath which no changes can be made without unhappiness and mental disturbance of our mental health. Knowing this, we should be willing to accept others even though there may be uncongenital elements in their personalities. Knowing that each person has a fundamental need for acceptance should make it easier for to get along with those who have ugly personalities as well as those who have attractive ones. There is no perfection in the world hence we must expect all people to have some faults. The person who has the greatest number of faults will also experience the greatest amount of rejection by other people. As a consequence, his emotional need for acceptance will be greater than average.

3. Social needs

These include need for social affiliation, social recognition, social prestige, etc. Curriculum farmers should corporate various types of needs as they emerge at different age levels. Our curriculum shohld satisfy the needs of children. A curriculum which does not do so creates anxiety and tension which ultimately lead to maladjustment.

Discipline

Discipline in the classroom plays an important role in maintaining the mental health of students. A classical study, referred to above was conducted by Lipitt & White which proved that democratic discipline creates desirable characteristics in children and minimizes their mental tension. Therefore, it is suggested that the teacher must solve the problems of the classroom through mutual discussion with the students. The student should feel their responsibility towards each other and towards the institution.

Curricular activities

Curricular activities also play an important rule in providing opportunities for the expression of pent-up feelings. The teachers should organize various curricular activities to the needs of individual students. Some of the curricular activities. are: regular games, drama, southing, mutual discussion, educational exhibitions, excursions, picnics, student magazine, etc.

The school can initiate certain activities on experimental basis: (a) classes in human relation: the school can hold classes in human relations once a week. In these classes individual problems of the students should be discussed and solved. These classes encourage the students to express their problems without inhibition and promote good human relations.

(b) An experiment was conducted in USA which is popularly known as the 'Tulsa project'. According to the scheme, boys and girls are provided opportunities to freely their views in the absence of a teacher. It is assumed that this project provides opportunity for catharsis, and the students feel fresh. It is hoped that if schools supplement faithfully the suggestions given above we can hope that the mental health of the students will be promoted.

In brief we have described the conditions within the schools within affect the mental health of children. The teacher and the principle should try to create a conductive environment in the school for the promotion of the mental health of children.

Promotion of mental health

The following methods would be very effective:

1. Encounter groups

In recent years a wave of experiments has started to promote human relations for enhancing mental health. The most widely used word "encounter" will serve as a heading for the many variations that have been developed in recent years. These meetings which are aimed at improving human relations have a good deal in common with group therapy but their intent is different.

The main purpose of these encounter groups is training, not treatment. Groups (T groups) were started after World War I when world wide destructiveness necessitated the need to improve human relations. In 1946, the human relations conference was held at Bethel. A group of successful people discovered how much they could learn about social interaction simply by interacting and focussing attention on how they did it. Moment and Zales Zink called attention to two dimensions of competence: the technical and the interpersonal. Specialists contributed ideas about the objective features of the problem to be solved. The social specialists, less fertile with solutions to the problems, listened to others, expressed appreciation and respect, suggested compromise and thus maintained a harmonious atmosphere for work. The original purpose of the "T" group was to increase sensitivity to the human relations aspect of joint endeavours.

"T" groups were designed, according to Argyris, "To provide maximum possible opportunity for the individuals to expose their behaviour, give and receive feedback, experiment with new behaviour and develop awareness and acceptance of self and others". The goals of encounter group are:

(a) Incr easing self-awareness

(b) Increasing sensitivity

(c) Increasing understanding of humaan relations.

2. Biofeedback

Biofeedback is a recently developed technique of self-control the various viseceral responses of the body. The procedure of biofeedback is facilitated by moment-to-moment information about the state of such procees as blood pressure and heart behaviour to the individual. Let us explain it more clearly. The information or feedback is provided by electronic devices that augment biological signals. The following diagram explains how the feedback is provided.

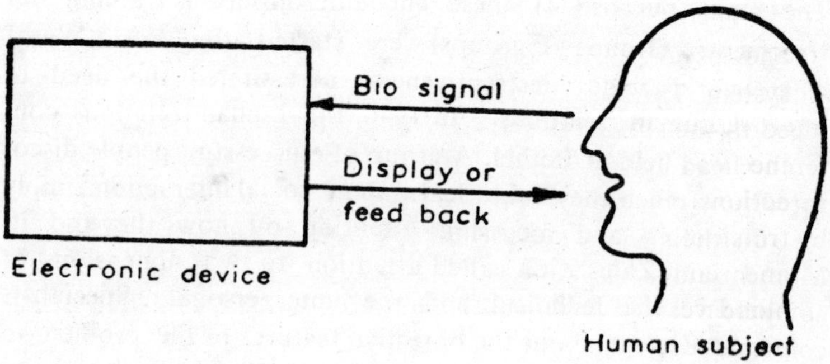

Fig.: 7

The following principal response measures are used in bio-feedback research:

(a) Electroencephalogram	measures of brain vaves
(b) Electrocardiogram	measure of heart behaviour
(c) Electromyograph	measure of muscle tension
(d) Galvanic skin response	measure of emotional responses
(e) Skin temperature	measure of dilation and constriction of small blood vessels

Biofeedback represents a major breakthrough in man-machine system. Human beings with the help of biofeedback can control their physiological systems, much like a musician can play on the piano.

The basic principles on which biofeedback is based have been known to psychologists for years but their use in controlling the physiological system is very recent The early learning theorist B.L, Thorndike, coined the 'principle of results', which states that learning is greatly facilitated if the learner is provided with information about the outcome of his actions. It has been proved beyond doubt that knowledge of results helps in shaping behaviour, dropping out those responses that do not contribute to learning goals and keeping in those responses that do.

There has been a traditional distinction between physiology and psychology, between the somatic and autonomic nervous system. The somatic nervous system controls the muscles attached to the skeleton actions as walking, moving a hand, turning the head and so forth and are voluntary. We can control these actions. On the other hand, the autonomic nervous system controls the smooth muscles associated with body's internal organs and endocrine glands and such internal events as heart rete, blood vessel changes, gastric juice secretion and thyroxince production that are involuntary actions. We cannot control these actions.

But the whole distinction between the voluntary and involuntary is breaking now-a-days. It was one of B.F. Skinner's accomplishment to demonstrate that voluntary behaviour could just be classed as involuntary. Instrumental conditioning deals with the conditioning of overt movements falling under voluntary behaviour. Many people feel that Skinner's work downgraded the importance of the conscious control of human will. But now biofeedback has made its appearance and has confined Skinner's view. The distinction between voluntary and involuntary is arbitrary. People can control involuntary process.

Principle

We understand our voluntary nervous system as that part of the nervous system directing the skeletal muscles which we can consiously control. The involuntary or automatic nervous sytem was previously believed unable to respond to conscious control. However, biofeedback and yoga show that conscious control of involuntary functions is possible. Blundell, an English psychologist, describes the biofeedback principle as : "If through the use of some device, one can become aware of an internal event of which one is not normally aware, e.g. the production of alpha rhythms is one's brain, then one can learn to control some aspect of the event". This principle speaks for itself about the use of biofeedback as an aid to the development of higher states of awareness. Biofeedback has made it possible to control the heart rate and is helpful in treating tension and headaches.

Anxiety can be reduces with EEG training and muscles relaxation.

It is hopped that EEG training will be useful in reducing the severity of some epileptic conditions.

Biofeedback training helps the individual to obtain self-control over emotional states and may alleviate some of the more severe symptoms of asthema.Biofeedback techniques allow the subject to gain control over automatic functions. It is clear that biofeedback training offers a large range of possible applications to control the voluntary and the involuntary actions of human beings. Many mental conditions that have been treated by psychosurgery and drugs may eventually fall within the domain of biofeedback technology.

Biofeedback technology is superior to treatments such as psychosurgery and chemotherapy with are fraught with side effects. Moreover, biofeedback enables the patients to participate actively in their own therapy and consequently develops their self-esteem. It offers some possiblities of maximizing human potentialities, Biofeedback as reasearches suggest, can help in the development of creativity, memory, perception and learning.

Brown in his book "New Mind, New Body" : concludes :

"The excitement that biofeedback has generated is deserved. It is a powerful and effective tool for the future of the mind. Its potential may be ultimited or it may be a step toward a new reality...."

Biofeedback is still in the initial stage of its development. Several research studies are being conducted to explore the possibility of applying feedback techniques to enhance the adjustment of the individual by reducing tension and other mental disorders.

Transcendental Meditation (T.M.)

Transcendental meditation, popularly known as TM, has revolutionized the technique of meditation in the last decades. It was developed by His Holiness Maharshi Mahesh Yogi of Shankara Ashram, Rishikesh, (India). This most ancient technique has been modified by His Holiness in accordance with the changed conditions in the world. T.M. is a simple, effortless mental technique which is very easy to practise by person of any age and sex. It is practised by sitting comfortably with eyes closed for 15-20 minutes in the morning and evening. It is unique in that the process is purely mechanical and requires no religious or philosophical beliefs on the part of individuals.

The technique of TM can be learnt by any one in four days, (an hour's session each day) from a qualified teacher of the TM.

Salient features of TM

— Extermely exact, systematic and scientific technique

— Entirely natural, effortless and easily mastered

— Gives immediate results

— Practice demands no change in ways of life.

— It requires no discipline, no concentration, contemplation nor is it emotionally demanding.

Method

The method of TM is very simple. A right thought is selected by the teacher of TM, according to the taste and temperament of the aspirant. The thought occupies the mind for sometime and then the aspirant dives deep in great relaxation, ceasing mental activity and creating a void in the mind, spontaneously cultivating a high degree of awareness.

The mind is just concentrated on a point, single thought and then directed towards its source. A real calmness and beatitude is attained when the mind transcends the thinking process. A thought is not perceptible as long as it is in the depth of the sub-conscious mind, like a small bubble which starts from the bottom of the pond. But as it slowly comes up to the surface, it is perceptible and becomes bigger and bigger, till it is recognized as a thought.

The TM practice takes a meditator into the deepest level of the sub-consious mind, expands the conscious mind and makes it powerful. The source of thought, the creative energy thus it powerful. The source of thought, the creative energy thus comes within the scope of the conscious mind fills it with strength over and above the strength gained by the conscious mind in fathoming the deeper level of sub-conscious.

Application

T.M. is the most widely used technique the world over to improve the physical and mental health of human beings. Tremendous research literature has been produced by conducting systematically controlled studies on TM and its application in different aspects of individual and social life. It has been established by almost all studies that TM systematically refines the nervous system by alternating deep rest with dynamic activity and develops the individual's full potential of mind and body. Though TM has greatly contributed to all walks of life, here we will mention only TM's contribution to psychology and education.

Psychology

(i) It decreases anxiety.

(ii) It improves behaviour in the following ways :

(a) Reduced nervousness, depression and irritability

(b) Increase self-confidence

(c) Increased sociability

(d) Decreased resistance to stress.

(e) Increased resistance to stress,

(iii) It increases self-actualization.

(iv) It increases mental health by reducing axiety.

(v) It helps harmonious development of personality as under :

(a) Increased spontaniety, inner and outer directedness capacity for intimate contact.

Education

(i) It increases the intelligence growth rate.

(ii) It increases learning ability.

(iii) It improves academic performance.

(iv) It widens comprehension, ability to focus attention and increases memory.

(v) In conclusion perceptual ability.

In conclusion it is suggested that an aspirant for TM should find out a suitable teacher who may properly initiate him into the discipline.

4. Yoga

Though reference to yoga has already been made in chapter Fourteenth under "Indian Psychotherapeutic Practices" here some Asanas (exercises) will be mentioned which may be very useful for enhancing physical and mental health if practised regularly under the guidance of a well-trained yoga teacher. The following exercises (asanas) are mentioned for the benefit of the readers:

(*i*) *Suryanamaskar Asana* : This is a simple and very easy asana which helps to energize the nervous system and the upper part of the body.

(*ii*) *Pawan Mukta Asana* : It is helpful for the concentration of mental energy. It is easy to perform and has no side effects, (*iii*) *Ekpada Utthan Asana* : This asana is very useful for correcting disorders of the stomach and intestines and eliminating the problems of wind and gas It also helps in developing power of concentration. Its regular practice energizes sex-glands and enhances potency.

(*iv*) *Shava Asana* : It is one of the most effective atanas and should be regularly practised by students and by those who perform mental work. It relaxes all the muscles of the body, nerves, the nervous system and the mind. This asana is very useful for persons suffering from tension, anxiety, insomania blood pressure, etc. because it gives immediately relief from the trouble and energizes physical as well as mental facilities. It helps in promoting resistance to diseases.

(*v*) *Bhujanga Asana* : This asana provides both physical and mental strength to the practitioner. It activates the spinal corde chest, shoulders, neck, face and head. It energizes the mind and maintains the body in sound physical health.

(*vi*) *Pashchimothan Asana* : This asana curestroubles of the head and stomach if regularly practised. It is a bit difficult, but by gradual practice one can acquire perfection.

(*vii*) *Trikona Asana* : This asana is very useful for correcting disorders of the neck and the shoulder joints. It is also very beneficial for improving the vision and mental alertness. It increases the decision making ability and creates firmness, concentration and positiveness.

(*viii*) *Yoga Mudra* : This asana has several benefits. It energizes the lungs and the central nervous system and helps in the smooth flow of blood.

(*ix*) *Ardhavakra Asana* : It is an easy asana and very useful. It activates the various organs of the body and keeps the person in sound physical as well as mental health.

(*x*) *Pranayama* : This *asana* corrects all disorders of the body relaxes the nervous system and removes tension and anxiety.

(*xi*) *Hala Asana* : This is one of the best and most effective asanas. It energizes the sex glands and increases their power. It activates the central nervous system and promotes mental health.

(*xii*) *Sarvanga Asana* : This asana is very effective for energizing and nourishing the whole body. It corrects the disorders of the mind and restores mental health. It also corrects all defects of sexual organs.

(*xiii*) *Matsya Asana* : This asana activates important organs of the body like chest, face, neck and shoulders. It gives them strength. It also energizes the central nervous system and promotes mental health.

(*xiv*) *Shalahba Asana* : This asana activates and energizes the whole body. It keeps the practitioner free from physical diseases of the internal system.

(*xv*) *Santulan Asana* : It is very useful asana to develop the power of concentration.

In conclusion it can be said that if yogic *asanas* are regularly practised, they will remove all physical and mental ailments of the practitioner, promote his mental health, and will enhance his resistance to diseases.

QUESTIONS FOR DISCUSSION

1. "Prevention is better than cure". Comment.
2. What is the role of the family in promoting the mental health of children ?
3. How can school help to preserve the mental health of students ?
4. What are the socio-cultural measures which may be helpful in preventing mental disorders among children ?

5. What is Transcendental Meditation ? What are its advantages ?
6. Write short notes on Biofeedback, Yoga and Encounter Group.

SUGGESTED READINGS

1. Caplan, G.: Principles of Preventive Psychiatry; Basic Books, NY, 1964.
2. Chaitow, L. : Relaxation and Meditation Techniques; Thorson Pub., 1983.
3. Corey, G. : Teachers Can Make a Difference; Merrill, Ohio, 1973.
4. Harris, G. G. (Ed.) : The Gronp Treatment of Human Problems; Grune and Straton, NY, 1977.
5. Mehar, Joseph : Abnormal Psychology; Holt, Rinehart and Winston, NY, 1983.
6. Sinha, Phulgenda : Yoga for Mental Power; Orient Paperbacks, Delhi, 1983.

CHAPTER 16

Mental Health of the Teacher

We have been talking in previous chapters about the mental health of students. The causes of maladjustment and remedial measures have been given in general. In this chapter, we will present the problems of maladjustment among teachers. A teachers' mental health plays an important role in the teaching-learning process. If the teacher is not in sound mental health, he can do incalculable harm to the nation in terms of poor guidance to the students. He cannot do justice to his job. His maladjustment will not only adversely affect his personality but will produce maladjustment in the children put under his charge.

In modern times, problems have also multiplied in proportion to rapid development in all walks of life. In ancient India, when education was confined to privileged communities, teaching was entrusted to great scholars and involved no problem. With the passage of time, education broke the barriers of caste and community and reached the masses. This new movement of mass education is fraught with certain problems for teachers. Before we discuss the problems of teachers which lead to maladjustment, let us, in brief, see what are the advantages of teaching as a profession.

Advantages of Teaching Profession

(1) **Teaching is clean work.** Teaching as a profession is clean and free from corrupt practices in comparison to other professions.

(2) **Contact with the youth.** A teacher remains in contact with the youth throughout his life. This interaction keeps the

teacher mentally alive and physically alert.

(3) Variety of work. Teaching involves a wide range of activities : physical, mental, social and emotional. Variation in activities eliminates boredom and releases tension.

(4) Income is steady and assured. Teaching provides a steady and assured income.

(5) Opportunity to meet professional workers. Teaching provides opportunities to meet professional workers. Teachers can discuss their academic problems and devise means to solve them. They can also plan their professional growth and achievement throughout their career.

(6) Personal satisfaction. Teaching gives personal satisfaction to the teacher. A teacher feels satisfied after teaching a class provided that he is a devoted teacher. He feels that he is doing something for the nation.

(7) Keeps the teacher abreast of the time. The greatest advantage of teaching is that it provides an opportunity to the teacher to move with the time. The teacher remains in touch with recent researches in his field of specialization.

Causes of Teacher's Maladjustment

A teacher is a member of the larger society. He also develops maladjustment as others do. There are many factors which cause maladjustment in teachers. Some of them are described below :

(1) Lack of professional aptitude and spirit

In our country teaching is accepted as a profession not because an individual is interested in teaching but because he has not been able to get entry into other professions. Young men and women have ambitions of joining administrative and executive posts irrespective of their personal competencies. But when they are rejected for these jobs, they accept teaching as a last resort to earn their livelihood. The author used to administer a simple question to B. Ed. teacher-trainees. The question was, "Did you ever want to become a teacher ?" 95% trainees replied negatively. In our country, most of the teachers lack professional aptitude and devotion to their profession.

(2) Occupational hazards

Every profession has frustrating conditions which lead to maladjustment. Teaching in our country has the following frustrating conditions :

(i) *Frequent criticisms.* It is the habit with people right from a peon to one in the highest rank, to criticize teaching and teachers. We read in newspapers that teachers do not work, that education is useless. etc.

(ii) *Restrictions.* Several types of restrictions are imposed on teachers. There are institutions which impose restrictions as regards clothing, food, religious affiliations and participation in politics.

(3) Extra work

Private institutions in our country are mostly run by politicians who in time of elections employ the services of teachers for canvassing and clerical work. Not only this, but every time a dignitary comes, teachers and students are ordered to welcome him.

(4) Lack of social prestige

All leaders and educationists give lip sympathy to the importance of teachers. All agree that they are the builders of the nation's future. The slogan sounds very sweet to the ears, but what is the importance of the teacher in the eyes of the society. The author conducted a survey to find out the importance of the teacher in the community with the help of questions administered to parents. The questions represented different social situations such as : you have to invite 4 persons at the birth anniversary of your son. Whom will yov invite ? You will be surprised to know that even the policeman and the patwari were preferred to teachers. It may have been due to the ignorance of illiterate parents from villages for whom the policeman and the patwari wield more power than the teacher. But even in the educated and richer classes, the social prestige of the teacher is not so high as it should be.

(5) Poor salaries

In spite of the high cost of living, the salaries of teachers have not been increased proportionately. As regards teachers engaged in higher education, their grades have been revised by some of the states. This revision of grades by the UGC has given relief to the teachers and enhanced the social prestige of the profession. We can now hope that better people will choose teaching as a profession.

(6) High moral expectations

Society expects that a teacher should be a saint. No doubt, the teacher must present a model of ideal behaviour to the students for imitation. But in actual practice how many students imitate or identify with the model or the ideals of the teacher ? He is a member of his society and it is natural that the evils of the social environment affect his personality.

(7) Work-load

In our schools, the work-load is excessive. The teacher has to teach 7 to 9 periods in a day. This excessive work develops emotional tensions and mental fatigue which if continued for a long period, leads to anxiety.

(8) Lack of recreational facilities

There is a dearth of recreational facilities for teachers in our schools.

(9) Relationship among teachers

It is said that there are fewer conflicts among illiterates than educated persons. This is quite true of teachers. Hardly, 20% of the schools in the country have perfect harmony, cooperation and good will among teachers. Most of them indulge in back-biting. This creates conflicts in the mind of a teacher.

(10) Relationship between the administrator and teachers

Some administrators are autocrats and impose their will on teachers.

(11) Feeling of caste, creed and religion

On paper discrimination and partial treatment, on the basis of religion and caste, have been done away with. But the evil exists in most institutions where preference is shown on the basis of caste and religion and not on the teaching competency of the individual. Teachers are unjustly accused, maltreated and sometimes dismissed because they do not flatter the authorities or they resent their malpractices and injustices.

(12) Insecurity of service

There are private institutions where the teachers feel insecure. This causes anxiety in the minds of the teachers which if it persists for a long period, may cause mental disturbances.

(13) Lack of facilities

There are many institutions which do not have good library facilities, audio-visual aids and a well-equipped science laboratory. This causes frustration in the minds of teachers.

Programmes to improve teacher's mental health

We have listed various factors in the school and outside which affect the mental health of the teacher. We will see how we can eliminate these factors and help the teacher to improve and maintain his mental health.

(1) Improving teacher-teacher relations

The success of the school depends upon the willingness, co-operation and the ability of its members to work together. The school should provide a better environment for creating good will among members of the teaching staff. Frequent meetings to discuss problems should be held to clarify any misunderstanding that may have arisen between members of staff. A teachers' club should be established in every institution to bring the teachers close to each other. Educational tours and excursion should be arranged to develop necessary skills to work with other teachers successfully.

(2) Improving teacher-principal relations

There is a tendency to blame each other in our school system. The administrator blames the teachers for any failure in school functioning and the teachers blame the administrator for his authoritarian attitude and partial treatment. The Principal works as a leader of the group and much of the success of the school depends on his quality of leadership and his personality. The Principal can do the following things to improve relations among sohool personnel.

(*i*) *Keep routines to a minimum* :

Unnecessary restrictions should not be imposed on teachers because they create tension.

(*ii*) *Listening* :

The Principal should listen to the problems of teachers in a free and frank environment.

(*iii*) *Use democratic administration* :

The Principal should take major decisions by holding discussion with members of the staff. He should not impose his decision on the staff in an authoritarian way. If there is misunderstanding between the Principal and staff, it should be discussed and clarified by mutual discussion.

(*iv*) *Impartiality* :

The Principal should remain impartial. He should not favour any member on the basis of his caste and creed.

(*v*) *Helping nature* :

The Principal can discuss school problems with the staff in the teachers' club meeting. He should respect all teachers. The principal should support the teachers when they need his help. He should not form cliques on the policy of "divide and rule". He should not create favourities because other teachers will resent this attitude.

(*vi*) *Making criticism in private* :

The Principal, if he has to correct any teacher regarding his method of teaching or behaviour should do so teacher in private. No teacher should be criticized before the students and his colleagues.

(*vii*) *Be flexible* :

The Principal should not be rigid and traditional in his think ing and ways of dealing with teachers' problems. He should change his strategy with the times. He should evaluate his own role as an administrator. He should set up example

(*viii*) *Plan in advance* :

Everything should be planned at the beginning of the academic year and should be communicated to teachers in advance for execution. He should work as a true leader of the team. A team spirit should be encouraged.

(3) Professional growth

The school should arrange for in-service programmes for teachers to refresh their knowledge of the matter and methods of teaching. The Principal should make arrangements for a good library and teaching materials. He should encourage his colleagues to experiment with innovative ideas in teaching methods. He should work as a friend and guide to his colleagues.

(4) Seminars, workshops and conference

Teachers from different schools should be invited to discuss problems of education in seminars and workshops. These activities provide an opportunity of knowing the points of view of other workers in the field through mutual discussion. They keep the teachers abreast of new trends and technology in the field of education.

(5) Service security

Some rules and regulations should be formed to check the exploitation of the teacher community by private managements who terminate the services of teachers on account of their personal whims. The teacher should feel secure about his service. Payment of salaries should be made regularly.

(6) Teacher-community relations

Excessive criticism of teachers occurs because there is a wide gap between the teacher and the community. A close relationship should be established between teachers and the community The following steps can be taken to strengthen teacher-community relationship.

(*i*) *Community service* :

The school should adopt the local community for improving sanitary conditions, road, and the supply of pure drinking water. If the students under the guidance of teachers go to local villages and do some useful work for the improvement of the villages, a close rapport will be established between the school and community which will enhance the prestige and importance of the teachers.

(*ii*) *Use criticism* :

The criticism made by society should be used by teachers in a constructive way to improve their existing conditions.

QUESTIONS FOR DISCUSSION

1. What are the common problems of secondary school teachers ?
2. How will you promote the mental health of teachers ?
3. Suggest some measures to improve the quality of secondary school teachers.
4. List any five problems of primary school teachers.

SUGGESTED READINGS

1. Averill, L.A.: The Hygiene of Instruction; Houghton, Mifflin, NY, 1934.
2. Bailey, C W,: Happiness in the School Blackie, London, 1919.
3. Chauhan, S.S.: Advanced Educational Psychology, Vikas Publishing House, New Delhi, 1987.

CHAPTER 17

Community Mental Health

There are no two opinions as regards the increasing percentage of mental disorders in our country after Independence. If we compare the statistics of mental disorders in pre-independence and post-independence periods we find a great difference in them. The question is : why have the incidences of mental disorders increased so alarmingly in our country ? The answer to this question is that the great changes have taken place in the socio-economic, technological and industrial areas of our society which have revolutionised the thinking of the people. These changes, coupled with the tremendous growth in our population have been accompainied by a sharp increase in deviant behaviour necessitating the evolvement of effective measures to cope with the changed conditions. Here one very important issue that needs our attention is : why do we need to pay attention to the mental health of the community ? Let us first answer this question. Some psychologists are of the opinion that mental abnormalities are restricted to individuals and therefore it is meaningless to refer to the total society as neurotic. But there are others who are of the opinion that individuals make up a society and are affected by the kind of society they live in. Hence problems of individual mental disorders cannot be understood, controlled and solved without reference to the society in which they occur. For example, if a society is strictly traditional it will inculcate traditional values in its members the violation of which may sometimes threaten the very existence of the individual and cause mental abnormality. The social environment, may suppress needs and demands and may cause frustration, conflicts communal disharmony, etc. This may well influence the relative severity and duration of disordered functioning as well as the relative predominance of certain types of symptoms in its members.

In India and in other developing countries of the world, traditional values and cultural norms are being challenged not only by scheduled castes and scheduled tribes but also by middle class youth and college students all over the country. The erosion of traditional values and consciousness of status in the members of weaker sections of the society have consequently resulted in a number of problems which have recently acquired unusual dimensions. There is increased delinquency among adolescents and a higher rate of crimes such as brides burning, agitation against reservation policy, use of drugs, communal riots, killings of leaders, rapes of women of weaker sections, hijacking of planes, banks robberies etc. All these acts of active and passive suggestions have been interpreted as symptoms of a sick society needing immediate attention of experts.

It is imperative that if we want to take our nation ahead in an increasingly competitive world we have to pay attention to the mental health problems of the society.

Mental health services were for the first time started during the second decade of the present century in western countries but in our country they have not yet attracted the attention of psychologists, educationists, social workers and the government. There is immediate need to start community mental health services. However, sporadic efforts by individuals to treat mental disorders have been made since the time of the Atharva-veda. Many community mental health services involve responsibility for prevention, treatment, and rehabilitation of mentally disordered people in society after recovery. Caplan suggests that responsibility must extend beyond the known cases of mental disorders to the unrecognized cases of current or future disorders.

Some of the programmes in the community mental health services, are as follows :

To develop programmes at centre, state and local levels to assist individuals in the betterment of their mental health in the following manners: (i) Promotion of mental health by helping people in the acquisition of knowledge, attitudes and behaviour that will foster, maintain and improve their mental health. (ii) Prevention of mental disorders by controlling biological, interpersonal and social factors that jeopardize the mental health of the community. (iii) Restoration of mental health to those who suffer from mental disorders by providing treatment, after care and rehabilitaton services. Community mental health centre can provide the following types of services :

(1) Inpatient care

(2) Partial hospitalization

(3) Outpatient therapy

(4) Emergency case treatment

(5) Consultation and education

Promotion of community mental health

There are three types of preventive measures which can be taken to prevent the occurrence of mental disorders in the community. They are :

A — Primary prevention measures aimed at identifying and eradicating the causes of mental disorders in order to lower their incidence in the community.

B — Secondary prevention measures involving early identification of the development of a problem in behaviour and implementation of such measures as will prevent the development of the mental disorder,

C — Tertiary prevention measures aimed at reducing the rate of residual defects in patients after treatment has been completed.

A brief description of all the above measures is as follows :

A. PRIMARY PREVENTION

1. Improving social environment

The social environment plays a crucial role in the development of a harmonious personality. The social environment has recently been contaminated by feelings of communal hatred, hostility and aggression culminating in mass murders of the people of a particular community. There is a great need to bring mutual understanding among different communities for the welfare of the nation. The social environment can be improved with the help of the mass media, radio, newspapers, TV, etc. The masses should be educated to preserve communal harmony.

2. Family welfare

Poverty is the root of all evils. It is unfortunate that more than 50 per cent of Indians live below the poverty line. The Government of India has launched programmes for family welfare with the specific purpose of reducing the birth rate in order to check the tremendous growth of population which has been negating the out-come of planning. The fewer the number of children, the better the care parents can provide. Family planning and welfare schemes will, in the long run, help to maintain mental health and prevent future mental disorders in the community.

3. Improving interpersonal relations

To improve interpersonal relations among members of different communities the following measures can be taken :

(i) Community centres :

In all big cities community centres should be established

where people can meet and discuss their problems daily or weekly.

(*ii*) *Lectures* :

In these community centres, lectures by religious leaders of different communities could be arranged to educate the masses about the fundamental principles of various religious. Lectures of mental health problems may also be occasionally arranged for the benefit of members.

(*iii*) *Cultural activities* :

Debates, dramas, games and other cultural activities may be organised in these centres.

(*iv*) *Neighbourhood clubs* :

These clubs may be started for adolescents and adults to bring them close to each other. In villages, panchayats should be made more effective.

4. Reduction of stresses

Modern society has been undergoing great stresses and strains due to constant fear of a nuclear war, economic problems, racial discrimination, unemployment and social alienation of the weaker sections of society. All these bring about social ills, and are major sources of needless sufferings and mental tension. The Government should pay immediate attention to eardicating these social evils. There should be no discrimination of individuals on the basis of caste, creed, religion and sex. The Indian constitution does not allow any type of discrimination but in practice it still continues. Therefore there is a need to enforce the law strictly with the help of community leaders.

5. Genetic counselling

Genetic counselling should be provided to members of the community to reduce incidence of mental retardation.

6. Educational programmes

The following types of educational programmes may be organized for the welfare of the community.

(a) Programmes on the dangers of the use of drugs and alcohol.

(b) Developing positive parenting skills in would be parents.

(c) Work-safety education programmes may be organized for workers in factories that deal with toxic chemicals.

(d) Programmes for old people may be organized to prevent social isolation.

Every individual should be given full opportunity for maximum personal growth and self-actualization. Mental health services hardly exist in our society. In fact, so far as may knowledge goes, there is hardly any mental health service centre. Therefore it is suggested that such centres must be opened. These centres will prove very useful because of their accessibility to the needy people, particularly in disadvantaged communities. The proximity factor also facilitates prompt intervention in a crisis.

B. SECONDARY PREVENTION

Secondary prevention of mental disorders involves early detection and rapid intervention. Here the main difficulty is to locate cases of mental disorders in the community.

According to Caplan, "The psychiatrist can no longer wait for patients to come to him because he carries equal responsibilities for all those who do not come. A significant part of his job consists in finding out who the mentally disordered are and where they are located. The following methods can be used.

(*i*) *Medical examination* :

Every year school children should be medically examined

by competent doctors. Any physical or mental abnormality should be properly treated to avoid further complications.

(ii) Early detection of childhood problems such as phobia, temper tentrum, refusal to go to school and withdrawal etc. will be very useful in planning the treatment at an early stage.

(iii) Crisis intervention for those who are faced with acute stressful experiences such as loss of job, a death in the family, prolonged illness and major disasters.

(iv) Hospitalizations of the patients who need it and effective treatment of their mental disorders.

(*v*) *Survey of mentally disordered* :

No doubt a survey of mentally disordered persons in the community is a huge and very difficult task but it can be started from the block level. After locating the mentally disordered persons at this level adequate arrangement for their treatment should be made to avoid further deterioration in their condition. Negihbourhood groups may be given basic courses to detect mentally disturbed persons.

(*vi*) *Child guidance clinic* :

Child guidance clinics may be established so that parents can seek guidance for behavioural problems of their children in the initial stage and prevent the evolution of more serious disorders. The child guidance clinic should be adequately equipped with staff and other material.

C. TERTIARY PREVENTION

It occurs once a person is in the treatment process. Efforts should be made to avoid the effects of chronicity, institutionalization in prisons which may lead to learning of patterns of behaviours that are not advantageous in the larger society. Mentally disordered people should be trained to earn their livelihood independently. Tertiary prevention may also aim at changing attitudes towards ex-psychiatric patients so that they may more readily resume their former place in society without any harassment.

It is hoped that if the above referred preventive measures are earnestly implemented, the mental health of the community will be improved and disorders will be reduced to the minimum.

QUESTIONS FOR DISCUSSION

1. What are the objectives community mental health services ?
2. Why have community mental health services become essential in modern society ?
3. What measures will you take to reduce the mental health problems of the community ?
4. How will family planning and adult education programmes help in preventing mental health problems in the community ?

SUGGESTED READINGS

1. Bloom, B.L. : Community Mental Health.
2. Magaro, P.A. : The Mental Health in Industry.
3. N.M.H. : The Mental Health of Urban America ; Washington, D.C., 1969.

Index